Essentials of Educational Technology

Essentials of Educational Technology

Vaishnavi Rajesh
Tanuja Patki

2026
Agri Horti Press
New Delhi-110 084

ISBN: 978-93-49690-22-6 (Hardbound)

Published By

Agri Horti Press

New Delhi

E-mail: agrihortipress@gmail.com

Digitally Printed at : Replika Press Pvt. Ltd.

Preface

Essentials of Educational Technology provides a comprehensive overview of the critical concepts, tools, and applications of technology in education. This book is designed for educators, instructional designers, researchers, and students who wish to understand how emerging technologies can enhance teaching, learning, and educational outcomes. It serves as a guide to both the theoretical foundations and practical applications of educational technology, covering key principles and best practices for integrating technology into educational settings.

The integration of technology into education has transformed the way teaching and learning processes are structured, executed, and experienced. From the use of digital learning tools and online platforms to the incorporation of interactive multimedia, virtual classrooms, and data analytics, educational technology is reshaping the landscape of education across all levels, from K-12 to higher education and beyond. This book aims to offer readers a deep understanding of how technology can be leveraged to improve student engagement, learning efficiency, and the overall educational experience.

This volume begins by addressing the fundamental theories and concepts behind educational technology, including its historical development, pedagogical implications, and the role it plays in fostering student-centered learning environments. The book explores various instructional design models and frameworks that guide the effective use of technology in curriculum development and delivery. It also examines the digital tools and platforms that are commonly used in modern education, such as Learning Management Systems (LMS), online assessment tools, and collaborative technologies.

A central focus of the book is the pedagogical value of different technologies and how they can be used to enhance specific learning objectives. Chapters explore the application of multimedia, interactive simulations, gamification, virtual reality (VR), augmented reality (AR), and artificial intelligence (AI) in educational settings, providing insights into how these technologies can be used to support diverse learning styles and needs. Furthermore, the book addresses the growing importance of digital literacy, both for students and educators, and the ways in which technology can help bridge educational gaps and promote inclusive learning.

In addition to examining the tools and technologies themselves, Essentials of Educational Technology also delves into the challenges and ethical considerations associated with the use of technology in education. Issues such as data privacy, accessibility, equity, and the digital divide are addressed in the context of ensuring that technology enhances educational opportunities for all learners.

The book also provides practical guidance on how educators can effectively implement and manage technology in their classrooms, including strategies for training teachers, evaluating the effectiveness of digital tools, and adapting to changing technological landscapes. Through case studies, real-world examples, and expert perspectives, the book offers valuable insights into the dynamic relationship between technology and education.

We are grateful to the contributors who have brought their expertise and experience to this volume. It is our hope that Essentials of Educational Technology will serve as a valuable resource for those looking to understand and apply the principles of educational technology in a rapidly evolving educational environment.

Vaishnavi Rajesh
Tanuja Patki

Contents

1

INTRODUCTION

Educational technology is most simply and comfortably defined as an array of tools that might prove helpful in advancing student learning. Educational Technology relies on a broad definition of the word "technology". Educational technology is the study and ethical practice of facilitating learning and improving performance by creating, using and managing appropriate technological processes and resources." The term educational technology is often associated with, and encompasses, instructional theory and learning theory.

While instructional technology covers the processes and systems of learning and instruction, educational technology includes other systems used in the process of developing human capability. Educational Technology includes, but is not limited to, software, hardware, as well as Internet applications and activities. But there is still debate on what these terms mean.

Technology can refer to material objects of use to humanity, such as machines or hardware, but it can also encompass broader themes, including systems, methods of organization, and techniques. Some modern tools include but are not limited to overhead projectors, laptop computers, and calculators. Newer tools such as "smartphones" and games (both online and offline) are beginning to draw serious attention for their learning potential.

Those who employ educational technologies to explore ideas and communicate meaning are learners or teachers.

Consider the *Handbook of Human Performance Technology*. The word technology for the sister fields of Educational and Human Performance Technology means "applied science." In other words, any valid and reliable process or procedure that is derived from basic research using the "scientific method" is considered a "technology." Educational or Human Performance Technology may be based purely on algorithmic or heuristic processes, but neither necessarily implies physical technology. The word technology comes from the Greek "techne" which means craft or art. Another word, "technique," with the same origin, also may be used when considering the field Educational Technology. So Educational Technology may be extended to include the techniques of the educator.

A classic example of an Educational Psychology text is Bloom's 1956 book, *Taxonomy of Educational Objectives*. Bloom's Taxonomy is helpful when designing learning activities to keep in mind what is expected of—and what are the learning goals for—learners. However, Bloom's work does not explicitly deal with educational technology *per se* and is more concerned with pedagogical strategies.

PSYCHOLOGICAL RESEARCH

According to some, an Educational Technologist is someone who transforms basic educational and psychological research into an evidence-based applied science (or a technology) of learning or instruction. Educational Technologists typically have a graduate degree (Master's, Doctorate, Ph.D., or D.Phil.) in a field related to educational psychology, educational media, experimental psychology, cognitive psychology or, more purely, in the fields of Educational, Instructional or Human Performance Technology or Instructional (Systems) Design. But few of those listed below as theorists would ever use the term "educational technologist" as a term to describe themselves, preferring terms such as "educator". The transformation of educational technology from a cottage industry to a profession is discussed by Shurville, Browne, and Whitaker.

A Short History

Educational technology in a way could be traced back to the emergence of very early tools, e.g., paintings on cave walls. But usually its history starts with educational film (1900s) or Sidney Pressey's mechanical teaching machines in the 1920s.

The first large scale usage of new technologies can be traced to US WWII training of soldiers through training films and other mediated materials. Today, presentation-based technology, based on the idea that people can learn through aural and visual reception, exists in many forms, e.g., streaming audio and video, or PowerPoint presentations with voice-over. Another interesting invention of the 1940s was hypertext, i.e., V. Bush's memex.

The 1950s led to two major, still popular designs. Skinners work led to "programmed instruction" focusing on the formulation of behavioral objectives, breaking instructional content into small units and rewarding correct responses early and often. Advocating a mastery approach to learning based on his taxonomy of intellectual behaviors, Bloom endorsed instructional techniques that varied both instruction and time according to learner requirements. Models based on these designs were usually referred to as computer-based training" (CBT), Computer-aided instruction or computer-assisted instruction (CAI) in the 1970s through the 1990s.

In a more simplified form they correspond to today's "e-contents" that often form the core of "e-learning" set-ups, sometimes also referred to as web-based training (WBT) or e-instruction. The course designer divides learning contents into smaller chunks of text augmented with graphics and multimedia presentation. Frequent Multiple Choice questions with immediate feedback are added for self-assessment and guidance. Such e-contents can rely on standards defined by IMS, ADL/Scorm and IEEE.

The 1980s and 1990s produced a variety of schools that can be put under the umbrella of the label Computer-based learning (CBL). Frequently based on constructivist and cognitivist learning theories, these environments focused on teaching both abstract and domain-specific problem solving. Preferred technologies were micro-worlds (computer environments were learners could explore and build), simulations (computer environments where learner can play with parameters of dynamic systems) and hypertext.

Digitized communication and networking in education started in the mid 80s and became popular by the mid-90's, in particular through the World-Wide Web (WWW), eMail and Forums. There is a difference between two major forms of online learning. The earlier type, based on either Computer Based Training (CBT) or Computer-based learning (CBL), focused on the interaction between the student and computer drills plus tutorials on one hand or micro-worlds and simulations on the other. Both can be delivered today over the WWW. Today, the prevailing paradigm in the regular school system is Computer-mediated communication (CMC), where the primary form of interaction is between students and instructors, mediated by the computer. CBT/CBL usually means individualized (self-study) learning, while CMC involves teacher/tutor facilitation and requires scenarization of flexible learning activities. In addition, modern ICT provides education with tools for sustaining learning communities and associated knowledge management tasks. It also provides tools for student and curriculum management.

In addition to classroom enhancement, learning technologies also play a major role in full-time distance teaching. While most quality offers still rely on paper, videos and occasional CBT/CBL materials, there is increased use of e-tutoring through forums, instant messaging, video-conferencing etc. Courses addressed to smaller groups frequently use blended or hybrid designs that mix presence courses (usually in the beginning and at the end of a module) with distance activities and use various pedagogical styles (e.g., drill & practise, exercises, projects, etc.).

The 2000s emergence of multiple mobile and ubiquitous technologies gave a new impulse to situated learning theories favoring learning-in-context scenarios. Some literature uses the concept of integrated learning to describe blended learning scenarios that integrate both school and authentic (e.g., workplace) settings.

Theories and Practices

Three main theoretical schools or philosophical frameworks have been present in the educational technology literature. These are Behaviorism, Cognitivism and Constructivism. Each of these schools of thought are still present in today's literature but have evolved as the Psychology literature has evolved.

Behaviorism

This theoretical framework was developed in the early 20th century with the animal learning experiments of Ivan Pavlov, Edward Thorndike, Edward C. Tolman, Clark L. Hull, B.F. Skinner and many others. Many psychologists used these theories to describe and experiment with human learning. While still very useful this philosophy of learning has lost favor with many educators.

Skinner's Contributions

B.F. Skinner wrote extensively on improvements of teaching based on his functional analysis of Verbal Behavior and wrote "The Technology of Teaching", an attempt to dispel the myths underlying contemporary education as well as promote his system he called programmed instruction. Ogden Lindsley also developed the Celeration learning system similarly based on behavior analysis but quite different from Keller's and Skinner's models.

Cognitivism

Cognitive science has changed how educators view learning. Since the very early beginning of the Cognitive Revolution of the 1960s and 1970s, learning theory has undergone a great deal of change. Much of the empirical framework of Behaviorism was retained even though a new paradigm had begun. Cognitive theories look beyond behavior to explain brain-based learning. Cognitivists consider how human memory works to promote learning.

After memory theories like the Atkinson-Shiffrin memory model and Baddeley's Working memory model were established as a theoretical framework in Cognitive Psychology, new cognitive frameworks of learning began to emerge during the 1970s, 1980s, and 1990s. It is important to note that Computer Science and Information Technology have had a major influence on Cognitive Science theory. The Cognitive concepts of working memory (formerly known as short term memory) and long term memory have been facilitated by research and technology from the field of Computer Science. Another major influence on the field of Cognitive Science is Noam Chomsky. Today researchers are concentrating on topics like Cognitive load and Information Processing Theory.

Constructivism is a learning theory or educational philosophy that many educators began to consider in the 1990s. One of the primary tenets of this philosophy is that learners construct their own meaning from new information, as they interact with reality or others with different perspectives.

Constructivist learning environments require students to utilize their prior knowledge and experiences to formulate new, related, and/or adaptive concepts in learning. Under this framework the role of the teacher becomes that of a facilitator, providing guidance so that learners can construct their own knowledge. Constructivist educators must make sure that the prior learning experiences are appropriate and related to the concepts being taught. Jonassen (1997) suggests "well-structured" learning environments are useful for novice learners and that "ill-structured" environments are only useful for more advanced learners. Educators utilizing technology when teaching with a constructivist perspective should choose technologies that reinforce prior learning perhaps in a problem-solving environment.

INSTRUCTIONAL TECHNIQUE AND TECHNOLOGIES

Problem Based Learning and Inquiry-based learning are active learning educational technologies used to facilitate learning. Technology which includes physical and process applied science can be incorporated into project, problem, inquiry-based learning as they all have a similar educational philosophy. All three are student centered, ideally involving real-world scenarios in which students are actively engaged in critical thinking activities. The process that students are encouraged to employ (as long as it is based on empirical research) is considered to be a technology. Classic examples of technologies used by teachers and Educational Technologists include Bloom's Taxonomy and Instructional Design.

Theorists

This is an area where new thinkers are coming to the forefront everyday. Many of the ideas spread from theorists, researchers, and experts through their blogs. Extensive lists of educational bloggers by area of interest are available at Steve Hargadon's "SupportBloggers" site or at the "movingforward" wiki started by Scott McLeod.

Many of these blogs are recognized by their peers each year through the edublogger awards. Web 2.0 technologies have led to a huge increase in the amount of information available on this topic and the number of educators formally and informally discussing it. Most listed below have been around for more than a decade, however, and few new thinkers mentioned above are listed here.

- Alan November
- Alex Jones
- Seymour Papert
- George Siemens
- Will Richardson
- David Wiley
- John Sweller
- David Wilson

Benefits

Educational technology is intended to improve education over what it would be without technology. Some of the claimed benefits are listed below:

- **Easy-to-access Course Materials**: Instructors can post the course material or important information on a course website, which means students can study at a time and location they prefer and can obtain the study material very quickly
- **Student Motivation**: Computer-based instruction can give instant feedback to students and explain correct answers. Moreover, a computer is patient and

non-judgmental, which can give the student motivation to continue learning. According to James Kulik, who studies the effectiveness of computers used for instruction, students usually learn more in less time when receiving computer-based instruction and they like classes more and develop more positive attitudes toward computers in computer-based classes. The American educator, Cassandra B. Whyte, researched and reported about the importance of locus of control and successful academic performance and by the late 1980s, she wrote of how important computer usage and information technology would become in the higher education experience of the future.

- **Wide Participation**: Learning material can be used for long distance learning and are accessible to a wider audience
- **Improved Student Writing**: It is convenient for students to edit their written work on word processors, which can, in turn, improve the quality of their writing. According to some studies, the students are better at critiquing and editing written work that is exchanged over a computer network with students they know
- **Subjects Made Easier to Learn**: Many different types of educational software are designed and developed to help children or teenagers to learn specific subjects. Examples include pre-school software, computer simulators, and graphics software
- A structure that is more amenable to measurement and improvement of outcomes. With proper structuring it can become easier to monitor and maintain student work while also quickly gauging modifications to the instruction necessary to enhance student learning.
- **Differentiated Instruction:** Educational technology provides the means to focus on active student participation and to present differentiated questioning strategies. It broadens individualized instruction and promotes the development of personalized learning plans. Students are encouraged to use multimedia components and to incorporate the knowledge they gained in creative ways.

Criticism

Although technology in the classroom does have many benefits, there are clear drawbacks as well. Lack of proper training, limited access to sufficient quantities of a technology, and the extra time required for many implementations of technology are just a few of the reasons that technology is often not used extensively in the classroom.

Similar to learning a new task or trade, special training is vital to ensuring the effective integration of classroom technology. Since technology is not the end goal of education, but rather a means by which it can be accomplished, educators must have a good grasp of the technology being used and its advantages over more traditional methods. If there is a lack in either of these areas, technology will be seen as a hindrance and not a benefit to the goals of teaching.

Another difficulty is introduced when access to a sufficient quantity of a resource is limited. This is often seen when the quantity of computers or digital cameras for classroom use is not enough to meet the needs of an entire classroom. It also occurs in less noticed forms such as limited access for technology exploration because of the high cost of technology and the fear of damages. In other cases, the inconvenience of resource placement is a hindrance, such as having to transport a classroom to a computer lab instead of having in-classroom computer access by means of technology such as laptop carts.

Technology implementation can also be time consuming. There may be an initial setup or training time cost inherent in the use of certain technologies. Even with these tasks accomplished, technology failure may occur during the activity and as a result teachers must have an alternative lesson ready.

Another major issue arises because of the evolving nature of technology. New resources have to be designed and distributed whenever the technological platform has been changed. Finding quality materials to support classroom objectives after such changes is often difficult even after they exist in sufficient quantity and teachers must design these resources on their own.

Research from the Alberta Initiative for School Improvement (AISI) indicates that inquiry and project-based approaches, combined with a focus on curriculum, effectively supports the infusion of educational technologies into the learning and teaching process.

There are various types of technologies currently used in traditional classrooms. Among these are:

- **Computer in the Classroom:** Having a computer in the classroom is an asset to any teacher. With a computer in the classroom, teachers are able to demonstrate a new lesson, present new material, illustrate how to use new programs, and show new websites.
- **Class Website:** An easy way to display your student's work is to create a web page designed for your class. Once a web page is designed, teachers can post homework assignments, student work, famous quotes, trivia games, and so much more. In today's society, children know how to use the computer and navigate their way through a website, so why not give them one where they can be a published author. Just be careful as most districts maintain strong policies to manage official websites for a school or classroom. Also, most school districts provide teacher webpages that can easily be viewed through the school district's website.
- **Class Blogs and Wikis:** There are a variety of Web 2.0 tools that are currently being implemented in the classroom. Blogs allow for students to maintain a running dialogue, such as a journal,thoughts, ideas, and assignments that also provide for student comment and reflection. Wikis are more group focused to allow multiple members of the group to edit a single document and create a truly collaborative and carefully edited finished product.

- **Wireless Classroom Microphones:** Noisy classrooms are a daily occurrence, and with the help of microphones, students are able to hear their teachers more clearly. Children learn better when they hear the teacher clearly. The benefit for teachers is that they no longer lose their voices at the end of the day.
- **Mobile Devices:** Mobile devices such as clickers or smartphone can be used to enhance the experience in the classroom by providing the possibility for professors to get feedback.
- **Smart Boards:** An interactive whiteboard that provides touch control of computer applications. These enhance the experience in the classroom by showing anything that can be on a computer screen. This not only aids in visual learning, but it is interactive so the students can draw, write, or manipulate images on the SmartBoard.
- **Online Media:** Streamed video websites can be utilized to enhance a classroom lesson (e.g. United Streaming, Teacher Tube, etc.)

There are many other tools being utilized depending on the local school board and funds available. These may include: digital cameras, video cameras, interactive whiteboard tools, document cameras, or LCD projectors.

- **Podcasts:** Podcasting is a relatively new invention that allows anybody to publish files to the Internet where individuals can subscribe and receive new files from people by a subscription. The primary benefit of podcasting for educators is quite simple. It enables teachers to reach students through a medium that is both "cool" and a part of their daily lives. For a technology that only requires a computer, microphone and internet connection, podcasting has the capacity of advancing a student's education beyond the classroom.
- When students listen to the podcasts of other students as well as their own, they can quickly demonstrate their capacities to identify and define "quality." This can be a great tool for learning and developing literacy inside and outside the classroom. Podcasting can help sharpen students' vocabulary, writing, editing, public speaking, and presentation skills. Students will also learn skills that will be valuable in the working world, such as communication, time management, and problem-solving.

Societies

Learned societies concerned with educational technology include:

- Association for the Advancement of Computing in Education (AACE)
- Association for Educational Communications and Technology
- Association for Learning Technology
- International Society for Performance Improvement
- International Society for Technology in Education - (ISTE)

ADDIE Model

The ADDIE model is the generic process traditionally used by instructional designers and training developers. The five phases—Analysis, Design, Development,

Implementation, and Evaluation—represent a dynamic, flexible guideline for building effective training and performance support tools.

It is an Instructional Systems Design (ISD) model. Most of the current instructional design models are spin-offs or variations of the ADDIE model; other models include the Dick & Carey and Kemp ISD models. One commonly accepted improvement to this model is the use of rapid prototyping. This is the idea of receiving continual or formative feedback while instructional materials are being created. This model attempts to save time and money by catching problems while they are still easy to fix.

Instructional theories also play an important role in the design of instructional materials. Theories such as behaviorism, constructivism, social learning and cognitivism help shape and define the outcome of instructional materials.

Analysis Phase

In the analysis phase, the instructional problem is clarified, the instructional goals and objectives are established and the learning environment and learner's existing knowledge and skills are identified. Below are some of the questions that are addressed during the analysis phase:

- Who are the learners and what are their characteristics?
- What is the new behavioral outcome?
- What types of learning constraints exist?
- What are the delivery options?
- What are the online pedagogical considerations?
- What are the Adult Learning Theory considerations?
- What is the timeline for project completion?

Design Phase

The design phase deals with learning objectives, assessment instruments, exercises, content, subject matter analysis, lesson planning and media selection. The design phase should be systematic and specific. *Systematic* means a logical, orderly method of identifying, developing and evaluating a set of planned strategies targeted for attaining the project's goals. *Specific* means each element of the instructional design plan needs to be executed with attention to details.

These are steps involved in design phase:

- Document the project's instructional, visual and technical design strategy
- Apply instructional strategies according to the intended behavioral outcomes by domain (cognitive, affective, and psychomotor).
- Design the user interface and/or user experience
- Create prototype
- Apply visual design (graphic design)

Development Phase

The development phase is where instructional designers and developers create and assemble the content assets that were blueprinted in the design phase. In this phase, storyboards and graphics are designed. If elearning is involved, programmers develop and/or integrate technologies. Testers perform debugging procedures. The project is reviewed and revised according to the feedback received.

Implementation Phase

During the implementation phase, a procedure for training the facilitators and the learners is developed. The facilitators' training should cover the course curriculum, learning outcomes, method of delivery, and testing procedures. Preparation of the learners includes training them on new tools (software or hardware) and student registration.

This is also the phase where the project manager ensures that the books, hands-on equipment, tools, CD-ROMs and software are in place, and that the learning application or website is functional.

Evaluation Phase

The evaluation phase consists of two parts: formative and summative. Formative evaluation is present in each stage of the ADDIE process. Summative evaluation consists of tests designed for domain specific criterion-related referenced items and providing opportunities for feedback from the users which were identified.

Learning

Learning is acquiring new or modifying existing knowledge, behaviors, skills, values, or preferences and may involve synthesizing different types of information. The ability to learn is possessed by humans, animals and some machines. Progress over time tends to follow learning curves.

Human learning may occur as part of education, personal development, or training. It may be goal-oriented and may be aided by motivation. The study of how learning occurs is part of neuropsychology, educational psychology, learning theory, and pedagogy.

Learning may occur as a result of habituation or classical conditioning, seen in many animal species, or as a result of more complex activities such as play, seen only in relatively intelligent animals.

Learning may occur consciously or without conscious awareness. There is evidence for human behavioral learning prenatally, in which habituation has been observed as early as 32 weeks into gestation, indicating that the central nervous system is sufficiently developed and primed for learning and memory to occur very early on in development.

Play has been approached by several theorists as the first form of learning. Children play, experiment with the world, learn the rules, and learn to interact.

Vygotsky agrees that play is pivotal for children's development, since they make meaning of their environment through play.

Simple Non-associative Learning

Habituation

In psychology, habituation is an example of non-associative learning in which there is a progressive diminution of behavioral response probability with repetition stimulus. An animal first responds to a stimulus, but if it is neither rewarding nor harmful the animal reduces subsequent responses. One example of this can be seen in small song birds—if a stuffed owl (or similar predator) is put into the cage, the birds initially react to it as though it were a real predator.

Soon the birds react less, showing habituation. If another stuffed owl is introduced (or the same one removed and re-introduced), the birds react to it again as though it were a predator, demonstrating that it is only a very specific stimulus that is habituated to (namely, one particular unmoving owl in one place). Habituation has been shown in essentially every species of animal, including the large protozoan *Stentor coeruleus*.

Sensitization

Sensitization is an example of non-associative learning in which the progressive amplification of a response follows repeated administrations of a stimulus (Bell et al., 1995). An everyday example of this mechanism is the repeated tonic stimulation of peripheral nerves that will occur if a person rubs his arm continuously.

After a while, this stimulation will create a warm sensation that will eventually turn painful. The pain is the result of the progressively amplified synaptic response of the peripheral nerves warning the person that the stimulation is harmful. Sensitization is thought to underlie both adaptive as well as maladaptive learning processes in the organism.

Associative Learning

Associative learning is the process by which an element is taught through association with a separate, pre-occurring element. It is also referred to as classical conditioning. Honeybees display associative learning through the proboscis extension reflex paradigm.

Operant conditioning is the use of consequences to modify the occurrence and form of behavior. *Operant conditioning* is distinguished from *Pavlovian conditioning* in that operant conditioning uses reinforcement/punishment to alter an action-outcome association. In contrast Pavlovian conditioning involves strengthening of the stimulus-outcome association.

Behaviorism is a psychological movement that seeks to alter behavior by arranging the environment to elicit successful changes and to arrange consequences to maintain or diminish a behavior. Behaviorists study behaviors that can be measured and changed by the environment. However, they do not eliminate that there are thought processes that interact with those behaviors.

Delayed discounting is the process of devaluing rewards based on the delay of time they are presented. This process is thought to be tied to impulsivity. Impulsivity is a core process for many behaviors (e.g., substance abuse, problematic gambling, OCD). Making decisions is an important part of everyday functioning.

How we make those decisions is based on what we perceive to be the most valuable or worthwhile actions. This is determined by what we find to be the most reinforcing stimuli. So when teaching an individual a response, you need to find the most potent reinforcer for that person. This may be a larger reinforcer at a later time or a smaller immediate reinforcer.

Classical Conditioning

The typical paradigm for classical conditioning involves repeatedly pairing an unconditioned stimulus (which unfailingly evokes a reflexive response) with another previously neutral stimulus (which does not normally evoke the response). Following conditioning, the response occurs both to the unconditioned stimulus and to the other, unrelated stimulus (now referred to as the "conditioned stimulus").

The response to the conditioned stimulus is termed a *conditioned response*. The classic example is Pavlov and his dogs. Meat powder naturally will make a dog salivate when it is put into a dog's mouth; salivating is a reflexive response to the meat powder. Meat powder is the unconditioned stimulus (US) and the salivation is the unconditioned response (UR). Then Pavlov rang a bell before presenting the meat powder.

The first time Pavlov rang the bell, the neutral stimulus, the dogs did not salivate, but once he put the meat powder in their mouths they began to salivate. After numerous pairings of the bell, and then food the dogs learned that the bell was a signal that the food was about to come and began to salivate just when the bell was rang. Once this occurs the bell becomes the conditioned stimulus (CS) and the salivation to the bell is the conditioned response (CR).

Another influential person in the world of Classical Conditioning is John B. Watson. Watson's work was very influential and paved the way for B. F. Skinner's radical behaviorism. Watson's behaviorism (and philosophy of science) stood in direct contrast to Freud. Watson's view was that Freud's introspective method was too subjective, and that we should limit the study of human development to directly observable behaviors.

In 1913, Watson published the article "Psychology as the Behaviorist Views," in which he argued that laboratory studies should serve psychology best as a science. Watson's most famous, and controversial, experiment, "Little Albert," where he demonstrated how psychologists can account for the learning of emotion through classical conditioning principles.

Imprinting

Imprinting is the term used in psychology and ethology to describe any kind of phase-sensitive learning (learning occurring at a particular age or a particular life stage) that is rapid and apparently independent of the consequences of behavior. It was first used to describe situations in which an animal or person learns the characteristics of some stimulus, which is therefore said to be "imprinted" onto the subject.

Observational Learning

The learning process most characteristic of humans is imitation; one's personal repetition of an observed behavior, such as a dance. Humans can copy three types of information simultaneously: the demonstrator's goals, actions, and environmental outcomes (results, see Emulation (observational learning)). Through copying these types of information, (most) infants will tune into their surrounding culture.

Play

Play generally describes behavior which has no particular end in itself, but improves performance in similar situations in the future. This is seen in a wide variety of vertebrates besides humans, but is mostly limited to mammals and birds. Cats are known to play with a ball of string when young, which gives them experience with catching prey. Besides inanimate objects, animals may play with other members of their own species or other animals, such as orcas playing with seals they have caught.

Play involves a significant cost to animals, such as increased vulnerability to predators and the risk of injury and possibly infection. It also consumes energy, so there must be significant benefits associated with play for it to have evolved. Play is generally seen in younger animals, suggesting a link with learning. However, it may also have other benefits not associated directly with learning, for example improving physical fitness.

Enculturation

Enculturation is the process by which a person learns the requirements of their native culture by which he or she is surrounded, and acquires values and behaviors that are appropriate or necessary in that culture. The influences which as part of this process limit, direct or shape the individual, whether deliberately or not, include parents, other adults, and peers.

If successful, enculturation results in competence in the language, values and rituals of the culture. (compare acculturation, where a person is within a culture different to their normal culture, and learns the requirements of this different culture).

Multimedia Learning

Multimedia learning is where a person uses both auditory and visual stimuli to learn information (Mayer 2001). This type of learning relies on dual-coding theory (Paivio 1971).

E-learning and Augmented Learning

Electronic learning or e-learning is a general term used to refer to Internet-based networked computer-enhanced learning. A specific and always more diffused e-learning is mobile learning (m-learning), which uses different mobile telecommunication equipment, such as cellular phones.

When a learner interacts with the e-learning environment, it's called augmented learning. By adapting to the needs of individuals, the context-driven instruction can be dynamically tailored to the learner's natural environment.

Augmented digital content may include text, images, video, audio (music and voice). By personalizing instruction, augmented learning has been shown to improve learning performance for a lifetime.

Rote Learning

Rote learning is a technique which avoids understanding the inner complexities and inferences of the subject that is being learned and instead focuses on memorizing the material so that it can be recalled by the learner exactly the way it was read or heard.

The major practice involved in rote learning techniques is *learning by repetition*, based on the idea that one will be able to quickly recall the meaning of the material the more it is repeated. Rote learning is used in diverse areas, from mathematics to music to religion. Although it has been criticized by some schools of thought, rote learning is a necessity in many situations.

Informal Learning

Informal learning occurs through the experience of day-to-day situations (for example, one would learn to look ahead while walking because of the danger inherent in not paying attention to where one is going). It is learning from life, during a meal at table with parents, play, exploring, etc.

Formal Learning

Formal learning is learning that takes place within a teacher-student relationship, such as in a school system.

Non-formal Learning

Non-formal learning is organized learning outside the formal learning system. For example: learning by coming together with people with similar interests and exchanging viewpoints, in clubs or in (international) youth organizations, workshops.

Non-formal Learning and Combined Approaches

The educational system may use a combination of formal, informal, and nonformal learning methods. The UN and EU recognize these different forms of learning (cf. links below). In some schools students can get points that count in the formal-learning systems if they get work done in informal-learning circuits.

They may be given time to assist international youth workshops and training courses, on the condition they prepare, contribute, share and can proof this offered valuable new insight, helped to acquire new skills, a place to get experience in organizing, teaching, etc.

In order to learn a skill, such as solving a Rubik's cube quickly, several factors come into play at once:

- Directions help one learn the patterns of solving a Rubik's cube.
- Practicing the moves repeatedly and for extended time helps with "muscle memory" and therefore speed.
- Thinking critically about moves helps find shortcuts, which in turn helps to speed up future attempts.
- The Rubik's cube's six colors help anchor solving it within the head.
- Occasionally revisiting the cube helps prevent negative learning or loss of skill.

Tangential Learning

Tangential learning is the process by which some portion of people will self-educate if a topic is exposed to them in something that they already enjoy such as playing a musical instrument.

Dialogic Learning

Dialogic learning is a type of learning based on dialogue.

Domains of Learning

Benjamin Bloom has suggested three domains of learning:

- Cognitive – To recall, calculate, discuss, analyze, problem solve, etc.
- Psychomotor – To dance, swim, ski, dive, drive a car, ride a bike, etc.
- Affective – To like something or someone, love, appreciate, fear, hate, worship, etc.

These domains are not mutually exclusive. For example, in learning to play chess, the person will have to learn the rules of the game (cognitive domain); but he also has to learn how to set up the chess pieces on the chessboard and also how to properly hold and move a chess piece (psychomotor). Furthermore, later in the game the person may even learn to love the game itself, value its applications in life, and appreciate its history (affective domain).

New Literacies

New literacies generally refers to new forms of literacy made possible by digital technology developments, although new literacies do not necessarily have to involve use of digital technologies to be recognized as such. The term "new literacies" itself is relatively new within the field of literacy studies (the first documented mention of it in an academic article title dates to 1993 in a text by David Buckingham). Its definition remains open, with new literacies being conceptualized in different ways by different groups of scholars.

Accompanying the varying conceptualizations of new literacies, we find a range of terms used by different researchers when referring to new literacies, including *21st century literacies*, *internet literacies*, *digital literacies*, *new media literacies*, *multiliteracies*, *information literacy*, *ICT literacies*, and *computer literacy*. In the *Handbook of New Literacies Research*, Coiro, Knobel, Lankshear, and Leu (2008) note that all these terms "are used to refer to phenomena we would see as falling broadly under a new literacies umbrella" (pg. 10).

Commonly recognized examples of new literacies include such practices as instant messaging, blogging, maintaining a website, participating in online social networking spaces, creating and sharing music videos, podcasting and videocasting, photoshopping images and photo sharing, emailing, shopping online, digital storytelling, participating in online discussion lists, emailing and using online chat, conducting and collating online searches, reading, writing and commenting on fan fiction, processing and evaluating online information, creating and sharing digital mashups, etc.

The field of new literacies studies is characterized by two theoretically distinct approaches that overlap to some extent. One is informed by cognitive and language processing theories such as cognitive psychology, psycholinguistics, schema theory, metacognition, constructivism, and other similar theories. This orientation includes a particular focus on examining the cognitive and decoding processes involved in comprehending online or digital texts.

Donald Leu, a prominent researcher in the field of new literacies, has outlined four defining characteristics of new literacies, according to a largely psycholinguistic orientation. First, new technologies (such as the internet) and the novel literacy tasks that pertain to these new technologies require new skills and strategies to effectively use them. Second, new literacies are a critical component of full participation—civic, economic, and personal—in our increasingly global society. A third component to this approach is new literacies are *deictic*—that is, they change regularly as new technology emerges and older technologies fade away.

With this in mind, "what may be important in reading instruction and literacy education is not to teach any single set of new literacies, but rather to teach students how to learn continuously new literacies that will appear during their lifetime." Finally, new literacies are "multiple, multimodal, and multifaceted," and as such, multiple points of view will be most beneficial in attempting to comprehensively analyze them.

The second approach to studying new literacies is overtly grounded in a focus on social practices. According to Colin Lankshear and Michele Knobel from this "social practice" perspectives, "new literacies" can refer to "new socially recognized ways of generating, communicating and negotiating meaningful content through the medium of encoded texts within contexts of participation in Discourses (or, as members of Discourses) ". From this perspective "new" refers to the presence of two dominant features of contemporary literacy practices. The first is the use of digital technologies as the means of producing, sharing, accessing and interacting with meaningful content.

New literacies typically involve screens and pixels rather than paper and type, and digital code (that renders texts as image, sound, conventional text, and any combination of these within a single process) rather than material print. The second defining feature of new literacies is their highly collaborative, distributed, and participatory nature, as expressions of what Henry Jenkins calls engagement in participatory culture, and Lankshear and Knobel refer to as a distinctive *ethos*.

RESEARCH IN NEW LITERACIES

Research within the field of new literacies is also diverse. A wide range of topics and issues are focused upon, and a broad range of methodologies are used.

Reading and Online Comprehension

One aspect of new literacies that has attracted researchers' attention is school-age children's online reading comprehension. Specifically, researchers are interested in finding the answers to questions such as how reading online differs from traditional print-based reading. In their research, Donald Leu and Julie Coiro attempt to understand how students become adept at online reading, and how students acquire the necessary skills, strategies, and dispositions to comprehend online texts.

According to Leu and colleagues, the new literacies of online reading comprehension are based around five defining functions: "These new literacies allow us to use the Internet and other ICT to identify important questions, locate information, critically evaluate the usefulness of that information, synthesize information to answer those questions, and then communicate the answers to others"

Online Fan Fiction and Adolescents

Recent research in the field of new literacies has focused on fan fiction on the internet, especially those stories published online by adolescents. Online fan fiction websites, such as FanFiction.Net, are spaces where fans of all ages, but especially adolescents and younger school-age fans, are able to use these new information and communication technologies (ICTs) to write and craft fictional stories based on their favorite characters in popular media such as movies, television, and graphic novels. Adolescents are participating more and more on these kinds of sites, not only engaging with "pop culture and media, but also with a broad array of literate activities that are aligned with many school-based literacy practices"

Of course, adults are just as able to spend time in such online environments—and they do. However, it is interesting to consider that young people were born into a digitally rich world, and thus could be seen as "digital natives," and therefore interact with the online environment in a fundamentally distinct way than an older generation of people, so-called "digital immigrants."

As digital natives, adolescents "use the online world to share, evaluate, create, report and program with each other differently to digital immigrants," and they engage easily and readily with new digital technologies such as instant messaging, file sharing songs and videos, and post all kinds of 'texts,' stories, photos, and videos among them.

A central characteristic of digital natives is their "desire to create." Digital natives are engaged in "programming to some extent, whether it be by including a piece of HTML code that personalizes a MySpace page or creating a Flash animation. They are creating web pages, blogs, avatars and worlds; and, in stark contrast to digital immigrants, digital natives readily report and share their ideas."

Video Games

James Paul Gee described video gaming as a new literacy "in virtue of the ways game design involves a multimodal code comprising images, actions, words, sounds, and movements that players interpret according to gaming conventions". Gee notes that game players participate in their game's world as a form of social practice, especially in real-time strategy games in which players can compete with each other to build on land masses, for instance, and in which they can shape and convey their virtual identities as a certain kind of strategist. Video games continue to use new digital technologies to create the symbols players interpret to encode and decode the meanings that constitute the game.

Other researchers have expanded the body of knowledge about video games as a new literacy, particularly as they relate to classroom learning. In one study, researchers examined how video games, supported by discussions and dramatic performances in the classroom, can contribute to the development of narrative thought as demonstrated in written compositions in various contexts.

Namely, the researchers engaged primary school children in activities designed to teach them to tell, play out, and write stories based on the most popular video game in their classroom, *Tomb Raider*. Although it was a challenging process at times, researchers discovered that the use of new digital media such as video games actually "complements the use of other written or audiovisual methods [in the classroom] and permits the development of multiple literacies in the classroom."

New Literacies and the Classroom

It has become clear to many researchers in the field that we need to better understand new literacies so that we can answer one critical question: How can educators best incorporate new literacies into the classroom? Kist (2007) observes that in the literature, there are examples of how new literacies can be used in classroom settings—from the use of rap music to anime to digital storytelling, there are already instances of teachers attempting to blend new literacies with traditional literacy practices in the classroom. Kist asks: "Can new literacies indeed 'fit' into how we currently 'do' school?" Kist notes that "the new literacies instruction that does exist often comes only out of the fortitude of lonely pioneers of new literacies."

Knobel and Lankshear (2006) argue that if educators and prospective teachers engage in blogging, or participate in "affinity spaces" devoted to practices like fan fiction, video game-playing, music and video remixing, photosharing, and the like, they will better understand how new literacies can better be integrated into worthwhile classroom learning.

Leu, Coiro, Castek, Hartman, Henry, & Reinking (2008) have begun to explore the use of a modified instructional model of reciprocal teaching that reflects some of the differences between offline and online reading contexts. In an instructional model known as Internet Reciprocal Teaching, each student has his/her own laptop with access to the Internet and students work in small groups to facilitate interactive group work and discussions about strategy use.

In addition, Internet Reciprocal Teaching with online informational resources (as opposed to narrative texts) and strategy instruction on both the common and unique processes by which students navigate through multiple and different texts, rather than the reading of one common text. Teachers and students model their choices about which links are most relevant to a group or individual question through think-alouds.

They discuss how to efficiently locate information within different kinds of websites, how to synthesize ideas across multiple texts and media, how to make judgments about the quality of the information and the author's level of expertise, and how to best represent the answers to their questions.

Responsibility for monitoring and effectively using these strategies to solve online information problems is gradually released to the students using an instructional scheme with three phases: Phase 1 includes direct, whole class instruction of basic skills and strategies of Internet use; Phase 2 includes group work and the reciprocal exchange of online reading comprehension strategies by students with their peers; and Phase 3 includes online individual inquiry units, sometimes with collaborative efforts involving other students in other classes, perhaps even in other parts of the world, and periodic strategy sessions with groups.

2

THEORISTS AND EDUCATIONAL TECHNOLOGISTS

An educational technologist is someone who is trained in the field of educational technology. Educational technologists try to analyze, design, develop, implement and evaluate process and tools for to enhance learning.

LYNDA WILLIAMS

Lynda Williams (born February 17, 1958) is a science fiction author, blogger and an educational technologist. Williams' fiction is centered around a series of ten novels set in the fictional Okal Rel Universe and published by Edge Science Fiction and Fantasy Publishing. Additional works by Williams and votary authors writing in her universe are published by the Absolute XPress imprint of Hades Publications, Inc. She is the founder of the online journal Reflections on Water. Williams lives in Quesnel, British Columbia where she is an Administrator at the College of New Caledonia.

NED KOCK

Ned Kock is best known for employing biological evolution ideas to the understanding of human behavior toward technologies, particularly information technologies. He developed media naturalness theory, an evolutionary communication media theory.

He has conducted research and written on the topic of academic plagiarism. His research and writings in this area have been discussed in The Chronicle of Higher Education, and contributed to considerable debate on the topic within the Association for Computing Machinery, and to the establishment of an ethics committee within the Association for Information Systems.

Kock has also been a proponent of the use of action research in the study of human behavior toward technologies, arguing that it can be used in investigations aimed at testing hypotheses in a postpositivist fashion. As a result of his action research investigations, he developed a method for systems analysis and business process redesign that places emphasis on the optimization of communication interactions in business processes.

He is a Professor of Information Systems at Texas A&M International University, and Founding Editor-in-Chief of the International Journal of e-Collaboration. He holds a B.E.E. in electronics engineering from the Federal Technological University of Parana at Curitiba, Brazil, a M.Sc. in computer science from the Institute of Aeronautical Technology, Brazil, and a Ph.D. in management with a concentration in information systems from the School of Management Studies, University of Waikato, New Zealand.

MURRAY GOLDBERG

Murray Goldberg (born October, 1962) is a noted educational technologist and a faculty member in the department of Computer Science at the University of British Columbia in Vancouver Canada. Goldberg is best known for being the founder of the e-learning companies WebCT, Silicon Chalk, and Brainify. Goldberg was born in Calgary, Alberta, Canada and raised in Edmonton until he moved to British Columbia to attend the University of Victoria in 1980. Murray graduated from UVic in 1985 and then went on to earn an MSc from the University of British Columbia.

Professional History

University of British Columbia

Murray began as a faculty member in the Department of Computer Science at UBC in 1993 and was awarded tenure there in 1998. In 1994, his first year as a faculty member at UBC, Goldberg won the Killiam Teaching Prize at UBC. Goldberg took a leave of absence from UBC in 1998 to lead WebCT full time.

WebCT

In 1995, as a UBC faculty member, Goldberg was researching the effectiveness of Web-Based learning environments. Golberg found that the experience of building the courses for this experimentation was sufficiently time consuming and expensive that he decided to create a platform to enable the simple and rapid creation of web-based learning environments, WebCT. WebCT was widely accepted as a catalyst in the world-wide boom of on-line learning that accelerated beginning in 1997. By November, 2000 WebCT was purportedly serving 6 million students in 57 countries, and by late 2001 10 million students in 80 countries at 2250 universities and colleges. In 1999, Goldberg sold most of his stake in WebCT to Boston-Based Universal Learning Technology. The combined company took on the WebCT name. Goldberg remained as president of the Canadian division of WebCT until 2002 when he left to co-found Silicon Chalk.

Silicon Chalk

In 2002 Goldberg co-founded Silicon Chalk and served as the president and CEO. Silicon Chalk created software for use in laptop or computer enabled higher education classrooms. The software facilitated the recording of classroom presentations, student note taking, polling, file sharing, and other features. The company never achieved wide spread success, though did have users in 70 universities and colleges when it was sold to Horizon Wimba

Brainify

In 2007 Goldberg began work on Brainify(website), an academic social bookmarking and networking site for university and college students and professors. Brainify was launched in January 2009 and Goldberg acts as the President and CEO. Members from 250 institutions had joined in the first 20 days since the launch.

Selected Awards and Distinctions

- 2004 - $100,000 National Manning Innovation Awards Principal Award for Innovation. This is a Canadian National award, awarded once per year for innovation in any human endeavor Award video can be found here.
- 2004 - Honorary Ph.D., Southern Cross University, Gold Coast, Australia
- 2001 - New Media Hyperion Award. This award for excellence is awarded annually to those who have made a significant contribution in the creation or development of software tools, hardware or connectivity innovations.
- 2000 - National CANARIE IWAY Award. This is awarded to nominees who have pioneered innovative uses of technology related to the development of Canada's information highway.
- 1994 - Killiam Teaching Prize. These prizes are awarded annually for excellence in teaching.

MICHAEL ALLEN

Dr. Michael Allen is a recognized leader in the architecture and design of interactive multimedia learning strategies and authoring tools. He has over 25 years of professional, academic, and corporate experience in the development, sales, and marketing of interactive learning and performance support systems. He has headed teams of doctorate level specialists in learning research, instructional design, computer-based training, and human engineering.

In recent years, he has concentrated on defining unique methods of instructional application design and development that provide meaningful and memorable learning experiences through "true" cognitive interactivity.

He was the primary architect of Authorware Professional, the founder, and former chairman of Authorware, Inc. (which merged with Macromind/Paracomp to form Macromedia, Inc.). He was a principal tools architect and designer of Control Data Corporation's famous PLATO computer-based education system used around the world. Dr. Allen has become widely respected for his abilities to define, design, and build tools which allow creative individuals to harness the potential of interactive multimedia technologies.

He is currently Chairman & CEO of Allen Interactions Inc., which builds custom interactive e learning applications and provides consulting and training for interactive multimedia professionals. Dr. Allen personally provides high level consulting for multimedia design and production groups who are looking to take greater advantage of interactive technologies. His clients include major public corporations and industry associations. He has been called upon by the press for individual interviews at Time, Fortune, Washington Post, US News and World Report, U.S.A. Today, (and many others) on the state and future of interactive educational simulations.

Dr. Allen was the founding editor of the Journal of Computer-Based Instruction, sponsored and published by the Association for the Development of Computer-based Instructional Systems (ADCIS). After many years of service in this position, he was named Editor Emeritus for the publication. He was elected president of the international ADCIS twice and has received many association awards and commendations. He is a frequently requested conference speaker at associations such the American Society of Training and Development (ASTD) and the e-Learning Guild, as well as the Corporate University Week.

In his first book, Michael Allen's Guide to e-Learning, Dr. Allen speaks out about his frustrations with e-learning and brings fundamental issues to light. Challenging both business leaders and instructional designers alike, he demonstrates that e-learning can be a powerful business solution that enables people to do "the right things at the right time." But this won't happen, he says, unless common practices in e-learning are aborted.

Creating Successful e-Learning: A Rapid System For Getting It Right First Time, Every Time was published in May 2006 and is the first book in Michael Allen e-Learning Library Series. The second book in the six volume series, Designing Successful e-Learning: Forget What You Know about Instructional Design and Do Something Interesting was published in May 2007. Michael Allen is also the editor of Michael Allen's 2008 e-Learning Annual, an essential source of guidance, opinions, and best practices on issues of interest and concern to e-learning professionals, which was published in February 2008.

Career Highlights

Allen Interactions Inc.

1993-Present Chairman & CEO

Allen Interactions is an innovator in the interactive multimedia industry. Founded by Dr. Michael Allen (creator of Authorware), Allen Interactions designs, develops and implements highly interactive educational simulations for the world's largest corporations. Through a proven process and skills born from experience, Allen Interactions delivers exciting interactive solutions that enhance knowledge, skills and performance.

Allen Interactions is one of the most successful and highly regarded providers of custom e-learning, training, and consulting, with studios in Minneapolis, Tampa, and San Francisco.

Lifetouch Learning

Dr. Allen joined Lifetouch as Executive Vice President in October 1992 when they purchased his company (MediaPros, Ltd.) and offered him the top position in the newly formed Lifetouch Learning corporation with a mission to become one of the top three companies providing multimedia education and training products and services for schools.

Dr. Allen headed the corporation and directed all its operations including technology and product development, sales, and marketing. After getting production costs and schedules under control, he upgraded the management team by bringing in key people in sales, marketing, project management, and programming. They finished the fiscal year with costs under budget and revenues over projections for the first time in the company's history. (Since Lifetouch is not public, numbers are held in confidence, but are in the millions.)

MediaPros, Ltd.

1992 Chairman & CEO

Dr. Allen was the principal co-founder of MediaPros, a spin-off of Authorware Inc.'s professional services division, which designed and developed interactive multimedia applications for Fortune 500 companies. Very shortly after being formed and securing a number of top clients, MediaPros was bought out by Lifetouch.

All employees of MediaPros Ltd. went to Lifetouch with Dr. Allen. MediaPros developed outstanding multimedia applications. Customers included Microsoft, British Petroleum, and Dahlberg (makers of Miracle Ear hearing devices).

Authorware, Inc.: A Short History

Start-up: Dr. Allen founded Authorware in 1984, incorporating it in 1985. He established an outstanding external professional team which included legal counsel, accounting, PR and advertising, and banking services all with experience in software ventures and a commitment to the company's success. After carrying the effort on personal financing for some time, he secured financial, technical, and marketing support from Apple Computer, a Japanese firm-Sundai Advanced Teaching Technologies, and private investors.

His developing products won "Best Designed Product Award-Software Category" at COMTEC '87 held in Singapore and released versions have won nearly all of the industry's top awards. Version 1.0 of the e-learning authoring product line began shipping in January 1988, a small network of Value Added Resellers was built, and advertising was placed in major periodicals.

Funding: In July 1988, Dr. Allen secured major financial capitalization from three leading groups of venture capitalists: Investment Advisors Inc., Don Lucas

Associates (Sand Hill Financial Group), and Vanguard Associates.

Product Design: As the visionary for Authorware, Inc., Dr. Allen led the design of Authorware products from feature specifications to human interface. Authorware Professional was based on his extensive research on creativity and creative problem-solving resulting in a ground-breaking product of both power and ease of use. It won many awards and praises, such as "The Premier Object-Oriented Multimedia Authoring System" (Macworld). It has held, by far, the dominant market share (Dataquest) for over a decade.

SELECTED PROFESSIONAL POSITIONS/ACTIVITIES

- 2007 to present: Board of Directors, Preventive Medicine, LLC
- 2007: Named among "top 20 most influential training professionals" by Training Industry, Inc.
- 2006: Adjunct Associate Professor, Division of Epidemiology and Community Health, School of Public Health, The University of Minnesota
- 2004-present: Curriculum Author and Faculty Member, ASTD Professional Certificate Programs
- 2002-2005: Advisory Board, VNU Online Learning conferences
- 1994-1996: Adjunct Professor, Graduate Programs in Software Engineering, St. Thomas University
- 1993: Distinguished Lecturer, Utah State University
- 1993-1997: Corporate Advisory Board, Macromedia, Inc.
- 1994-2000: Director, Double Impact, Inc.
- 1991-2002: Director, International Institute for Effective Communications
- 1985-1992: Founder and Chairman, Authorware, Inc.
- 1985-1989: Editorial Board, Education & Computing, North Holland
- 1986: Information Resources Advisory Council, The University of Maryland
- 1983-1986: Faculty Fellow in Educational Computing, Curricular and Instructional Systems Graduate Degree Program, The University of Minnesota
- 1983-1984: Advisory Board, National Demonstration Center for Technology in Medical Education, Lister Hill Center, National Library of Medicine
- 1982-1983: Re-elected President, Association for the Development of Computer-Based Instructional Systems
- 1980-1981: President, Association for the Development of Computer-Based Instructional Systems
- 1974-present: Editorial Board, Journal of Computer-Based Instruction, ADCIS
- 1974-1978: Founding Editor, Journal of Computer-Based Instruction, ADCIS

STEPHEN MOLYNEUX

Steve Molyneux, (born Walton, Liverpool, 24 February, 1955) is a British educational technologist and Apple Distinguished Educator. His recent fame results from him resigning as a Justice of the Peace on 25 April 2009 due to an issue over his use of Twitter in reporting the outcome of public case hearings.

In 1995, whilst holding the Microsoft Chair of Advanced Learning Technologies at the University of Wolverhampton, he developed one of the first Virtual Learning Environments.

In 1996, as a British Association for the Advancement of Science (now the British Science Association) media fellow, he developed with Ed Briffa, Editor of the BBC Science programme Tomorrow's World, one of the first real-time online science magazines. The magazine was set up to report live from the Annual Festival of Science held at University of Birmingham and reporters included Vivienne Parry, Philippa Forrester and Craig Doyle.

In 2002 he was appointed by Estelle Morris, the then Secretary of Education as a member of the Post-16 eLearning Strategy Taskforce. The taskforce was chaired by Steve Morrison, CEO of ITV. The report was published in July 2002 under the title "Getting on with IT".

In 2005 he was appointed advisor to the UK Deputy Chief of Defence Staff to monitor the evaluation of a Defence Training Review initiative.

He is a patron of Shropshire Young Enterprise and from 2003-2006 was Mayor of Oakengates where he currently resides. He broadcasts occasionally on BBC Radio Shropshire Morning Show on issues relating to technology and in October 2009 was elected to the West Midlands regional committee of the British Science Association.

WILL RICHARDSON

Will Richardson is the author of the highly ranked and read edublog Weblogged and author of the book, Blogs, Wikis, Pod casts, and other Powerful Web Tools for Classrooms. Formerly a teacher at Hunterdon Central Regional High School in Flemington, N.J, Will was recognized for his use of blogs in the classroom as a "trendsetter in education" by the New York Times.

Richardson is now an independent presenter and owner of Connective Learning, LLC. He promotes the implementation of Read/Write technologies in K-12 classrooms. He is also an advocate for school reform which encourages the integration of technology in learning. He was also recently named to the National Advisory Board for the George Lucas Education Foundation. Along with Sheryl Nussbaum-Beach, he is co-owner of Powerful Learning Practice, a company that delivers job-embedded, year-long professional development to schools worldwide around the pedagogies of Web 2.0 tools.

District Administration magazine publishes a column by Richardson, who also contributes to their blog, The Pulse.

Richardson has been part of a panel presentation at the 2006 Milken Global Conference and has given presentations all over the world.

DAVID A. WILEY

David A. Wiley, is currently Associate Professor of Instructional Psychology & Technology at Brigham Young University. He is also Chief Openness Officer of Flat World Knowledge and Founder of the Open High School of Utah. He was previously Associate Professor of Instructional Technology, and was also the Founder and Director of the Center for Open and Sustainable Learning, (COSL), at Utah State University. He is best known for having coined the term Open Content and creating the first open source-style license for non-software. His work on open content, open education, and informal online learning communities has been reported in many international outlets, including the New York Times, the London Financial Times, The Hindu, The Globe and Mail, The Economist, MIT Technology Review, and WIRED. Wiley is also a member of the Advisory Committee of University of the People, tuition free online University]

He has received the National Science Foundation's CAREER award and served as a Nonresident Fellow of the Center for Internet and Society at Stanford Law School, served as the Chair of the NSF's National Science Digital Library's (NSDL) Standards Committee, presented at AERA, AECT, Internet2, WebNet and recently at the 6th IEEE International Conference on Advanced Learning Technologies (ICALT).

Wiley earned his Ph. D., in Instructional Psychology and Technology, from Brigham Young University in 2000 and a BFA in vocal performance from Marshall University in Music in 1997. He has expressed personal interests in, among other things, superstring theory, Japanese music, world religions, and musical theater.

Reusability and Learning Objects

Much of Wiley's work has focused on the development of learning objects. On one website, reusability.org, he explains that learning objects , are developed to be reused as a solution to the problem of "teacher bandwidth". The "teacher bandwidth" problem is defined as "the number of students we are capable of serving with our distance education offerings". Fast Company Magazine rated Wiley #78 in a list of the top 100 creative people for 2009.

Works

A list (last updated in 2004) of Wiley's publications is available on his blog at His work includes:

- Conversations About Learning Objects: The Instructional Use of Learning Objects, available online in its entirety.
- OSOSS (Online Self-Organizing Social Systems) - Crisis / Response.
- Learning objects: difficulties and opportunities.

- Online self-organizing social systems: The decentralized future of online learning. Quarterly Review of Distance Education. (With Erin Brewer).
- Learning objects need instructional design theory. In A. Rossett (Ed.) The 2001/2002 ASTD Distance Learning Yearbook. New York: McGraw-Hill.
- Learning objects - a definition. In A. Kovalchick & K. Dawson (Eds.) Educational Technology: An Encyclopedia. Santa Barbara: ABC-CLIO.
- The Instructional Architect: A System for Discovering, Recommending, and Using Learning

Objects

- Another hypermedia biography on David Wiley, done as an assignment this semester (Fall 2006) by a student in David Wiley's Foundations of Instructional Technology course.

ALAN NOVEMBER

Alan November is an American educator and educational consultant. He currently lives in Marblehead, Massachusetts. Alan November is notable in that he is believed to be the first major educator to embrace modern web technologies commonly referred to as Web 2.0 in elementary, middle, and high schools. Alan was one of the initial five Christa McAuliffe Educators, co-founded the Institute for education leadership and technology at Stanford, and is the author of Empowering Students with Technology.

He runs November Learning educational consulting as well as the educational blogging software NLCommunities. His annual summer conference Building Learning Communities is very popular.

Mr. November was educated at Marblehead High School, Marblehead, Mass and the University of Massachusetts and Harvard University and the University of Edinburgh.

JOHN SWELLER

John Sweller is an Australian educational psychologist who is best known for formulating an influential theory of cognitive load. He has a Ph.D. from the University of Adelaide's Department of Psychology - his thesis was titled "Effects of initial discrimination training on subsequent shift learning in animals and humans" - and also has a B.A. (Hons.) from the same institution.

He has authored over 80 academic publications, mainly reporting research on cognitive factors in instructional design, with specific emphasis on the instructional implications of working memory limitations and their consequences for instructional procedures.

Sweller is a Fellow of the ASSA (Academy of the Social Sciences in Australia), and is currently Professor Emeritus at the University of New South Wales.

SEYMOUR PAPERT

Seymour Papert (born February 29, 1928 in Pretoria, South Africa) is an MIT mathematician, computer scientist, and educator. He is one of the pioneers of artificial intelligence, as well as an inventor of the Logo programming language.

Early Years and Education

Papert attended the University of Witwatersrand, receiving a B.A. in 1949 and a Ph.D. in mathematics in 1952. He then went on to receive another Ph.D., also in mathematics, at Cambridge University in 1959. He was a leading figure in the revolutionary socialist circle around Socialist Review while living in London in the 1950s.

Career

Papert worked as a researcher in a variety of places, including St. John's College, Cambridge, the Henri Poincare Institute at the University of Paris, the University of Geneva and the National Physical Laboratory in London before becoming a research associate at MIT in 1963. He held this position until 1967, when he became professor of applied math and director of the MIT Artificial Intelligence Laboratory, until 1981; he also served as Cecil & Ida Green professor of education at MIT from 1974-1981.

Research and Theories

Papert worked on learning theories, and is known for focusing on the impact of new technologies on learning in general and in schools as learning organizations in particular.

Constructionism

At MIT, Papert went on to create the Epistemology and Learning Research Group at the MIT Architecture Machine Group. Here, he was the developer of an original and highly influential theory on learning called constructionism, built upon the work of Jean Piaget in Constructivism learning theories. Papert worked with Jean Piaget during the 1960s and is widely considered the most brilliant and successful of Piaget's proteges; Piaget once said that "no one understands my ideas as well as Papert." Papert has rethought how schools should work based on these theories of learning.

Logo

Papert used Piaget's work in his development of the Logo programming language whilst at MIT. He created Logo as a tool to improve the way that children think and solve the problems. A small robot called the "Logo Turtle" was developed and children used it to solve problems. A main purpose of the Logo Foundation research group is to strengthen the ability to learn knowledge. Papert insists a simple language or program that children can learn-like Logo-can also have advanced functionality for expert users.

Other work

As part of his work with technology, Papert has been a proponent of the Knowledge Machine. He is also currently one of the principals for the One Laptop Per Child initiative to manufacture and distribute The Children's Machine in developing nations.

Influence and Awards

Papert's work has been highly influential to other researchers in the fields of education and computer science. He influenced the work of Uri Wilensky in the design of NetLogo and collaborated with him on the study of knowledge restructurations, as well as the work of Andrea diSessa and the development of dynaturtles. In 1981, Papert along with several others in the Logo group at MIT, started Logo Computer Systems Inc., of which he was Board Chair for over 20 years. Working with LCSI, Papert designed a number of award-winning programs, including LogoWriter and Lego/Logo (marketed as Lego Mindstorms). He also influenced the research of Idit Harel Caperton, coauthoring articles and the book Constructionism and chairing the advisory board of the company MaMaMedia. He also influenced Alan Kay and the Dynabook concept, and worked with Kay on various projects.

Papert won a Guggenheim fellowship in 1980, a Marconi International fellowship in 1981, the Software Publishers Association Lifetime Achievement Award in 1994, and the Smithsonian Award from Computerworld in 1997. Papert has been called by Marvin Minsky "the greatest living mathematics educator."

3

Learning

A learning management system (LMS) is a software application for the administration, documentation, tracking, and reporting of training programs, classroom and online events, e-learning programs, and training content. A robust LMS should be able to do the following:

- centralize and automate administration
- use self-service and self-guided services
- assemble and deliver learning content rapidly
- consolidate training initiatives on a scalable web-based platform
- support portability and standards
- personalize content and enable knowledge reuse.

LMSs range from systems for managing training and educational records, to software for distributing courses over the Internet with features for online collaboration. Corporate training use LMSs to automate record-keeping and employee registration. Student self-service (e.g., self-registration on instructor-led training), training workflow (e.g., user notification, manager approval, wait-list management), the provision of on-line learning (e.g., computer-based training, read & understand), on-line assessment, management of continuous professional education (CPE), collaborative learning (e.g., application sharing, discussion threads), and training resource management (e.g., instructors, facilities, equipment), are dimensions to Learning Management Systems.

Some LMSs are Web-based to facilitate access to learning content and administration. LMSs are used by regulated industries (e.g. financial services and biopharma) for compliance training. They are also used by educational institutions to enhance and support classroom teaching and offering courses to a larger population of learners across the globe.

Some LMS providers include "performance management systems", which encompass employee appraisals, competency management, skills-gap analysis, succession planning, and multi-rater assessments (i.e., 360 degree reviews). Modern techniques now employ competency-based learning to discover learning gaps and guide training material selection.

For the commercial market, some Learning and Performance Management Systems include recruitment and reward functionality.

LMSs cater to educational, administrative, and deployment requirements. While an LMS for corporate learning, for example, may share many characteristics with a VLE, or virtual learning environment, used by educational institutions, they each meet unique needs. The virtual learning environment used by universities and colleges allow instructors to manage their courses and exchange information with students for a course that in most cases will last several weeks and will meet several times during those weeks. In the corporate setting a course may be much shorter in length, completed in a single instructor-led event or online session.

The characteristics shared by both types of LMSs include:

- Manage users, roles, courses, instructors, facilities, and generate reports
- Course calendar
- Learning Path
- Student messaging and notifications
- Assessment and testing handling before and after testing
- Display scores and transcripts
- Grading of coursework and roster processing, including wait listing
- Web-based or blended course delivery

Characteristics more specific to corporate learning, which sometimes includes franchisees or other business partners, include:

- Auto enrollment (enrolling Students in courses when required according to predefined criteria, such as job title or work location)
- Manager enrollment and approval
- Boolean definitions for prerequisites or equivalencies
- Integration with performance tracking and management systems
- Planning tools to identify skill gaps at departmental and individual level
- Curriculum, required and elective training requirements at an individual and organizational level
- Grouping students according to demographic units (geographic region, product line, business size, etc.)
- Assign corporate and partner employees to more than one job title at more than one demographic unit

Learning content management system (LCMS)

A learning content management system (LCMS) is a related technology to the learning management system in that it is focused on the development, management and publishing of the content that will typically be delivered via an LMS. An LCMS is a multi-user environment where developers may create, store, reuse, manage, and deliver digital learning content from a central object repository. The LMS cannot create and manipulate courses; it cannot reuse the content of one course to build another. The LCMS, however, can create, manage and deliver not only training modules but also manage and edit all the individual pieces that make up a catalog of training. LCMS applications allow users to create, import, manage, search for and reuse small units or "chunks" of digital learning content and assets, commonly referred to as learning objects. These assets may include media files developed in other authoring tools, assessment items, simulations, text, graphics or any other object that makes up the content within the course being created. An LCMS manages the process of creating, editing, storing and delivering e-learning content, ILT materials and other training support deliverables such as job aids.

LCMS have the ability to assemble and consolidate learning objects into lengthier "learning paths" or learning experiences that are personalized to a learner's profile, job description, assessment results, or requests.

By separating content, style, and flow, and integrating extensibility, an extended Learning Content Management System allows courseware authors to leverage their learning content and present it in countless different ways for a wide variety of target platforms and in a remarkably short timeframe.

Drawbacks to Learning Management Systems

Certain learning tasks are well suited for an LMS (centralized functions like learner administration and content management). Learning itself is different - it is not a process to be managed. Learning is by nature multi-faceted and chaotic. Organizations that now lock into enterprise-level systems will be able to do an excellent job of delivering courses. They won't, however, be positioning themselves well for informal learning, performance support, or knowledge management. The concept is simple: one tool can't do it all without losing functionality. The more feature-rich an individual tool becomes, the more it loses its usefulness to the average user. Connected specialization, modularization, and decentralization are learning foundations capable of adjusting to varied information climate changes.

Learning management systems compared to learning content management systems

Some systems have tools to deliver and manage instructor-led synchronous and asynchronous online training based on learning object methodology. These systems are called learning content management systems or LCMSs. LCMSs provide tools for authoring and reusing or re-purposing content (mutated learning objects, or MLOs) as well as virtual spaces for student interaction (such as discussion forums, live chat rooms and live web-conferences). Despite this distinction, the term LMS is often used to refer to both an LMS and an LCMS, although the LCMS is a further development of the LMS. Due to this conformity issue, the acronym CLCIMS (Computer Learning Content Information Management System) is now widely used to create a uniform phonetic way of referencing any learning system software based on advanced learning technology methodology.

In essence, an LMS is software for planning, delivering, and managing learning events within an organization, including online, virtual classroom, and instructor-led courses. For example, an LMS can simplify global certification efforts, enable entities to align learning initiatives with strategic goals, and provide a means of enterprise-level skills management. The focus of an LMS is to manage students, keeping track of their progress and performance across all types of training activities. It performs administrative tasks, such as reporting to instructors, HR and other ERP systems but isn't used to create course content.

By contrast, an LCMS is software for managing learning content across an organization's various training development areas. It provides developers, authors, instructional designers, and subject matter experts the means to create and re-use e-learning content and reduce duplicated development efforts. In the remote AICC hosting approach, an LCMS may host the content in a central repository and allow multiple LMSs to access it.

Primary business problems an LCMS solves are

- centralized management of an organization's learning content for efficient searching and retrieval,
- productivity gains around rapid and condensed development timelines,
- productivity gains around assembly, maintenance and publishing / branding / delivery of learning content.

Criticism of LMS is that it is not content centric. In this sense, the technology is used for organizational control rather than the empowerment of the learner. The platform is usually poor in its content, and is part of a hierarchical bureaucratic (Max Weber) rather than socially oriented system. A/R/D/T is a term referring to its implementation in complex organizations sometimes replacing regular web sites.

Rather than developing entire courses and adapting them to multiple audiences, an LCMS provides the ability for single course instances to be modified and republished for various audiences maintaining versions and history. The objects stored in the centralized repository can be made available to course developers and content experts throughout an organization for potential reuse and repurpose. This eliminates duplicate development efforts and allows for the rapid assembly of customized content.

To look at this another way, an LMS is learner?centric. It focuses on e-learning process management and content delivery. In essence, an LMS is software for planning, delivering and managing learning events within an organization, including online, virtual classroom, and instructor-led courses. For example, an LMS can simplify global certification efforts, enable entities to align learning initiatives with strategic goals and provide a means for enterprise-level skills management. The focus of an LMS is to manage students, keeping track of their progress and performance across all types of training activities. It performs administrative tasks, such as reporting to instructors, HR and other ERP systems but it isn't used to create course content.

An LCMS is content-centric. Here, the focus is on the authoring and management of e-learning reusable content.

By contrast, LCMS solutions are ideally suited to create content-centric learning strategies, supporting multiple methods for gathering and organizing content, leveraging content for multiple purposes, and operation for mission critical purposes. LCMS technology can either be used in tandem with an LMS, or as a standalone application for learning initiatives that require rapid development and distribution of learning content.

Rather than developing entire courses and adapting them to multiple audiences, an LCMS is designed for managing learning content across an organization's various training development areas. It provides developers, authors, instructional designers, and subject matter experts the means to create and re-use e-learning content and reduce duplicated development efforts. An LCMS provides the ability for single course instances to be modified and republished for various audiences maintaining versions and history. The objects stored in the centralized repository can be made available to course developers and content experts throughout an organization for potential reuse and repurpose. This allows for the rapid assembly of customized content.

In addition, Brandon Hall believes that:

when LCMS technology is appropriately applied and matched to an orchestrated e-learning strategy, with a complete instructional design plan for designing and using learning objects, great efficiencies can and will be achieved, such as:

- The ability to make instantaneous, company-wide changes to critical learning content
- Rapid and productive content development efforts
- Seamless collaboration among subject matter experts and course designers
- The ability to create multiple, derivative versions of content applicable to different audiences from senior management to line-level workers
- Access to find and reuse learning content, 'just-in-time' and 'just enough'
- Ultimate reusability of content by making it available through a wide array of output types such as structured e-learning courses, CD-ROM courses, learning material available from a Palm device or PocketPC, print-based learning for use in classroom settings, and so on.

Technical aspects

Most LMSs are web-based, built using a variety of development platforms, like Java/J2EE, Microsoft .NET or PHP. They usually employ the use of a database like MySQL, Microsoft SQL Server or Oracle as back-end. Although most of the systems are commercially developed and have commercial software licenses there are several systems that have an open-source license.

Learning management industry

In the relatively new LMS market, commercial vendors for corporate and education applications range from new entrants to those that entered the market in the nineties. In addition to commercial packages, many open source solutions are available, including Moodle, Sakai Project and LRN.

LMSs represent an $860 million market, made up of more than 60 different providers. The six largest LMS product companies constitute approximately 50% of the market. In addition to the remaining smaller LMS product vendors, training outsourcing firms, enterprise resource planning vendors, and consulting firms all compete for part of the learning management market. Approximately 40 percent of US training organizations reported that they have an LMS installed, a figure that has not changed significantly over the past two years. The small business market offers the greatest opportunity for growth, as only 36 percent of these companies are using an LMS. Many of these businesses would like a low-cost, easy-to-use, easy-to-maintain system - but, as yet, they are not willing to make the commitment. An LMS is still a nontrivial investment in money and resources.

According to a 2009 report by American Society for Training and Development (ASTD) 91 percent of ASTD respondents are using LMSs in their organizations, with more than half purchasing rather than building their systems, and one-fifth of respondents opting to go with a hosted platform. And whether built or bought, the majority of respondents are satisfied with their current LMS, with 22.2 percent very satisfied, 31.1 percent satisfied, and 25.6 percent somewhat satisfied. Still, some 13.3 said they were unsatisfied, and 8.8 said they were very unsatisfied.

Most buyers of LMSs utilize an authoring tool to create their e-learning content, which is then hosted on an LMS. In many cases LMSs include a primitive authoring tool for basic content manipulation. For advanced content creation buyers must choose an authoring software that integrates with their LMS in order for their content to be hosted. There are authoring tools on the market, which meet AICC and SCORM standards and therefore content created in tools such as these can be hosted on an AICC or SCORM certified LMS. By May 2010, ADL had validated 301 SCORM-certified products while 329 products were compliant.

Evaluation of LMSs is a complex task and significant research supports different forms of evaluation, including iterative processess where students' experiences and approaches to learning are evaluated.

Trends

Another upcoming trend in this technology is 'Channel Learning' where organizations are sharing online contents and learning from their partner firms. According to a survey by trainingindustry.com, for many buyers channel learning is not their number one priority, but often there is a gap when the HR department oversees training and development initiatives, where the focus is consolidated inside traditional corporate boundaries. Software technology companies are at the front end of this curve, placing higher priority on channel trainings.

Today the biggest trend in the e-learning market is for these systems to be integrated with 'Talent Management Systems'. A talent management software serves towards the process of recruiting, managing, assessing, developing and maintaining an organization's most important resources. Bersin research shows that in 2009 more than 70 percent of large companies have an LMS already and almost one third of these companies are considering replacing or upgrading these systems with integrated talent management systems.

A growing trend in today's market is the ability for publishers to sell training/ courses on their site with syndicated training. Syndicated training courses are hosted by a third party learning management system. This allows publishers to sell their courses via a turn key syndication process . The rise and popularity of social media has allowed many content/course creators to syndicate content on their own sites.

Learning Object

A learning object is "a collection of content items, practice items, and assessment items that are combined based on a single learning objective". The term is credited to Wayne Hodgins when he created a working group in 1994 bearing the name though the concept was first described by Gerard in 1967. Learning objects go by many names, including content objects, chunks, educational objects, information objects, intelligent objects, knowledge bits, knowledge objects, learning components, media objects, reusable curriculum components, nuggets, reusable information objects, reusable learning objects, testable reusable units of cognition, training components, and units of learning.

Learning objects offer a new conceptualization of the learning process: rather than the traditional "several hour chunk", they provide smaller, self-contained, re-usable units of learning.

They will typically have a number of different components, which range from descriptive data to information about rights and educational level. At their core, however, will be instructional content, practice, and assessment. A key issue is the use of metadata.

Learning object design raises issues of portability, and of the object's relation to a broader learning management system.

The following is a list of some of the types of information that may be included in a learning object and its metadata:

- General Course Descriptive Data, including: course identifiers, language of content (English, Spanish, etc.), subject area (Maths, Reading, etc.), descriptive text, descriptive keywords
- Life Cycle, including: version, status
- Instructional Content, including: text, web pages, images, sound, video
- Glossary of Terms, including: terms, definition, acronyms
- Quizzes and Assessments, including: questions, answers
- Rights, including: cost, copyrights, restrictions on Use
- Relationships to Other Courses, including prerequisite courses
- Educational Level, including: grade level, age range, typical learning time, and difficulty. [IEEE 1484.12.1:2002]
- Typology as defined by Churchill (2007): presentation, practice, simulation, conceptual models, information, and contextual representation

Metadata

One of the key issues in using learning objects is their identification by search engines or content management systems. This is usually facilitated by assigning descriptive learning object metadata. Just as a book in a library has a record in the card catalog, learning objects must also be tagged with metadata. The most important pieces of metadata typically associated with a learning object include:

1. objective: The educational objective the learning object is instructing
2. prerequisites: The list of skills (typically represented as objectives) which the learner must know before viewing the learning object
3. topic: Typically represented in a taxonomy, the topic the learning object is instructing
4. interactivity: The Interaction Model of the learning object.
5. technology requirements: The required system requirements to view the learning object.

Mutability

A mutated learning object is, according to Michael Shaw, a learning object that has been "re-purposed and/or re-engineered, changed or simply re-used in some way different from its original intended design". Shaw also introduces the term "contextual learning object", to describe a learning object that has been "designed to have specific meaning and purpose to an intended learner".

Portability

Before any institution invests a great deal of time and energy into building high-quality e-learning content (which can cost over $10,000 per classroom hour), it needs to consider how this content can be easily loaded into a Learning Management System. It is possible for example, to package learning objects with SCORM specification and load it at Moodle Learning Management System.

If all of the properties of a course can be precisely defined in a common format, the content can be serialized into a standard format such asXML and loaded into other systems. When you consider that some e-learning courses need to include video, mathematical equations usingMathML, chemistry equations using CML and other complex structures the issues become very complex, especially if the systems needs to understand and validate each structure and then place it correctly in a database.

Instructional Design

Instructional Design (also called Instructional Systems Design (ISD)) is the practice of creating "instructional experiences which make the acquisition of knowledge and skill more efficient, effective, and appealing." The process consists broadly of determining the current state and needs of the learner, defining the end goal of instruction, and creating some "intervention" to assist in the transition. Ideally the process is informed by pedagogically (process of teaching) and andragogically (adult learning) tested theories of learning and may take place in student-only, teacher-led or community-based settings. The outcome of this instruction may be directly observable and scientifically measured or completely hidden and assumed. There are many instructional design models but many are based on the ADDIE model with the five phases: 1) analysis, 2) design, 3) development, 4) implementation, and 5) evaluation. As a field, instructional design is historically and traditionally rooted in cognitive and behavioral psychology, though recently Constructivism (learning theory) has influenced thinking in the field.

Learning design

The concept of learning design arrived in the literature of technology for education in the late nineties and early 2000s with the idea that "designers and instructors need to choose for themselves the best mixture of behaviourist and constructivist learning experiences for their online courses". But the concept of learning design is probably as old as the concept of teaching. Learning design might be defined as "the description of the teaching-learning process that takes place in a unit of learning (eg, a course, a lesson or any other designed learning event)".

As summarized by Britain, learning design may be associated with:

- The concept of learning design
- The implementation of the concept made by learning design specifications like PALO, IMS Learning Design, LDL, SLD 2.0, etc...
- The technical realisations around the implementation of the concept like TELOS, RELOAD LD-Author, etc...

Instructional design models

ADDIE process

Perhaps the most common model used for creating instructional materials is the ADDIE Model. This acronym stands for the 5 phases contained in the model:

- Analyze - analyze learner characteristics, task to be learned, etc.

Identify Instructional Goals, Conduct Instructional Analysis, Analyze Learners and Contexts

- Design - develop learning objectives, choose an instructional approach

Write Performance Objectives, Develop Assessment Instruments, Develop Instructional Strategy

- Develop - create instructional or training materials

Design and selection of materials appropriate for learning activity, Design and Conduct Formative Evaluation

- Implement - deliver or distribute the instructional materials
- Evaluate - make sure the materials achieved the desired goals

DESIGN AND CONDUCT SUMMATIVE EVALUATION

Most of the current instructional design models are variations of the ADDIE process. Dick,W.O,.Carey, L.,&Carey, J.O.(2004)Systematic Design of Instruction. Boston,MA:Allyn&Bacon.

Rapid prototyping

Sometimes utilized adaptation to the ADDIE model is in a practice known as rapid prototyping.

Proponents suggest that through an iterative process the verification of the design documents saves time and money by catching problems while they are still easy to fix. This approach is not novel to the design of instruction, but appears in many design-related domains including software design, architecture, transportation planning, product development, message design, user experience design, etc. In fact, some proponents of design prototyping assert that a sophisticated understanding of a problem is incomplete without creating and evaluating some type of prototype, regardless of the analysis rigor that may have been applied up front. In other words, up-front analysis is rarely sufficient to allow one to confidently select an instructional model. For this reason many traditional methods of instructional design are beginning to be seen as incomplete, naive, and even counter-productive.

However, some consider rapid prototyping to be a somewhat simplistic type of model. As this argument goes, at the heart of Instructional Design is the analysis phase. After you thoroughly conduct the analysis-you can then choose a model based on your findings. That is the area where most people get snagged-they simply do not do a thorough-enough analysis. (Part of Article By Chris Bressi on LinkedIn)

Dick and Carey

Another well-known instructional design model is The Dick and Carey Systems Approach Model. The model was originally published in 1978 by Walter Dick and Lou Carey in their book entitled The Systematic Design of Instruction.

Dick and Carey made a significant contribution to the instructional design field by championing a systems view of instruction as opposed to viewing instruction as a sum of isolated parts. The model addresses instruction as an entire system, focusing on the interrelationship between context, content, learning and instruction. According to Dick and Carey, "Components such as the instructor, learners, materials, instructional activities, delivery system, and learning and performance environments interact with each other and work together to bring about the desired student learning outcomes". The components of the Systems Approach Model, also known as the Dick and Carey Model, are as follows:

- Identify Instructional Goal(s): goal statement describes a skill, knowledge or attitude(SKA) that a learner will be expected to acquire

- Conduct Instructional Analysis: Identify what a learner must recall and identify what learner must be able to do to perform particular task
- Analyze Learners and Contexts: Identify general characteristics of the target audience including prior skills, prior experience, and basic demographics; identify characteristics directly related to the skill to be taught; and perform analysis of the performance and learning settings.
- Write Performance Objectives: Objectives consists of a description of the behavior, the condition and criteria. The component of an objective that describes the criteria that will be used to judge the learner's performance.
- Develop Assessment Instruments: Purpose of entry behavior testing, purpose of pretesting, purpose of posttesting, purpose of practive items/practive problems
- Develop Instructional Strategy: Pre-instructional activities, content presentation, Learner participation, assessment
- Develop and Select Instructional Materials
- Design and Conduct Formative Evaluation of Instruction: Designer try to identify areas of the instructional materials that are in need of improvement.
- Revise Instruction: To identify poor test items and to identify poor instruction
- Design and Conduct Summative Evaluation

With this model, components are executed iteratively and in parallel rather than linearly.

Instructional Development Learning System (IDLS)

Another instructional design model is the Instructional Development Learning System (IDLS). The model was originally published in 1970 by Peter J. Esseff, PhD and Mary Sullivan Esseff, PhD in their book entitled IDLS-Pro Trainer 1: How to Design, Develop, and Validate Instructional Materials.

Peter (1968) & Mary (1972) Esseff both received their doctorates in Educational Technology from the Catholic University of America under the mentorship of Dr. Gabriel Ofiesh, a Founding Father of the Military Model mentioned above. Esseff and Esseff contributed synthesized existing theories to develop their approach to systematic design, "Instructional Development Learning System" (IDLS).

Also see: Managing Learning in High Performance Organizations, by Ruth Stiehl and Barbara Bessey, from The Learning Organization, Corvallis, Oregon. ISBN: 0-9637457-0-0.

The components of the IDLS Model are:

- Design a Task Analysis
- Develop Criterion Tests and Performance Measures
- Develop Interactive Instructional Materials
- Validate the Interactive Instructional Materials

Other models

Some other useful models of instructional design include: the Smith/Ragan Model, the Morrison/Ross/Kemp Model and the OAR Model of instructional design in higher education, as well as, Wiggins' theory of backward design.

Learning theories also play an important role in the design of instructional materials. Theories such as behaviorism, constructivism, social learning and cognitivism help shape and define the outcome of instructional materials.

How to Implement LMS Systems Successfully

Now that your company has chosen a learning management system, the implementation plan must have some important components in place. Even small systems deserve caution and attention during implementation. The largest areas of the implementation plan are teams, the business rules and the business policies

Teams

- Assign the appropriate members of the business team to the project. This team will determine the business rules and handle the overall decisions for the LMS program. Governance teams or focus groups may assist in steering the direction of the program, but the business team is the final decision point.
- Work with the information technology group to secure the appropriate members of the technical team to the project. This team handles all aspects of the implementation from the information technology perspective. It will work with the vendor directly to ensure smooth operations and availability of the system.
- Choose the method of support available after implementation and roll out. This team will interact with the users of the LMS to provide support with technical questions and issue troubleshooting. Part of the decision is whether you will provide support from in-house, or use a vendor outside of the company.
- Determine the domain structure to be configured in the LMS installation. This can potentially be a difficult step. All of the teams should be involved in this discussion. The domain structure determines who can access content within the LMS. In addition to the domain, other filters may exist that are used by the system to constrain or allow content to certain users.
- Determine if the LMS should be made available solely on the intranet, or also on the Internet. Keep in mind that if the content is on a separate server it can be restricted to the intranet, even if the user accesses it from the Internet. Consider consulting with your information security personnel if you decide to allow access from the Internet. They can work with your technical team and vendor to ensure the most secure configuration.
- Schedule a series of meetings to work with the teams to determine the business rules of your LMS. Business rules are options that are chosen during the initial installation of your LMS. The vendor is an important member of these meetings and should drive the process. The vendor should discuss which decisions cannot be changed once the installation is complete. These should be seriously considered since it affects certain operations of the system.
- Lead a meeting with all the teams to discuss the support structure after the implementation. Many options are available for support. One option is in-

house support by creating or utilizing an existing group to handle questions and issues. Your company may also decide to outsource the support to a vendor. Service- level agreements should be discussed and documented. The service-level agreement describes the response time and resolution quality that users can expect from their support personnel. It is a quality control measure.

- Create the business policies that will govern the usage and support of the LMS. Multiple areas require policies. When creating policies, it is imperative to keep the business rules in mind. The business rules affect the functionality of the LMS. The entire team should consider taking responsibility for a section of the policies.

Content management policies include the naming conventions to be used, as well as the version process when a course significantly changes. Certifications should also be given considerable attention. They require guidelines on the setup and version processes.

Protocol policies will guide both internal and external instructional designers (those who create web-based training) on the settings that should be used for their courses. Your vendor can provide insight into best practices and what has successfully integrated with its system.

- Compile all of the defined policies and distribute to all team members. Carefully review these policies with team support to ensure they do not conflict with other policies or business rules.

Schedule user acceptance testing for all people in the system, including administrators, end-users and managers. A help-desk should be set up to assist users during the testing period. Each participant should document any issues or user-friendliness feedback.

Review and troubleshoot each of the issues reported during the user acceptance testing. The technical team should report any issues that need additional decisions to the business team.

Create a marketing and roll-out plan. Roll out the LMS once the support team is in place.

How to Choose an LMS

A LMS, or Learning Management System, is a specialized software application used in the administration and reporting of online and offline curricula, training programs, and other educational content. Learning Management Systems range from open-source management systems to enterprise class propriety management systems. With so many options available, it is important to clarify your requirements and your goals before finding a Learning Management System that is a strong fit for your organization or institution

- Determine the learning strategy and demographic of your target audience. While most institutions have already put considerable legwork into this area, make sure this is outlined well in advance before thinking about implementing a Learning Management System.

- Determine your document and reporting requirements. Rate each of your requirements in priority from critical to low priority. It is easier to work with an LMS that is already equipped to handle your core requirements rather than reorganizing your course and reporting structure to fit the LMS.
- Figure out the technology requirements for you LMS. This includes both the back end administration and the end user experience. For example, if you are looking to have users access the system across platforms, then you will need a system that will be supported by all operating systems. In addition, make sure you already have the computer infrastructure and software in place to run the LMS, or have the budget to install the components it needs.
- Draft a request for proposal from available LMS software developers. Using the requirements you determined earlier, your RFP (request for proposal) will be the document you present to potential vendors to collect quotes and implementation time frames. Your RFP does not need to list your requirements in any particular order, but it does need to thoroughly outline your core demographic, scenarios where the LMS will be utilized, and what the system needs to accomplish. When drafting your RFP, try to be as specific as possible, because this will help your potential vendors address your specific questions.
- Review the proposals. Once you have sent your RFP to a few vendors, you will begin to get bids for your project. Screen the potential contractors on their experience, former satisfied clients, and their proposed time frame and cost.
- Schedule software demos. Once you have screened you bids and chosen a few top candidates, schedule product demos where you can see how the LMS works. When viewing the demo, you want to see whether the software is hosted or licensed, and make sure the software is easy to use and meets all your core requirements.
- Finally, select an LMS which is the best fit to your needs and fits within your working budget.

A Learning Management System (or LMS) is a software package, usually on a large scale (that scale is decreasing rapidly), that enables the management and delivery of learning content and resources to students. Most LMS systems are web-based to facilitate "anytime, anywhere" access to learning content and administration.

At a minimum, the LMS usually allows for student registration, the delivery and tracking of e-learning courses and content, and testing, and may also allow for the management of instructor-led training classes. In the most comprehensive of LMSs, one may find tools such as competency management, skills-gap analysis, succession planning, certifications, virtual live classes, and resource allocation (venues, rooms, textbooks, instructors, etc.). Most systems allow for learner self-service, facilitating self-enrollment, and access to courses.

Some LMS vendors do not distinguish between LMS and LCMS, preferring to refer to both under the term "LMS", but there is a difference. The LCMS, which stands for "Learning Content Management System", facilitates organization of content from authoring tools, and presentation of this content to students via the LMS.

LMSs are based on a variety of development platforms, from Java EE based architectures to Microsoft .NET, and usually employ the use of a robust database back-end. While most systems are commercially developed, free and open-source models do exist. Other than the most simplistic, basic functionality, all LMSs cater to, and focus on different educational, administrative, and deployment requirements.

FUNCTIONAL FEATURES OF LMS

Assessment capabilities

It's a good idea to have an assessment feature that enables authoring within the product and includes assessments as part of each course. Evaluation, testing, and assessment engines help developers build a program that becomes more valuable over time.

Adherence to standards

An LMS should attempt to support standards, such as SCORM. Support for standards means that the LMS can import and manage content and courseware that complies with standards regardless of the authoring system that produced it. Beware: Unless the supplier certifies that the content will work on your LMS, plan on additional expenses.

Administration tools

The LMS must enable administrators to manage user registrations and profiles, define roles, set curricula, chart certification paths, assign tutors, author courses, manage content, and administer internal budgets, user payments, and chargebacks. Administrators need complete access to the training database, enabling them to create standard and customized reports on individual and group performance. Reports should be scalable to include the entire workforce. The system should also be able to build schedules for learners, instructors, and classrooms. Most important, all features should be manageable using automated, user-friendly interfaces. In addition, the system should be able to identify employees who need a particular course and tell them how it fits into their overall career path, when it's available, how it's available (classroom, online, CD-ROM), if there are prerequisites, and when and how they can fulfill those prerequisites. Once learners complete a course, the LMS can administer tests based on proficiency requirements, report test results, and recommend next steps. In that capacity, LMSs are instrumental in assuring that organizations meet rigid certification requirements in such vertical markets as healthcare, finance, and government.

Configurability

If an organization needs to completely re-engineer its internal processes to install an LMS or employ expensive programming resources to make changes to the LMS, then it's probably not a good fit. Also, it's helpful if IT and designers can access the LMS behind the scenes; they need to set processes and standards based on company policy. To make some systems IT- and user-friendly, some LMS providers have user groups or customer advisory councils that provide insight into installing or upgrading systems.

Content access

This involves the medium (e.g., classroom, CD-ROM, online, etc.) in which the content is delivered, the method (e.g., instructor-led, selfpaced, blended) in which the content is delivered, the languages in which the content is delivered and to whom the content is being delivered (e.g., employees, customers, partners, etc.).

Content development

Content development encompasses authoring, maintaining, and storing the learning content. This is where the issues of authoring-tool compatibility, version control, and re-usable learning objects are considered.

Content integration

It's important for an LMS to provide native support to a wide range of third-party courseware. When shopping for an LMS, keep in mind that some LMSs are compatible only with the supplier's own courseware, and others do little more than pay lip-service to learning content standards. An LMS supplier should be able to certify that third-party content will work within their system, and accessing courses should be as easy as using a drop-down menu.

Integration with HR

LMSs that aren't synchronized with HR systems miss the boat. When systems are integrated, a human resources employee can enter a new hire's information into the HR system, and the employee is automatically signed up for training tailored to his or her role within the company.

Security

Security is a priority in any data system containing employee information and proprietary content. Security measures typically include passwords and encryption.

Skills management

Skill assessment and management capabilities revolve around learners assessing their competency gaps. Skills assessments can be culled from multiple sources, including peer reviews and 360-feedback tools. Managers must be able to determine whether results are weighted, averaged, or compared to determine a skill gap. Businesses also might use this feature to search their employee base for specialized skills.

THE BEST LEARNING MANAGEMENT SYSTEMS

Learning management systems (LMS) are content publishing platforms that allow publishers and educational institutions to create online educational courses. LMS systems can create presentations, manage classroom courses, track subscriber progress and create customized training programs. LMS software applications allow businesses and educational institutions to connect with their employees and students

Benefits

- LMS software applications are typically quite affordable for businesses and educational institutions. The software serves as a template to produce and publish training, presentations and courses. Businesses can reduce travel costs. Rather than having trainers travel to multiple company locations, employees can quickly access company training online. Educational institutions can reach a larger number of students online versus in a classroom setting. LMS systems have built-in monitoring applications for performance management.

Selection

- Choosing a LMS system for your institution or business depends on your budget and the features you require. When selecting a LMS system, you need a programmer who can update, edit or add new features to customize the program. Programmers may not be necessary when using a hosted version. In choosing the best LMS system, make sure it's scalable, web-based and allows you to add your own custom branding.

Software

- LMS software applications are deployed as a web-based solution or as a desktop package. Web-based LMS systems can be quickly updated through the online administration panel. Consumers who use a desktop solution may have to receive system upgrades through downloads or in the mail. The software includes a calendar module, enrollment management system, transcript and scoring system and student profiling system.

Systems

- There are numerous Learning Management Systems available that can be categorized into two types. Your selection would depend on your organization's requirements or needs. An open-source learning management system is geared towards installation and administration of your own system. Open source systems include Moodle, Latitude Learning and Mind Flash. The other solution is a hosted system, meaning you can use a third party's LMS software to create and publish your educational course. Hosted LMS applications include Taleo Business Edition and Silk Road technology.

Pros and Cons from Employer Perspective

- The LMS may be fed information from a Human Resources' database to include employee work location, supervisor, title, department name, job description and education in addition to the employee's name. This combination of data can be used to generate reports based on specific office locations, supervisors or departments within the company. An LMS system can be setup to be accessible by employees so they can access their records and so supervisors can monitor training completed by their people. This easy access can encourage a healthy rivalry among employees to finish more training.

An LMS is as useful as the information it contains. Attending instructor-led training or participating in any other non-computerized form of training requires someone to manually input attendance. f the data is not entered in a timely manner, not entered at all or entered into the system incorrectly, it can impact the query results.

Pros and Cons from Employee Perspective

- Being able to access the LMS to see their records is rewarding and encouraging to some employees. An opposite affect of viewing training records occurs for employees who are not located in an area where they can get training, do not have time for training or are not finding training offered that meets their needs.

Pros and Cons from Management Perspective

- An LMS system can be setup to allow high level management access to training reports of employees in their division. This managerial oversight can be subdivided down to lower level supervisors to have access to their employees' records. This ready access to training records can be a benefit when reviewing an employee's performance to note training that they have or have not completed, or to ensure that mandatory training has been completed.

The system will prevent supervisors on up to high level management from viewing training records outside their realm of authority. This lack of access means management is unable to see where their people stand in relationship to the rest of the company. For upper management in particular, that lack of company-wide knowledge for comparison could mean that the data has little value to them. This potential issue can be rectified with company-wide statistics generated from and provided by the training department.

Training Data

- The data included in an LMS can include available instructor-led training, giving employees the option to register for the training. If the class has a pre-requisite, the LMS can confirm that requirement has been met or alert the employee that other training is needed first. The LMS option to register employees for instructor-led training can be setup to email the employee a confirmation and a subsequent reminder the day before class. The instructor can also receive an email as registrations are confirmed and can printout a roster the day of class.

Companies offering employees online training in the form of self-paced courses over the Internet or Intranet can electronically migrate the records into the LMS avoiding the need to manually input them.

Mandatory Training

- A company may have a requirement that certain types of training be completed within a specified time-frame from their hire date, like sexual harassment awareness. The system can be setup to alert the employee via email as to when and where the training will be conducted. The system can also be setup to alert the employee's supervisor at the same time.

Tracking Budgets

- If training is conducted internally but by outside vendors, the expense of that training can be recorded in the LMS. With expenditures recorded in the LMS, reports can be run to see where the training dollars are being spent and how many employees were covered in the learning event to help determine return on investment.

ADVANTAGES OF LMS CLASSROOMS

Due to the increasing popularity and availability of the Internet, Learning Management System (LMS) classes have steadily become a more viable option for both professors and students. These are comprehensive online "classrooms" that have all the resources of an active classroom -- peer discussions, lesson summaries, assignments and even tests can be administered through these systems. Consider the following advantages and determine whether taking an LMS course is appropriate for you

Individual Review

- Some professors and students have a hard time trying to schedule review sessions and conduct feedback sessions, especially in larger classes. LMS integrated classes allow these processes to be brought online and handled on a person-by-person basis. Scheduling tools allow students to book individual appointment times with professors even outside of school hours. Professors have easy access to data and reports on an individual student even if the class has more than 100 students. Typical LMS courses are designed with large class sizes in mind.

Student Interaction

- A particular selling point of LMS is that it is designed to encourage student-to-student interaction just as much as student-to-professor interaction. There are specific tools integrated into an LMS class, such as discussion boards and chat rooms, to accommodate peer reviews and group study. These tools also have relevant resources linked for easier access to reference material.

Course-Material Delivery

- One of the main features of an LMS course is that all course material can be uploaded and downloaded in its interface. This allows professors to save time in making copies of multiple-page materials and simply upload them for students to view. This is particularly effective for classrooms with Internet access, as students can read the online content, follow along and take notes all within the LMS. Students can also submit their assignments electronically, complete with a time stamp and proper formatting for the professor's grading convenience.

Expert Insight: Replacing the Classroom

- More universities are starting to integrate LMS courses into their curriculum. However, full integration -- creating purely online classrooms -- is still a debatable issue. LMS courses still have their share of disadvantages, such as the technical level of skill required to interact with them, as well as the lack of a consistent support system. The learning curve in fully utilizing an LMS course remains high. As such, students and professors must carefully consider when it is applicable to use this technology.

EFFECTIVENESS OF LMS INSTRUMENTS

Many educational institutes use learning management system (LMS) software with the goals of flexibility, scalability of all teaching programs, training, support and cost effectiveness. All instruments used in LMS will create a stable but versatile infrastructure for any educational institute. However no set parameters exist as to the effectiveness of the different instruments within the system

Simulation Software

- Institutions have used simulation software determine which instruments and practices make LMS more effective and which do not. Learning effectiveness depends on resources and network strength, making it impossible to investigate the many factors that influence these two items beyond the standard program content and accessibility to information. Simulation software will produce models based on historical information. Once you have input the different items and factors, the software will produce results specifically for your needs. Learn which factors improve effectiveness and which are simply a waste of time and money. In eliminating the need for extensive trial and error, simulation shortens the time of implementing and perfecting LMS.

Online Education Environment

- The online education environment supports face-to-face interaction over the LMS system, including online classes, lectures and discussions. This type of program also provides access to class notes and slides as well as additional assignments to help better cement concepts presented in class. Students have found this system extremely effective, as it helps with organization and preparation for classes. This program helps provide clarity on assignments, allows for students to plan and prepare in advance and supplements learning through the availability of class notes and slides.

Communication Tools

- Educational LMS systems offer much more extensive communication tools than corporate LMS. Students can reach instructors through the LMS system using email, instant messaging, video chat and even Web-based phone calls. Other means of communication include blogs and chat rooms. Students find these LMS-based communication tools extremely effective --- particularly those students who may be shy and avoid speaking up in class. The ability to set meetings can increase communication between instructors and students.

Course Authoring

- Though LMS systems normally do not include course authoring tools and instruments, you can generally add them on. Course authoring provides different websites to help individuals learn; examples include PowerPoint presentations on different subjects or a series of detailed videos based on specific concept and topics. These tools make it much easier for instructors to organize and provide resources that relate to the curriculum and to collect feedback on which resources are the most effective.

Leading Learning Management Systems

Learning management systems are programs or templates for organizing learning materials, delivering information to students, tracking student attendance and responses, tracking teacher responses and, finally, awarding grades to students. Some management systems deliver portions of these functions, while others deliver all of them. Some are designed primarily as a lesson plan and grading system that can be shared with parents, while others provide ways for the teacher to post complete lessons, share discussions and even host online, interactive sessions

TeacherEase

- TeacherEase is used in elementary and high schools. It provides lesson planning tools for the teacher, access to local, state and national standards on which to base lessons and tracking for attendance, grades and even behavior. It includes a centralized database through which parents can access lesson plans and student grades, as well as teacher comments.

Blackboard

- Blackboard is a learning system used by many colleges. It includes online bulletin boards through which the instructor can post instruction and assignments, and receive materials from students. It also provides chat-type functions, which allow for groups to meet in real-time. Many colleges also include access to reference resources for students.

Moodle

- Moodle is an open-source learning system. It includes many of the same features as Blackboard at a more modest licensing cost. It allows instructors to post material, open student discussion groups, receive student material and track grades.

Desire2Learn

- Desire2Learn was founded in 1999. It is sufficiently flexible to be used by elementary and high schools, as well as by institutes of higher learning. It has many of the same features as the other three systems, but emphasizes that it can also be accessed through mobile media, such as Blackberry or Android.

4

SYSTEMS APPROACH TO EDUCATION

Goal setting involves the development of an action plan designed to motivate and guide a person or group toward a goal. Goal setting can be guided by goal-setting criteria (or rules) such as SMART criteria. Goal setting is a major component of personal-development and management literature. Studies by Edwin A. Locke and his colleagues have shown that more specific and ambitious goals lead to more performance improvement than easy or general goals. The goals should be specific, difficult, and have time constraints. As long as the person accepts the goal, has the ability to attain it, and does not have conflicting goals, there is a positive linear relationship between goal difficulty and task performance.

History of goal setting

Edwin A. Locke began to examine goal setting in the mid-1960s and continued researching goal setting for more than 30 years. Locke derived the idea for goal-setting from Aristotle's form of final causality. Aristotle speculated that purpose can cause action; thus, Locke began researching the impact goals have on human activity. Locke developed and refined his goal-setting theory in the 1960s, publishing his first article on the subject, "Toward a Theory of Task Motivation and Incentives", in 1968. This article established the positive relationship between clearly identified goals and performance.

Goal commitment

People perform better when they are committed to achieving certain goals. Through an understanding of the effect of goal setting on individual performance, organizations are able to use goal setting to benefit organizational performance. Locke and Latham (2002) have indicated three moderators that indicate goal setting success:

1. The importance of the expected outcomes of goal attainment,
2. Self-efficacy: one's belief that they are able to achieve the goals,
3. Commitment to others: promises or engagements to others can strongly improve commitment.

Expanding the three from above, the level of commitment is influenced by external factors. Such as the person assigning the goal, setting the standard for the person to achieve/perform. This influences the level of commitment by how compliant the individual is with the one assigning the goal. An external factor can also be the role models of the individual. Say if they strive to be like their favorite athlete, the individual is more likely to put forth more effort to their own work and goals.

Internal factors can derive from their participation level in the work to achieve the goal. What they expect from themselves can either flourish their success, or destroy it. Also, the individual may want to appear superior to their peers or competitors. They want to achieve the goal the best and be known for it. The self-reward of accomplishing a goal, is usually one of the main keys that keep individuals committed.

Goal–performance relationship

Locke and colleagues (1981) examined the behavioral effects of goal-setting, concluding that 90% of laboratory and field studies involving specific and challenging goals led to higher performance than did easy or no goals.

Locke and Latham (2006) argue that it is not sufficient to urge employees to "do their best". "Doing one's best" has no external referent, which makes it useless in eliciting specific behavior. To elicit some specific form of behavior from another person, it is important that this person has a clear view of what is expected from him/her. A goal is thereby of vital importance because it helps an individual to focus his or her efforts in a specified direction. In other words, goals canalize behavior. (However, when faced with complex tasks and directions that are difficult to specify, telling someone to "do their best", with a focus on learning, can sometimes lead to the discovery of better strategies whereby specific goals can then be set.)

Feedback

Without proper feedback channels it is impossible for employees to adapt or adjust to the required behavior. Managers should keep track of performance to allow employees to see how effective they have been in attaining their goals. Providing feedback on short-term objectives helps to sustain motivation and commitment to the goal and without it, goal setting is unlikely to be successful. Feedback should be provided on the strategies followed to achieve the goals and the final outcomes achieved, as well. Feedback on strategies used to obtain goals is very important, especially for complex work, because challenging goals put focus on outcomes rather than on performance strategies, so they impair performance. Properly delivered feedback is also very essential, and the following hints may help for providing a good feedback:

- Create a positive context for feedback.
- Use constructive and positive language.
- Focus on behaviors and strategies.
- Tailor feedback to the needs of the individual worker.
- Make feedback a two-way communication process.

Advances in technology can facilitate providing feedback. Systems analysts have designed computer programs that track goals for numerous members of an organization. Such computer systems may maintain every employee's goals, as well as their deadlines. Separate methods may check the employee's progress on a regular basis, and other systems may require perceived slackers to explain how they intend to improve.

More difficult goals require more cognitive strategies and well-developed skills. The more difficult the tasks, the smaller the group of people who possess the necessary skills and strategies. From an organizational perspective, it is thereby more difficult to successfully attain more difficult goals, since resources become more scarce.

In personal life

Common personal goals include losing weight, achieving good grades, and saving money. The strategy for goal setting begins with the big picture; taking a look at the big picture before breaking it into smaller components allows one to focus on the primary goal. Once the main goal is set, breaking it up into smaller, more achievable components helps in the planning portion of setting the goal. These smaller, more obtainable objectives promote self-esteem and provide instant feedback to keep the individual on task.

Time management is the practice of systematically finishing tasks assigned by superiors or one's self in an efficient and timely manner. Time management steps require identifying the objective and laying out a plan that maximizes efficiency and execution of the objective. There are many useful mobile apps that help with personal goal setting; some of the categories include budgeting, wellness, calendar and productivity apps.

Limitations

Goal-setting theory has limitations. In an organization, a goal of a manager may not align with the goals of the organization as a whole. In such cases, the goals of an individual may come into direct conflict with the employing organization. Without aligning goals between the organization and the individual, performance may suffer.

For complex tasks, goal-setting may actually impair performance. In these situations, an individual may become preoccupied with meeting the goals, rather than performing tasks.

Some evidence suggests that goal-setting can foster unethical behavior when people do not achieve specified goals.

Goal setting may have the drawback of inhibiting implicit learning: goal setting may encourage simple focus on an outcome without openness to exploration, understanding, or growth.A solution to this limitation is to set learning goals as well as performance goals, so that learning is expected as part of the process of reaching goals.

Developments in theory

Goal choice

Self-efficacy, past performance, and various other social factors influence goal setting. Failure to meet previous goals often leads to setting lower (and more likely achievable) goals.

LEARNING GOALS

There are times when having specific goals is not a best option; this is the case when the goal requires new skills or knowledge. Tunnel vision is a consequence of specific goals; if a person is too focused on attaining a specific goal, he or she may ignore the need to learn new skills or acquire new information. This concept is illustrated well by the "basketball game task" study in which observers watched a video of a group of people wearing white shirts and black shirts who are passing a basketball back and forth, and the observers were instructed to count the number of times a basketball is passed between only the players wearing white shirts. During the video, a woman carrying an open umbrella walks across the screen. Of 28 observers who were focused on counting the number of passes between only the players wearing white shirts, only 6 reported noticing the woman carrying the umbrella. When observers watched the video without focusing on a specific task, all of the observers noticed the umbrella woman. In situations where the risk of tunnel vision is high, the best option is to set a learning goal. A learning goal is a generalized goal to achieve knowledge in a certain topic or field, but it can ultimately lead to better performance in specific goals related to the learning goals.

Locke and Latham (2006) attribute this response to metacognition. They believe that "a learning goal facilitates or enhances metacognition—namely, planning, monitoring, and evaluating progress toward goal attainment". This is necessary in environments with little or no guidance and structure. Although jobs typically have set goals, individual goals and achievement can benefit from metacognition.

Framing

Framing, or how goals are viewed, influences performance. When one feels threatened and or intimidated by a high goal they perform poorer than those who view the goal as a challenge. The framing of a goal as a gain or a loss influences one's eventual performance.

Affect

Realization of goals has an effect on affect—that is, feelings of success and satisfaction. Achieving goals has a positive effect, and failing to meet goals has negative consequences. However, the effect of goals is not exclusive to one realm. Success in one's job can compensate for feelings of failure in one's personal life.

Group goals

The relationship between group goals and individual goals influences group performance; when goals are compatible there is a positive effect, but when goals are incompatible the effects can be detrimental to the group's performance. There is another factor at work in groups, and that is the sharing factor; a positive correlation exists between sharing information within the group and group performance. In the case of group goals, feedback needs to be related to the group, not individuals, in order for it to improve the group's performance.

Goals and traits

On a basic level, the two types of goals are learning goals and performance goals; each possesses different traits associated with the selected goal.

Learning goals involve tasks where skills and knowledge can be acquired, whereas performance goals involve easy-to-accomplish tasks that will make one appear successful (thus tasks where error and judgment may be possible are avoided).

A more complex trait-mediation study is the one conducted by Lee, Sheldon, and Turban (2003), which yielded the following results:

- Amotivated orientation (low confidence in one's capabilities) is associated with goal-avoidance motivation, and more generally, associated with lower goals levels and lower performance.
- Control orientation (extrinsic motivation) is associated with both avoidance and approach goals. Approach goals are associated with higher goal levels and higher performance.
- Autonomy goals (intrinsic motivation) leads to mastery goals, enhanced focus, and therefore enhanced performance.

Macro-level goals

Macro-level goals refer to goal setting that is applied to the company as a whole. Cooperative goals reduce the negative feelings that occur as a result of alliances and the formation of groups. The most common parties involved are the company and its suppliers. The three motivators for macro-level goals are: self-efficacy, growth goals, and organizational vision.

Goals and subconscious priming

The effects of subconscious priming and conscious goals are independent, although a conscious goal has a larger effect. The interaction effect is that priming can enhance the effects of difficult goals, but it has no effect on easy goals. There is also the situation in which priming and conscious goals conflict with one another, and in this situation the conscious goals have a greater effect on performance.

General action and inaction goals

Action goals are believed to promote the sense of action, whereas inaction goals are considered to reduce people's tendency to take actions. Common action goals can be to do something, perform a certain act, or to go someplace, whereas typical inaction goals can take the form of having a rest or to stop doing something.

Goal-regulated overall activity and inactivity tendency result from both biological conditions and social-cultural environment. Recent research revealed that most nations hold more favorable attitude towards action rather than inaction, even though some countries value action and inaction slightly differently than others.

Recent research suggested that people tend to choose inaction goals when they are making decisions among choices where uncertainty could result in negative outcomes, but they prefer action over inaction in their daily behaviors when no deliberation is needed.Timothy D. Wilson and colleagues found that many people "preferred to administer electric shocks to themselves instead of being left alone with their thoughts".

TASK ANALYSIS

Task analysis is the analysis of how a task is accomplished, including a detailed description of both manual and mental activities, task and element durations, task frequency, task allocation, task complexity, environmental conditions, necessary clothing and equipment, and any other unique factors involved in or required for one or more people to perform a given task.

Information from a task analysis can then be used for many purposes, such as personnel selection and training, tool or equipment design,procedure design (e.g., design of checklists, or decision support systems) and automation. Though distinct, task analysis is related to user analysis.

Applications

The term "task" is often used interchangeably with activity or process. Task analysis often results in a hierarchical representation of what steps it takes to perform a task for which there is a goal and for which there is some lowest-level "action" or interaction among humans and/or machines: this is known as hierarchical task analysis. Tasks may be identified and defined at multiple levels of abstraction as required to support the purpose of the analysis. A critical task analysis, for example, is an analysis of human performance requirements which, if not accomplished in accordance with system requirements, will likely have adverse effects on cost, system reliability, efficiency, effectiveness, or safety. Task analysis is often performed by human factors and ergonomics professionals.

Task analysis may be of manual tasks, such as bricklaying, and be analyzed as time and motion studies using concepts from industrial engineering. Cognitive task analysis is applied to modern work environments such as supervisory control where little physical work occurs, but the tasks are more related to situation assessment, decision making, and response planning and execution.

Task analysis is also used in education. It is a model that is applied to classroom tasks to discover which curriculum components are well matched to the capabilities of students with learning disabilities and which task modification might be necessary. It discovers which tasks a person hasn't mastered, and the information processing demands of tasks that are easy or problematic. In behavior modification, it is a breakdown of a complex behavioral sequence into steps. This often serves as the basis for chaining.

The results of task analysis are often represented in task models, which clearly indicate the relations among the various tasks, An example notation used to specify task models is ConcurTaskTrees (by Fabio Paternò), which is also supported by tools that are freely available.

Versus work domain analysis

If task analysis is likened to a set of instructions on how to navigate from Point A to Point B, then Work domain analysis (WDA) is like having a map of the terrain that includes Point A and Point B. WDA is broader and focuses on the environmental constraints and opportunities for behavior, as in Gibsonianecological psychology and ecological interface design (Vicente, 1999; Bennett & Flach, 2011, p. 61)

Documentation

Since the 1980s, a major change in technical documentation has been to emphasize the tasks performed with a system rather than documenting the system itself. In software documentation particularly, long printed technical manuals that exhaustively describe every function of the software are being replaced by online help organized into tasks. This is part of the new emphasis on usability and user-centered design rather than system/software/product design.

This task orientation in technical documentation began with publishing guidelines issued by IBM in the late 1980s. Later IBM studies led to John Carroll's theory of minimalism in the 1990s.

With the development of XML as a markup language suitable for both print and online documentation (replacing SGML with its focus on print), IBM developed the Darwin Information Typing Architecture XML standard in 2000. Now an OASIS standard, DITA has a strong emphasis on task analysis. Its three basic information types are Task, Concept, and Reference. Tasks are analyzed into steps, with a main goal of identifying steps that are reusable in multiple tasks.

Hierarchical task analysis

Hierarchical task analysis (HTA) is a task description method and a variant of task analysis. Task description is a necessary precursor for other analysis techniques, including critical path analysis (CPA). HTA is used to produce an exhaustive description of tasks in a hierarchical structure of goals, sub-goals, operations and plans. In HTA, tasks are broken down into progressively smaller units.

Operations and plans

Operations are the actions performed by people interacting with a system or by the system itself, and plans explain the conditions necessary for these operations. Operations describe the smallest individual task steps in the HTA, i.e. those which cannot be broken down into plans and further operations. They are the individual actions, such as 'visually locate control' or 'move hand to control', which the user must perform in a particular combination to achieve the goal of task completion.

Applying

The following steps should be followed when conducting a HTA:

1. Define the task under investigation and identify the purpose of the task analysis. The analyst should have some further evaluation methods in mind for which the HTA will be useful and should have reason for needing this type of analysis to be performed.
2. Data collection – In order to carry out the HTA it is necessary to obtain data on how the task is performed. This could be collected via observation of the task in question or from a detailed specification of the device under analysis. Alternatively, interviews or questionnaires with people that have first-hand experience of performing that task could be conducted to gather the necessary detail.
3. Define the overall task goal, which will be presented as the top level in the HTA. An example might be "increase fan speed by two steps". This describes what is being achieved by performing the task; however, at this stage there is no indication of how the task will be performed.
4. Determine the next level of sub-goals by breaking down the overall goal. A sub-goal for the above example might be "open the climate menu". This provides more information about how to accomplish the task; however, it can still be broken down into smaller units, which will describe the individual operations (performed via the visual, manual or cognitive modes) that need to be performed.
5. Continue breaking down the sub-goals until all operations are identified. Operations in the "reduce fan speed task" will include "move finger to climate menu button" and "touch climate menu button".
6. Define plans to describe how to perform the operations in each sub-goal level of the hierarchy. In the fan speed example, the two operations will have to be performed in series, one after the other. The plan will instruct the user to "perform 1, then 2". Operations can also be performed in parallel, and in this case the plan would instruct the user to "perform 1 and 2 together". Numbers should be assigned to the different levels in the hierarchy.

Organising the hierarchy

Each level in the HTA should be numbered according to its hierarchical level:

The overall goal is the highest hierarchical level and should be numbered 0. The first sub-goal in the hierarchy will be 1, also with plan 1. Further levels just extend this system - third hierarchical level: 1.1, fourth hierarchical level: 1.1.1, and so on. A HTA can be represented in list or diagram form. In list form lines should be indented to denote the different hierarchical levels. In diagram form each operation should be placed within a box and links should be made between them: a lower hierarchical level should branch from underneath a higher level operation. Plans should be written next to the branches to describe the way in which the branched operations should be carried out.

Applications and limitations

HTA is a task description method which is most commonly used as a starting point for further analyses such as multimodal CPA and SHERPA. On its own, HTA does not provide results for usability evaluation; however, you should be able to study the HTA in order to learn about the structure of different tasks. It may also allow you to highlight unnecessary task steps or potential errors that might occur in task performance. HTA is a fairly time-consuming method to carry out as each individual operation in a task needs to be analysed; however, creating a comprehensive HTA can considerably reduce the time required for other modelling methods.

Content analysis

History of content analysis

Over the years, content analysis has been applied to a variety of scopes. Hermeneutics and philology have long used content analysis to interpret sacred and profane texts and, in many cases, to attribute texts' authorship and authenticity.

In recent times, particularly with the advent of mass communication, content analysis has known an increasing use to deeply analyze and understand media content and media logic. The political scientist Harold Lasswell formulated the core questions of content analysis in its early-mid 20th-century mainstream version: "Who says what, to whom, why, to what extent and with what effect?". The strong emphasis for a quantitative approach started up by Lasswell was finally carried out by another "father" of content analysis, Bernard Berelson, who proposed a definition of content analysis which, from this point of view, is emblematic: "a research technique for the objective, systematic and quantitative description of the manifest content of communication".

Quantitative content analysis has enjoyed a renewed popularity in recent years thanks to technological advances and fruitful application in of mass communication and personal communication research. Content analysis of textual big data produced by new media, particularly social media and mobile devices has become popular. These approaches take a simplified view of language that ignores the complexity of semiosis, the process by which meaning is formed out of language. Quantitative content analysts have been criticized for limiting the scope of content analysis to simple counting, and for applying the measurement methodologies of the natural sciences without reflecting critically on their appropriateness to social science. Conversely, qualitative content analysts have been criticized for being insufficiently systematic and too impressionistic. Krippendorff argues that quantitative and qualitative approaches to content analysis tend to overlap, and that there can be no generalisable conclusion as to which approach is superior.

Recently, Arash Heydarian Pashakhanlou has argued for a combination of quantitative, qualitative, manual and computer-assisted in a single study to offset the weaknesses of a partial content analysis and enhance the reliability and validity of a research project.

Content analysis can also be described as studying traces, which are documents from past times, and artifacts, which are non-linguistic documents. Texts are understood to be produced by communication processes in a broad sense of that phrase—often gaining mean through abduction.

Content analysis is a research method for studying documents and communication artifacts, which might be texts of various formats, pictures, audio or video. Social scientists use content analysis to examine patterns in communication in a replicable and systematic manner. One of the key advantages of using content analysis to analyse social phenomena is its non-invasive nature, in contrast to simulating social experiences or collecting survey answers.

Practices and philosophies of content analysis vary between academic disciplines. They all involve systematic reading or observation of texts or artifacts which are assigned labels (sometimes called codes) to indicate the presence of interesting, meaningful pieces of content. By systematically labeling the content of a set of texts, researchers can analyse patterns of content quantitatively using statistical methods, or use qualitative methods to analyse meanings of content within texts.

Computers are increasingly used in content analysis to automate the labeling (or coding) of documents. Simple computational techniques can provide descriptive data such as word frequencies and document lengths. Machine learning classifiers can greatly increase the number of texts that can be labeled, but the scientific utility of doing so is a matter of debate.

Computational tools

More generally, content analysis is research using the categorization and classification of speech, written text, interviews, images, or other forms of communication. In its beginnings, using the first newspapers at the end of the 19th century, analysis was done manually by measuring the number of lines and amount of space given a subject. With the rise of common computing facilities like PCs, computer-based methods of analysis are growing in popularity. Answers to open ended questions, newspaper articles, political party manifestos, medical records or systematic observations in experiments can all be subject to systematic analysis of textual data. By having contents of communication available in form of machine readable texts, the input is analyzed for frequencies and coded into categories for building up inferences.

RELIABILITY

Robert Weber notes: "To make valid inferences from the text, it is important that the classification procedure be reliable in the sense of being consistent: Different people should code the same text in the same way". The validity, inter-coder reliability and intra-coder reliability are subject to intense methodological research efforts over long years. Neuendorf suggests that when human coders are used in content analysis two coders should be used. Reliability of human coding is often measured using a statistical measure of inter-coder reliability or "the amount of agreement or correspondence among two or more coders". Lacy and Riffe identify the measurement of inter-coder reliability as a strength of quantitative content analysis, arguing that, if content analysts do not measure inter-coder reliability, their data are no more reliable than the subjective impressions of a single reader.

Kinds of text

There are five types of texts in content analysis:

1. written text, such as books and papers
2. oral text, such as speech and theatrical performance
3. iconic text, such as drawings, paintings, and icons
4. audio-visual text, such as TV programs, movies, and videos
5. hypertexts, which are texts found on the Internet

Context analysis

Context analysis is a method to analyze the environment in which a business operates. Environmental scanning mainly focuses on the macro environment of a business. But context analysis considers the entire environment of a business, its internal and external environment. This is an important aspect of business planning. One kind of context analysis, called SWOT analysis, allows the business to gain an insight into their strengths and weaknesses and also the opportunities and threats posed by the market within which they operate. The main goal of a context analysis, SWOT or otherwise, is to analyze the environment in order to develop a strategic plan of action for the business.

Context analysis also refers to a method of sociological analysis associated with Scheflen (1963) which believes that 'a given act, be it a glance at [another] person, a shift in posture, or a remark about the weather, has no intrinsic meaning. Such acts can only be understood when taken in relation to one another.' (Kendon, 1990: 16). This is not discussed here; only Context Analysis in the business sense is.

Trend Analysis

The next step of the method is to conduct a trend analysis. Trend analysis is an analysis of macro environmental factors in the external environment of a business, also called PEST analysis. It consists of analyzing political, economical, social, technological and demographic trends. This can be done by first determining which factors, on each level, are relevant for the chosen subject and to score each item as to specify its importance. This allows the business to identify those factors that can influence them. They can't control these factors but they can try to cope with them by adapting themselves. The trends (factors) that are addressed in PEST analysis are Political, Economical, Social and Technological; but for context analysis Demographic trends are also of importance. Demographic trends are those factors that have to do with the population, like for example average age, religion, education etc. Demographic information is of importance if, for example during market research, a business wants to determine a particular market segment to target. The other trends are described in environmental scanning and PEST analysis. Trend analysis only covers part of the external environment. Another important aspect of the external environment that a business should consider is its competition. This is the next step of the method, competitor analysis.

Competitor Analysis

As one can imagine, it is important for a business to know who its competition is, how they do their business and how powerful they are so that they can be on the defense and offense. In Competitor analysis a couple of techniques are introduced how to conduct such an analysis. Here I will introduce another technique which involves conducting four sub analyses, namely: determination of competition levels, competitive forces, competitor behavior and competitor strategy.

Evaluation strategies

Definition

Evaluation is the structured interpretation and giving of meaning to predicted or actual impacts of proposals or results. It looks at original objectives, and at what is either predicted or what was accomplished and how it was accomplished. So evaluation can be formative, that is taking place during the development of a concept or proposal, project or organization, with the intention of improving the value or effectiveness of the proposal, project, or organisation. It can also be summative, drawing lessons from a completed action or project or an organisation at a later point in time or circumstance.

Evaluation is inherently a theoretically informed approach (whether explicitly or not), and consequently any particular definition of evaluation would have been tailored to its context – the theory, needs, purpose, and methodology of the evaluation process itself. Having said this, evaluation has been defined as:

- A systematic, rigorous, and meticulous application of scientific methods to assess the design, implementation, improvement, or outcomes of a program. It is a resource-intensive process, frequently requiring resources, such as, evaluate expertise, labor, time, and a sizable budget
- "The critical assessment, in as objective a manner as possible, of the degree to which a service or its component parts fulfills stated goals" (St Leger and Wordsworth-Bell) The focus of this definition is on attaining objective knowledge, and scientifically or quantitatively measuring predetermined and external concepts.
- "A study designed to assist some audience to assess an object's merit and worth" (Stufflebeam). In this definition the focus is on facts as well as value laden judgments of the programs outcomes and worth.

Discussion

However, the strict adherence to a set of methodological assumptions may make the field of evaluation more acceptable to a mainstream audience but this adherence will work towards preventing evaluators from developing new strategies for dealing with the myriad problems that programs face.

It is claimed that only a minority of evaluation reports are used by the evaluand (client) (Datta, 2006). One justification of this is that "when evaluation findings are challenged or utilization has failed, it was because stakeholders and clients found the inferences weak or the warrants unconvincing" (Fournier and Smith, 1993). Some reasons for this situation may be the failure of the evaluator to establish a set of shared aims with the evaluand, or creating overly ambitious aims, as well as failing to compromise and incorporate the cultural differences of individuals and programs within the evaluation aims and process.

None of these problems are due to a lack of a definition of evaluation but are rather due to evaluators attempting to impose predisposed notions and definitions of evaluations on clients. The central reason for the poor utilization of evaluations is arguably due to the lack of tailoring of evaluations to suit the needs of the client, due to a predefined idea (or definition) of what an evaluation is rather than what the client needs are (House, 1980).

The development of a standard methodology for evaluation will require arriving at applicable ways of asking and stating the results of questions about ethics such as agent-principal, privacy, stakeholder definition, limited liability; and could-the-money-be-spent-more-wisely issues.

Standards

Depending on the topic of interest, there are professional groups that review the quality and rigor of evaluation processes.

Evaluating programs and projects, regarding their value and impact within the context they are implemented, can be ethically challenging. Evaluators may encounter complex, culturally specific systems resistant to external evaluation. Furthermore, the project organization or other stakeholders may be invested in a particular evaluation outcome. Finally, evaluators themselves may encounter "conflict of interest (COI)" issues, or experience interference or pressure to present findings that support a particular assessment.

General professional codes of conduct, as determined by the employing organization, usually cover three broad aspects of behavioral standards, and include inter-collegial relations (such as respect for diversity and privacy), operational issues (due competence, documentation accuracy and appropriate use of resources), and conflicts of interest (nepotism, accepting gifts and other kinds of favoritism). However, specific guidelines particular to the evaluator's role that can be utilized in the management of unique ethical challenges are required. The Joint Committee on Standards for Educational Evaluation has developed standards for program, personnel, and student evaluation. The Joint Committee standards are broken into four sections: Utility, Feasibility, Propriety, and Accuracy. Various European institutions have also prepared their own standards, more or less related to those produced by the Joint Committee. They provide guidelines about basing value judgments on systematic inquiry, evaluator competence and integrity, respect for people, and regard for the general and public welfare.

The American Evaluation Association has created a set of Guiding Principles for evaluators. The order of these principles does not imply priority among them; priority will vary by situation and evaluator role. The principles run as follows:

- Systematic Inquiry: evaluators conduct systematic, data-based inquiries about whatever is being evaluated. This requires quality data collection, including a defensible choice of indicators, which lends credibility to findings. Findings are credible when they are demonstrably evidence-based, reliable and valid. This also pertains to the choice of methodology employed, such that it is consistent with the aims of the evaluation and provides dependable data. Furthermore, utility of findings is critical such that the information obtained by evaluation is comprehensive and timely, and thus serves to provide maximal benefit and use to stakeholders.
- Competence: evaluators provide competent performance to stakeholders. This requires that evaluation teams comprise an appropriate combination of competencies, such that varied and appropriate expertise is available for the evaluation process, and that evaluators work within their scope of capability.
- Integrity/Honesty: evaluators ensure the honesty and integrity of the entire evaluation process. A key element of this principle is freedom from bias in evaluation and this is underscored by three principles: impartiality, independence, and transparency.

Independence is attained through ensuring independence of judgment is upheld such that evaluation conclusions are not influenced or pressured by another party, and avoidance of conflict of interest, such that the evaluator does not have a stake in a particular conclusion. Conflict of interest is at issue particularly where funding of evaluations is provided by particular bodies with a stake in conclusions of the evaluation, and this is seen as potentially compromising the independence of the evaluator. Whilst it is acknowledged that evaluators may be familiar with agencies or projects that they are required to evaluate, independence requires that they not have been involved in the planning or implementation of the project. A declaration of interest should be made where any benefits or association with project are stated. Independence of judgment is required to be maintained against any pressures brought to bear on evaluators, for example, by project funders wishing to modify evaluations such that the project appears more effective than findings can verify.

Impartiality pertains to findings being a fair and thorough assessment of strengths and weaknesses of a project or program. This requires taking due input from all stakeholders involved and findings presented without bias and with a transparent, proportionate, and persuasive link between findings and recommendations. Thus evaluators are required to delimit their findings to evidence. A mechanism to ensure impartiality is external and internal review. Such review is required of significant (determined in terms of cost or sensitivity) evaluations. The review is based on quality of work and the degree to which a demonstrable link is provided between findings and recommendations.

Transparency requires that stakeholders are aware of the reason for the evaluation, the criteria by which evaluation occurs and the purposes to which the findings will be applied. Access to the evaluation document should be facilitated through findings being easily readable, with clear explanations of evaluation methodologies, approaches, sources of information, and costs incurred.

- Respect for People: Evaluators respect the security, dignity and self-worth of the respondents, programparticipants, clients, and other stakeholders with whom they interact.This is particularly pertinent with regards to those who will be impacted upon by the evaluation findings. Protection of people includes ensuring informed consent from those involved in the evaluation, upholding confidentiality, and ensuring that the identity of those who may provide sensitive information towards the program evaluation is protected. Evaluators are ethically required to respect the customs and beliefs of those who are impacted upon by the evaluation or program activities. Examples of how such respect is demonstrated is through respecting local customs e.g. dress codes, respecting peoples privacy, and minimizing demands on others' time. Where stakeholders wish to place objections to evaluation findings, such a process should be facilitated through the local office of the evaluation organization, and procedures for lodging complaints or queries should be accessible and clear.
- Responsibilities for General and PublicWelfare: Evaluators articulate and take into account the diversity of interests and values that may be related to the general and public welfare. Access to evaluation documents by the wider public should be facilitated such that discussion and feedback is enabled.

Furthermore, the international organizations such as the I.M.F. and the World Bank have independent evaluation functions. The various funds, programmes, and agencies of the United Nations has a mix of independent, semi-independent and self-evaluation functions, which have organized themselves as a system-wide UN Evaluation Group (UNEG), that works together to strengthen the function, and to establish UN norms and standards for evaluation. There is also an evaluation group within the OECD-DAC, which endeavors to improve development evaluation standards. The independent evaluation units of the major multinational development banks (MDBs) have also created the Evaluation Cooperation Group to strengthen the use of evaluation for greater MDB effectiveness and accountability, share lessons from MDB evaluations, and promote evaluation harmonization and collaboration.

PERSPECTIVES

The word "evaluation" has various connotations for different people, raising issues related to this process that include; what type of evaluation should be conducted; why there should be an evaluation process and how the evaluation is integrated into a program, for the purpose of gaining greater knowledge and awareness?

There are also various factors inherent in the evaluation process, for example; to critically examine influences within a program that involve the gathering and analyzing of relative information about a program. Michael Quinn Patton motivated the concept that the evaluation procedure should be directed towards:

- Activities
- Characteristics
- Outcomes
- The making of judgments on a program
- Improving its effectiveness,
- Informed programming decisions

Founded on another perspective of evaluation by Thomson and Hoffman in 2003, it is possible for a situation to be encountered, in which the process could not be considered advisable; for instance, in the event of a program being unpredictable, or unsound. This would include it lacking a consistent routine; or the concerned parties unable to reach an agreement regarding the purpose of the program. In addition, an influencer, or manager, refusing to incorporate relevant, important central issues within the evaluation

APPROACHES

There exist several conceptually distinct ways of thinking about, designing, and conducting evaluation efforts. Many of the evaluation approaches in use today make truly unique contributions to solving important problems, while others refine existing approaches in some way.

Classification of approaches

Two classifications of evaluation approaches by House and Stufflebeam and Webster can be combined into a manageable number of approaches in terms of their unique and important underlying principles.

House considers all major evaluation approaches to be based on a common ideology entitled liberal democracy. Important principles of this ideology include freedom of choice, the uniqueness of the individual and empirical inquiry grounded in objectivity. He also contends that they are all based on subjectivist ethics, in which ethical conduct is based on the subjective or intuitive experience of an individual or group. One form of subjectivist ethics is utilitarian, in which "the good" is determined by what maximizes a single, explicit interpretation of happiness for society as a whole. Another form of subjectivist ethics is intuitionist/pluralist, in which no single interpretation of "the good" is assumed and such interpretations need not be explicitly stated nor justified.

These ethical positions have corresponding epistemologies—philosophies for obtaining knowledge. The objectivist epistemology is associated with the utilitarian ethic; in general, it is used to acquire knowledge that can be externally verified (intersubjective agreement) through publicly exposed methods and data. The subjectivist epistemology is associated with the intuitionist/pluralist ethic and is used to acquire new knowledge based on existing personal knowledge, as well as experiences that are (explicit) or are not (tacit) available for public inspection. House then divides each epistemological approach into two main political perspectives. Firstly, approaches can take an elite perspective, focusing on the interests of managers and professionals; or they also can take a mass perspective, focusing on consumers and participatory approaches.

Stufflebeam and Webster place approaches into one of three groups, according to their orientation toward the role of values and ethical consideration. The political orientation promotes a positive or negative view of an object regardless of what its value actually is and might be—they call this pseudo-evaluation. The questions orientation includes approaches that might or might not provide answers specifically related to the value of an object—they call this quasi-evaluation. The values orientation includes approaches primarily intended to determine the value of an object—they call this true evaluation.

When the above concepts are considered simultaneously, fifteen evaluation approaches can be identified in terms of epistemology, major perspective (from House), and orientation. Two pseudo-evaluation approaches, politically controlled and public relations studies, are represented. They are based on an objectivist epistemology from an elite perspective. Six quasi-evaluation approaches use an objectivist epistemology. Five of them—experimental research, management information systems, testing programs, objectives-based studies, and content analysis—take an elite perspective. Accountability takes a mass perspective. Seven true evaluation approaches are included. Two approaches, decision-oriented and policy studies, are based on an objectivist epistemology from an elite perspective. Consumer-oriented studies are based on an objectivist epistemology from a mass perspective. Two approaches—accreditation/certification and connoisseur studies—are based on a subjectivist epistemology from an elite perspective. Finally, adversary and client-centered studies are based on a subjectivist epistemology from a mass perspective.

Summary of approaches

The following table is used to summarize each approach in terms of four attributes—organizer, purpose, strengths, and weaknesses. The organizer represents the main considerations or cues practitioners use to organize a study. The purpose represents the desired outcome for a study at a very general level. Strengths and weaknesses represent other attributes that should be considered when deciding whether to use the approach for a particular study. The following narrative highlights differences between approaches grouped together.

PSEUDO-EVALUATION®

Politically controlled and public relations studies are based on an objectivist epistemology from an elite perspective. Although both of these approaches seek to misrepresent value interpretations about an object, they function differently from each other. Information obtained through politically controlled studies is released or withheld to meet the special interests of the holder, whereas public relations information creates a positive image of an object regardless of the actual situation. Despite the application of both studies in real scenarios, neither of these approaches is acceptable evaluation practice.

Objectivist, elite, quasi-evaluation

As a group, these five approaches represent a highly respected collection of disciplined inquiry approaches. They are considered quasi-evaluation approaches because particular studies legitimately can focus only on questions of knowledge without addressing any questions of value. Such studies are, by definition, not evaluations. These approaches can produce characterizations without producing appraisals, although specific studies can produce both. Each of these approaches serves its intended purpose well. They are discussed roughly in order of the extent to which they approach the objectivist ideal.

- Experimental research is the best approach for determining causal relationships between variables. The potential problem with using this as an evaluation approach is that its highly controlled and stylized methodology may not be sufficiently responsive to the dynamically changing needs of most human service programs.

- Management information systems (MISs) can give detailed information about the dynamic operations of complex programs. However, this information is restricted to readily quantifiable data usually available at regular intervals.
- Testing programs are familiar to just about anyone who has attended school, served in the military, or worked for a large company. These programs are good at comparing individuals or groups to selected norms in a number of subject areas or to a set of standards of performance. However, they only focus on testee performance and they might not adequately sample what is taught or expected.
- Objectives-based approaches relate outcomes to prespecified objectives, allowing judgments to be made about their level of attainment. Unfortunately, the objectives are often not proven to be important or they focus on outcomes too narrow to provide the basis for determining the value of an object.
- Content analysis is a quasi-evaluation approach because content analysis judgments need not be based on value statements. Instead, they can be based on knowledge. Such content analyses are not evaluations. On the other hand, when content analysis judgments are based on values, such studies are evaluations.

Objectivist, mass, quasi-evaluation

- Accountability is popular with constituents because it is intended to provide an accurate accounting of results that can improve the quality of products and services. However, this approach quickly can turn practitioners and consumers into adversaries when implemented in a heavy-handed fashion.

Objectivist, elite, true evaluation

- Decision-oriented studies are designed to provide a knowledge base for making and defending decisions. This approach usually requires the close collaboration between an evaluator and decision-maker, allowing it to be susceptible to corruption and bias.
- Policy studies provide general guidance and direction on broad issues by identifying and assessing potential costs and benefits of competing policies. The drawback is these studies can be corrupted or subverted by the politically motivated actions of the participants.

Objectivist, mass, true evaluation

- Consumer-oriented studies are used to judge the relative merits of goods and services based on generalized needs and values, along with a comprehensive range of effects. However, this approach does not necessarily help practitioners improve their work, and it requires a very good and credible evaluator to do it well.

Subjectivist, elite, true evaluation

- Accreditation / certification programs are based on self-study and peer review of organizations, programs, and personnel. They draw on the insights, experience, and expertise of qualified individuals who use established guidelines to determine if the applicant should be approved to perform specified functions.

However, unless performance-based standards are used, attributes of applicants and the processes they perform often are overemphasized in relation to measures of outcomes or effects.

- Connoisseur studies use the highly refined skills of individuals intimately familiar with the subject of the evaluation to critically characterize and appraise it. This approach can help others see programs in a new light, but it is difficult to find a qualified and unbiased connoisseur.

  Subject, mass, true evaluation

- The adversary approach focuses on drawing out the pros and cons of controversial issues through quasi-legal proceedings. This helps ensure a balanced presentation of different perspectives on the issues, but it is also likely to discourage later cooperation and heighten animosities between contesting parties if "winners" and "losers" emerge.

  Client-centered

- Client-centered studies address specific concerns and issues of practitioners and other clients of the study in a particular setting. These studies help people understand the activities and values involved from a variety of perspectives. However, this responsive approach can lead to low external credibility and a favorable bias toward those who participated in the study.

5

MODELS OF EDUCATION

Teaching methods can best be defined as the types of principles and methods used for instruction. There are many types of teaching methods, depending on what information or skill the teacher is trying to convey. Class participation, demonstration, recitation, and memorization are some of the teaching methods being used. When a teacher is deciding on their method, they need to be flexible and willing to adjust their style according to their students. Student success in the classroom is largely based on effective teaching methods.

For effective teaching to take place, a good method must be adopted by a teacher. A teacher has many options when choosing a style by which to teach. The teacher may write lesson plans of their own, borrow plans from other teachers, or search online or within books for lesson plans.

When deciding what teaching method to use, a teacher needs to consider students' background knowledge, environment, and learning goals. Teachers are aware that students learn in different ways, but almost all children will respond well to praise. Students have different ways of absorbing information and of demonstrating their knowledge.

Teachers often use techniques which cater to multiple learning styles to help students retain information and strengthen understanding. A variety of strategies and methods are used to ensure that all students have equal opportunities to learn. A lesson plan may be carried out in several ways: Questioning, explaining, modeling, collaborating, and demonstrating.

A teaching method that includes questioning is similar to testing. A teacher may ask a series of questions to collect information of what students have learned and what needs to be taught. Testing is another application of questioning.

A teacher tests the student on what was previously taught in order to identify if a student has learned the material. Standardized testing is in about every middle school (i.e. Ohio Graduation Test (OGT), Proficiency Test, College entrance Tests (ACT and SAT). Learning can be done in three ways- Auditory, Visual, and Kinesthetic. It is important to try and include all three as much as possible into your lessons.

EXPLAINING

This form is similar to lecturing. Lecturing is teaching by giving a discourse on a specific subject that is open to the public, usually given in the classroom. This can also be associated with modeling. Modeling is used as a visual aid to learning.

Students can visualize an object or problem, then use reasoning and hypothesizing to determine an answer.

In your lecture you have the opportunity to tackle two types of learning. Not only can explaining (lecture) help the auditory learner through the speech of the teacher, but if the teacher is to include visuals in the form of overheads or slide shows, his/her lecture can have duality. Although a student might only profit substantially from one form of teaching, all students profit some from the different types of learning.

Demonstrating

Demonstrations are done to provide an opportunity to learn new exploration and visual learning tasks from a different perspective. A teacher may use experimentation to demonstrate ideas in a science class. A demonstration may be used in the circumstance of proving conclusively a fact, as by reasoning or showing evidence.

The uses of storytelling and examples have long since become standard practice in the realm of textual explanation. But while a more narrative style of information presentation is clearly a preferred practice in writing, judging by its' prolificacy, this practice sometimes becomes one of the more ignored aspects of lecture. Lectures, especially in a collegiate environment, often become a setting more geared towards factorial presentation than a setting for narrative and/or connective learning.

The use of examples and storytelling likely allows for better understanding but also greater individual ability to relate to the information presented. Learning a list of facts provides a detached and impersonal experience while the same list, containing examples and stories, becomes, potentially, personally relatable.

Furthermore, storytelling in information presentation may also reinforce memory retention because it provides connections between factorial presentation and real-world examples/personable experience, thus, putting things into a clearer perspective and allowing for increased neural representation in the brain. Therefore, it is important to provide personable, supplementary, examples in all forms of information presentation because this practice likely allows for greater interest in the subject matter and better information-retention rates.

Often in lecture numbers or stats are used to explain a subject but often when many numbers are being used it is difficult to see the whole picture. Visuals that are bright in color, etc. offer a way for the students to put into perspective the numbers or stats that are being used. If the student can not only hear but see what is being taught, it is more likely they will believe and fully grasp what is being taught. It allows another way for the student to relate to the material.

Collaborating

Having students work in groups is another way a teacher can direct a lesson. Collaborating allows students to talk with each other and listen to all points of view in the discussion. It helps students think in a less personally biased way. When this lesson plan is carried out, the teacher may be trying to assess the lesson by looking at the student's: ability to work as a team, leadership skills, or presentation abilities. It is one of the direct instructional methods.

A different kind of group work is the discussion. After some preparation and with clearly defined roles as well as interesting topics, discussions may well take up most of the lesson, with the teacher only giving short feedback at the end or even in the following lesson. Discussions can take a variety of forms, e.g. fishbowl discussions.

Collaborating (kinesthetic) is great in that it allows to actively participate in the learning process. These students who learn best this way by being able to relate to the lesson in that they are physically taking part of it in some way. Group projects and discussions are a great way to welcome this type of learning.

Learning by Teaching

Learning by teaching (German:LdL) is a widespread method in Germany, developed by Jean-Pol Martin. The students take the teacher's role and teach their peers.

This method is very effective when done correctly. Having students teach sections of the class as a group or as individuals is a great way to get the students to really study out the topic and understand it so as to teach it to their peers. By having them participate in the teaching process it also builds self-confidence, self-efficacy, and strengthens students speaking and communication skills. Students will not only learn their given topic, but they will gain experience that could be very valuable for life.

EVOLUTION OF TEACHING METHODS

Ancient Education

About 3000 BC, with the advent of writing, education became more conscious or self-reflecting, with specialized occupations requiring particular skills and knowledge on how to be a scribe, an astronomer, etc.

Philosophy in ancient Greece led to questions of educational method entering national discourse. In his *Republic*, Plato describes a system of instruction that he felt would lead to an ideal state. In his *Dialogues*, Plato describes the Socratic method.

It has been the intent of many educators since then, such as the Roman educator Quintilian, to find specific, interesting ways to encourage students to use their intelligence and to help them to learn.

Medieval Education

Comenius, in Bohemia, wanted all boys and girls to learn. In his *The World in Pictures*, he gave the first vivid, illustrated textbook which contained much that children would be familiar with in everyday life, and use it to teach the academic subjects they needed to know. Rabelais described how the student Gargantua learned about the world, and what is in it.

Much later, Jean-Jacques Rousseau in his *Emile*, presented methodology to teach children the elements of science and much more. In it, he famously eschewed books, saying the world is one's book. And so Emile was brought out into the woods without breakfast to learn the cardinal directions and the positions of the sun as he found his way home for something to eat.

There was also Johann Heinrich Pestalozzi of Switzerland, whose methodology during Napoleonic warfare enabled refugee children, of a class believed to be unteachable, to learn - and love to learn. He describes this in his account of the educational experiment at Stanz. He felt the key to have children learn is for them to be loved, but his method, though transmitted later in the school for educators he founded, has been thought "too unclear to be taught today". One result was when he would ask, "Children, do you want to learn more or go to sleep?" they would reply, "Learn more!"

19th Century - compulsory Education

The Prussian education system was a system of mandatory education dating to the early 19th century. Parts of the Prussian education system have served as models for the education systems in a number of other countries, including Japan and the United States. The Prussian model had a side effect of requiring additional classroom management skills to be incorporated into the teaching process.

20th Century

In the 20th century, the philosopher, Eli Siegel, who believed that all children are equally capable of learning regardless of ethnic background or social class, stated: "The purpose of all education is to like the world through knowing it." This is a goal which is implicit in previous educators, but in this principle, it is made conscious. With this principle at basis, teachers, predominantly in New York, have found that students learn the curriculum with the kind of eagerness that Pestalozzi describes for his students at Stanz centuries earlier.

Many current teaching philosophies are aimed at fulfilling the precepts of a curriculum based on Specially Designed Academic Instruction in English (SDAIE). Arguably the qualities of a SDAIE curriculum are as effective if not more so for all 'regular' classrooms.

Some critical ideas in today's education environment include:

- Instructional scaffolding
- Graphic organizers
- Standardized testing

According to Dr. Shaikh Imran, the teaching methodology in education is a new concept in the teaching learning process. New methods involved in the teaching learning process are television, radio, computer, etc.

Other educators believe that the use of technology, while facilitating learning to some degree, is not a substitute for educational method that brings out critical thinking and a desire to learn. Another modern teaching method is inquiry learning and the related inquiry-based science.

Elvis H. Bostwick recently concluded Dr. Cherry's quantitative study "The Interdisciplinary Effect of Hands On Science", a three-year study of 3920 middle school students and their Tennessee State Achievement scores in Math, Science, Reading and Social Studies. Metropolitan Nashville Public School is considered urban demographically and can be compared to many of urban schools nationally and internationally.

This study divided students on the basis of whether they had hands on trained teachers over the three-year period addressed by the study. Students who had a hands-on trained science teacher for one or more years had statistically higher standardized test scores in science, math and social studies.

Learning by Teaching

In professional education, learning by teaching designates currently the method by Jean-Pol Martin that allows pupils and students to prepare and to teach lessons, or parts of lessons. Learning by teaching should not be confused with presentations or lectures by students, as students not only convey a certain content, but also choose their own methods and didactic approaches in teaching classmates that subject. Neither should it be confused with tutoring, because the teacher has intensive control of, and gives support for, the learning process in learning by teaching as against other methods.

Seneca the Younger told in his letters to Lucilius that we are learning if we teach (epistulae morales I, 7, 8): *docendo discimus* (lat.: "by teaching we are learning"). At all times in the history of schooling there have been phases where students were mobilized to teach their peers. Frequently, this was to reduce the number of teachers needed, so one teacher could instruct 200 students. However, since the end of the 19th century, a number of didactic-pedagogic reasons for student teaching have been put forward.

Students as Teachers in Order to Spare Teachers

In 1795 the Scotsman Andrew Bell wrote a book about the mutual teaching method that he observed and used himself in Madras. The Londoner Joseph Lancaster picked up this idea and implemented it in his schools. This method was introduced 1815 in France in the "écoles mutuelles", because of the increasing number of students who had to be trained and the lack of teachers. After the French revolution of 1830, 2,000 "écoles mutuelles" were registered in France.

Due to a political change in the French administration, the number of écoles mutuelles shrank rapidly and these schools were marginalized. It is important to stress that the learning level in the Bell-Lancaster-schools was very low. In hindsight, the low level can probably be attributed to the fact that the teaching-process was delegated entirely to the tutors and that the teachers did not supervise and support the teaching process.

Students as Teachers in Order to Improve the Learning-process

The first attempts using the learning by teaching method in order to improve learning were started at the end of the 19th century.

Selective Descriptions and Researches

Systematic research – though initially only descriptive – began in the middle of the 20th century. For instance Gartner 1971 in the US, in Germany Krüger 1975, Wolfgang Steining 1985, Udo Kettwig 1986, Theodor F. Klassen 1988, Ursula Drews 1997 and A. Renkl 1997

LdL as a Comprehensive Method

The method received broader recognition starting in the early eighties, when Jean-Pol Martin developed the concept systematically for the teaching of French as a foreign language and gave it a theoretical background in numerous publications. 1987 he founded a network of more than a thousand teachers that employed learning by teaching (the specifical name: LdL = "Lernen durch Lehren") in many different subjects, documented its successes and approaches and presented their findings in various teacher training sessions. From 2001 on LdL has gained more and more supporters as a result of educational reform movements started throughout Germany.

Learning by Teaching by Martin (LdL)

LdL by Martin consists of two components: a general anthropological one and a subject-related one.

- The anthropological basis of LdL is related to the pyramid or hierarchy of needs introduced by Abraham Maslow, which consists, from base to peak, of 1) physiological needs, 2) safety/security, 3) social/love/belonging, 4) esteem/self-confidence and 5) being/growth through self-actualization and self-transcendence. Personal growth moves upward through hierarchy, whereas regressive forces tend to push downward. The act of successful learning, preparation and teaching of others contributes to items 3 through 5 above. Facing the problems of our world today and in the future, it is essential to mobilize as many intellectual resources as possible, which happens in LdL lessons in a special way. Democratic skills are promoted through the communication and socialization necessary for this shared discovery and construction of knowledge.
- The subject related component (in foreign language teaching) of LdL aims to negate the alleged contradiction between the three main components: automatization of speech-related behavior, teaching of cognitively internalized contents and authentic interaction/communication.

The LdL Approach

After intensive preparation by the teacher, students become responsible for their own learning and teaching. The new material is divided into small units and student groups of not more than three people are formed. Each group familiarizes itself with a strictly defined area of new material and gets the assignment to teach the whole group in this area. One important aspect is that LdL should not be confused with a student-as-teacher-centered method. The material should be worked on didactically and methodologically (impulses, social forms, summarizing phases etc.).

The teaching students have to make sure their audience has understood their message/topic/grammar points and therefore use different means to do so (e.g. short phases of group or partner exercises, comprehension questions, quizzes etc.). An important effect from LdL is to develop the students' "websensibility," defined as "a cognitive and emotional sensibility for interdependence."

Building Neural Network: Websensibility as Target

Martin attempted to transfer the brain structure, especially the operating model from neural networks – to classroom interactions. The activities conducted during the various lessons phases and their consequences are summarized in the following table:

Advantages and Disadvantages

Most teachers using the method do not apply it in all their classes or all the time. They state the following advantages and disadvantages:

Advantages

- Student work is more motivated, efficient, active and intensive due to lowered inhibitions and an increased sense of purpose
- By eliminating the class division of authoritative teacher and passive audience, an emotive solidarity is obtained.
- Students may perform many routine tasks, otherwise unnecessarily carried out by the instructor
- Next to subject-related knowledge students gain important key qualifications like
    - teamwork
    - planning abilities
    - reliability
    - presentation and moderation skills
    - self-confidence

Disadvantages

- The introduction of the method requires a lot of time.
- Students and teachers have to work more than usual.

- There is a danger of simple duplication, repetition or monotony if the teacher does not provide periodic didactic impetus.

Reception of Martin's Methods

Martin's work has been well received in teacher training and by practicing teachers: since 1985 more than 100 teacher students in all subjects wrote their ending thesis about LdL. Also the education administration received both the theory and the practice of LdL (vgl.Margret Ruep 1999). In didactics handbooks LdL has been described as an "*extreme form of learner centred teaching*"). On the university level, LdL has been disseminated by Joachim Grzega in Germany, Guido Oebel in Japan and Alina Rachimova in Russia.

Learning by Teaching Outside the LdL-context

Sudbury Schools

Sudbury schools, since 1968, do not segregate students by age, so that students of any age are free to interact with students in other age groups. One effect of this age mixing is that a great deal of the teaching in the school is done by students. Here are some statements about Learning by teaching in the Sudbury Schools:

"Kids love to learn from other kids. First of all, it's often easier. The child teacher is closer than the adult to the students' difficulties, having gone through them somewhat more recently. The explanations are usually simpler, better. There's less pressure, less judgment. And there's a huge incentive to learn fast and well, to catch up with the mentor.

Kids also love to teach. It gives them a sense of value, of accomplishment. More important, it helps them get a better handle on the material as they teach; they have to sort it out, get it straight. So they struggle with the material until it's crystal clear in their own heads, until it's clear enough for their pupils to understand."

Pupil-Team Learning: The Durrell Studies

In the 1950s Dr. Donald D. Durrell and his colleagues at Boston University pursued similar methods which they named Pupil-Team Learning. A year-long efficacy study in the schools of Dedham, Massachusetts, was published in the Boston University Journal of Education, Vol. 142, December, 1959, entitled "Adapting Instruction to the Learning Needs of Children in the Intermediate Grades" in which one of the authors, Walter J. McHugh, reported significant learning gains from the use of pupil teams.

Peer Learning and Teaching in Higher Education

Teaching and learning within a group or team context can be particularly effective in higher education. This cooperative atmosphere mimics potential workplace scenerios that students would expect to find in there careers after college. The skills learned in this group atmosphere, such as the ability to listen and learn from their peers, is essential in many vocations. Marbach-Ad and Sokolove found that in this peer-to-peer cooperative learning and teaching atmosphere resulted in students questioning and being involved at a higher-level.

The Vygotsky Connection

In the 1930s Lev Vygotsky wrote extensively, in Russian, on the profound connection between language and cognition, and in particular oral language (speech) and learning. The implication of Vygotsky's observations for Learning by Teaching would appear to be direct and apt. "The one who does the talking, does the learning" may best summarize the point: students learn by teaching their peers.

Teaching Machine

The teaching machine was a mechanical device whose purpose was to administer a curriculum of programmed instruction. It housed a list of questions, and a mechanism through which the learner could respond to each question. Upon delivering a correct answer, the learner would be rewarded.

Programmed Instruction

Programmed instruction is the name of the technology invented by the behaviorist B.F. Skinner to improve teaching. It is based on his theory of Verbal Behavior as a means to accelerate and increase conventional educational learning.

It typically consists of self-teaching with the aid of a specialized textbook or teaching machine that presents material structured in a logical and empirically developed sequence or sequences. Programmed instruction may be presented by a teacher as well, and it has been argued that the principles of Programmed Instruction can improve classic lectures and textbooks.

Programmed instruction allows students to progress through a unit of study at their own rate, checking their own answers and advancing only after answering correctly. In one simplified form of PI, after each step, they are presented with a question to test their comprehension, then are immediately shown the correct answer or given additional information.

However the objective of the instructional programming is to present the material in very small increments. The more sophisticated forms of programmed instruction may have the questions or tasks programmed well enough that the presentation and test model—an extropolation from traditional and classical instruction is not necessarily utilized.

Programmed Learning

This idea was later adapted by Robert M. Gagné, who invented programmed learning for use in teaching in schools. The difference between programmed instruction (PI) and programmed learning (PL) is that PI is intended to modify behavior, whereas PL is used for teaching facts and skills.

Personalized System of Instruction

Personalized System of Instruction or (PSI), developed by Fred S. Keller, was another idea for how to incorporate programmed learning into the classroom.

Errorless Discrimination

Programmed instruction resulted from early efforts to implement Skinner's basic research findings on learning at Harvard that led to "errorless discrimination" techniques being developed. Programmed instruction had some early success in aphasia rehabilation.

Programmed Instruction Today

While not popular, programmed instruction continues to be used today. Recently, the application of programmed instruction principles was applied to training in computer programs and combined with Benjamin Bloom's taxonomy to teach college students. Some have argued that there is a resurgence of research on programmed instruction due to use of computers and the internet.

Educational Technology

Many studies have found that effective classroom technology use positively affects students' motivation and self-esteem by offering a chance for students to work at their own pace (Underwood and Brown, 1997). Other studies have attributed improvements in school attendance, time-on-task, and pro-social behavior to technology use (Cotton, 1992). The resources below highlight the existing research about educational technology and help educators take on the many challenges of classroom integration.

Alliance for Community Technology (ACT)

Founded by the W. K. Kellogg Foundation and the University of Michigan, ACT promotes technology use in disadvantaged communities and pursues its goals through building partnerships among academic, business, and other community organizations.

Center for Technology in Learning (CTL)

Researchers at SRI International established CTL to focus their efforts on evaluating the efficacy of technology use in enhancing student achievement. The site contains articles about the organization's current research projects.

Computers for Learning (CFL)

CFL provides surplus federal technology to students in public or private schools, or home schools in the U.S. and its territories.

Digital Divide Network (DDN)

Originally created by the Benton Foundation (http://www.benton.org/),

DDN is now a project of the Center for Media and Community at the Educational Development Center (EDC). DDN provides news and research articles, email discussion groups, blogs, and tools to help educators reduce the digital divide.

Family Center on Technology and Disability (FCTD)

FCTD offers "assistive" technology designed to help families of children and youth with disabilities.

International Society for Technology in Education (ISTE)

ISTE provides leadership and service to educators, driven by the goal of improving education through classroom technology integration. ISTE's most well-known initiatives are the Center for Applied Research in Education Technology (CARET), National Educational Technology Standards (NETS), and the National Educational Computing Conference (NECC). Its key publications are Learning and Leading with Technology and the Journal of Research on Technology in Education.

Learning in Hand

This site, created by a classroom teacher who conducts professional development nationwide, contains a repository of articles about the effects of using handheld computers in enhancing children's learning.

Learning Point Associates, Inc. (formerly NCREL)

Learning Point Associates, Inc. provides resources on a vast array of educational topics, including technology integration. See the technology section for case studies, planning guides, research reports, and more.

National Center to Improve Practice Through Technology, Media and Materials (NCIP)

NCIP provides resources for promoting technology that enhances educational outcomes for students with sensory, cognitive, physical, and social/emotional disabilities.

The National Education Technology Plan

An initiative of the U.S. Department of Education's Office of Educational Technology, The National Education Technology Plan is meant to help motivate technology-driven transformation in America's schools. The plan uncovers the educational needs of today's students and reflects on the progress that has been made in connecting classrooms to the Internet, providing students with computers, and equipping teachers with the skills they need to use technology as an instructional tool.

Sun Associates

Professional Development specialists at Sun Associates provide free materials for evaluating the impact of technology on learning.

Tech Learning

Readers of this online magazine can find reviews of research about educational technology, book reviews, information about funding opportunities, and useful "how to" tips.

Ubiquitous Computing Evaluation Consortium

Created by researchers at SRI International, this site summarizes analyses of studies about ubiquitous computing in K-12 schools. Users will find scholarly literature reviews, reports about classroom technology use, and evaluation materials here.

Future Trends in Educational Technology

The development of the personal computer and the Internet has "enabled man to transcend the barriers of physical distance". People no longer limit their learning to an educational setting such as a school or university. Learning can take place at home or at the office, by online distance learning. The future of technology will enable people to be life-long learners. Learning will continue into the work place where there is a "need to keep up with current information."

Learners do not have to depend on their memories. They can store information on their personal computers and be able to retrieve it at all times. The concept of knowledge has changed from having information in the brain, to "having access to information about a particular topic and knowing how to use it". Teachers' roles will ultimately change since they will no longer be providers of information. They will be facilitators who concentrate "on the teaching of social skills rather than academic or technical expertise". However, "teacher-mediated classrooms do not foster computer-mediated learning". "Technology requires changes in the way humans work", yet schools are "adding computers to a traditional, authoritarian, classroom-centered" setting.

It won't work. "As General Electric CEO Jack Welch has said, "If the rate of change inside an institution is less than the rate of change outside, the end is in sight" Welch. Technology is developing at a very fast pace. If education fails to keep up with the current trends, will it keep up with those of the future? This paper will discuss two articles that deal with future trends of educational technology. The articles are: David Thornburg's "Reading the Future" (1999) and Aureo Castro's "Learning in a Digital Age: Current and Future Trends in Educational Technology" (2001).

Even though David Thornburg's article appeared in 1999, the trends he writes about are still relevant today. David Thornburg lists seven "trends and their consequences" (1999) while Aureo Castro mentions six. The former discusses the "rapid increase in the growth of information, the collapse of the information float, increasingly global marketplace, computers continue to increase in power while dropping in cost, the computer chips continue to follow Moore's Law, bandwidth is becoming free and finally network power continues to obey Metcalfe's Law as future trends that will have "implications for education" (1999). Aureo Castro's future trends include, an increase in web enabled courses, more home schoolers, new roles for teachers, a paradigm shift in primary education, new roles for schools and centralization of curriculum and instructional development" (2001).

According to David Thornburg, because the Internet is "doubling in size every year, the web is doubling in size every 90 days [there is need for] a complete rethinking of education". He suggests the need for "technological fluency [so that students] can sit down at a computer and use it as easily as can pick up and read a book in [their] native language".

Aureo Castro sees "home schooling [and] more web-enabled courses" as future trends in "rethinking education". He predicts "new roles for teachers [as] facilitators [who will] concentrate on the teaching of social skills rather than [on] academic or technical expertise". Aureo Castro predicts that there will be an increase in online courses "offered through the Internet". He suggests that "the only way to go with the fast increase in population and the physical constraint of the existing colleges and universities [is] in cyberspace".

Aureo Castro focuses on the Internet and "distance education" as a trend that will become even more popular in the future. He claims that future "schools will cease to become like a mill where students undergo academic processing but will evolve into becoming community centers where students engage in a variety of activities and projects". According to Aureo Castro, school "curriculum will shift from what used to be extra-curricular activities and become the main curriculum".

David Thornburg focuses on another trend for the future of schools. He worries about "the lack of technologically fluent workers" and getting prepared for jobs that have not been invented yet. David Thornburg claims that educators "must create an educational system that prepares students to work in fields that do not even exist. David Thornburg doesn't predict how educators would deal with the educational trends of the future.

However, he does claim that once "technologies become commonplace with all students, the tools for lifelong learning will be in place, the notion [of] lifelong learning is a survival skill". Future trends cannot be ignored. David Thornburg's final words are harsh. He claims that "Schools that ignore the trends shaping tomorrow will cease to be relevant in the lives of their students and will disappear quickly". The competition is tough. This reflects Jack Welch's statement that "if the rate of change inside an institution is less than the rate of change outside, the end is in sight".

"Truly global leaders are geo-strategic futurists who gaze across time and make extraordinary things happen". Aureo Castro and David Thornburg are educational futurists who have looked at future trends in technology and their impact on education. Technology can improve student learning and make teachers' work much easier. Educational technology will become "powerful low-cost, off the shelf tools that can make learning more engaging and knowledge more accessible". Educators "must work in partnership to break down the barriers of time, space, content and form so [learners] can collaborate, communicate, and share ideas".

EDUCATIONAL TECHNOLOGY RESEARCH AND DEVELOPMENT

It is the only scholarly journal in the field focusing entirely on research and development in educational technology. The *Research Section* assigns highest priority in reviewing manuscripts to rigorous original quantitative, qualitative, or mixed methods studies on topics relating to applications of technology or instructional design in educational settings.

Such contexts include K-12, higher education, and adult learning (e.g., in corporate training settings). Analytical papers that evaluate important research issues related to educational technology research and reviews of the literature on similar topics are also published. This section features well documented articles on the practical aspects of research as well as applied theory in educational practice and provides a comprehensive source of current research information in instructional technology.

The *Development Section* publishes research on planning, implementation, evaluation and management of a variety of instructional technologies and learning environments. Empirically-based formative evaluations and theoretically-based instructional design research papers are welcome, as are papers that report outcomes of innovative approaches in applying technology to instructional development.

Papers for the Development section may involve a variety of research methods and should focus on one or more aspect of the instructional development process; when relevant and possible, papers should discuss the implications of instructional design decisions and provide evidence linking outcomes to those decisions.

Computer-assisted Instruction

Computers are a familiar sight in classrooms in the twenty-first century, and technology has been used to streamline many educational tasks. There are different types of educational computer use, and not every use of a computer in the classroom is considered computer-assisted instruction. The educational uses of computers that are considered to be computer-assisted instruction (CAI) or computer-based instruction (CBI) are those cases in which either instruction is presented through a computer program to a passive student, or the computer is the platform for an interactive and personalized learning environment.

Within the broad definition, computer-assisted instruction may follow different paths to the same end. One example is how computer-assisted instruction is used in relation to other teaching presentations. CAI can be used either in isolation, bearing the whole responsibility for conveying instruction to students, or in combination with conventional, i.e., face-to-face, teaching methods. Research has shown that the combination of conventional and CAI instruction has been most effective in raising student achievement scores.

Computer-assisted instruction is used through the entire range of education from preschool to professional school. It has been offered in a wide variety of fields, including all the main school subjects taught in elementary and secondary schools. At CALI, the Center for Computer-Assisted Legal Instruction, law students from across the United States and other countries such as Belgium, Brazil, Canada, China, Denmark, Ireland, Kenya, Korea, Mexico, the Netherlands, Nigeria, Russia, Singapore, South Africa, Sweden, and Taiwan have access to CAI law school lessons to supplement their instruction.

Computer-assisted instruction has also been growing in use in a wide number of employment areas. It has been used to teach novice nurses how to perform intravenous injections, to teach jet engine mechanics in the US Air Force maintenance tasks, and to provide safety instruction for food service workers in an urban hospital.

CAI can also focus on smaller segments of the population. Computer-assisted instruction has also been used to personalize learning for people with learning disabilities, language limitations, and physical limitations. In the latter case, screen-reading programs may cater to sight-impaired users, and a variety of specialized interactive devices, such as roller balls, joysticks, and oversized keyboards may be used by a person when a mouse or standard keyboard present a challenge.

Formative Assessment

Formative assessment is a reflective process that Intends to promote student attainment. Cowie and Bell define it as the bidirectional process between teacher and student to enhance, recognize and respond to the learning. Black and Wiliam consider an assessment 'formative' when the feedback from learning activities is actually used to adapt the teaching to meet the learner's needs. Nicol and Macfarlane-Dick have re-interpreted research on formative assessment and feedback and shown how these processes can help students take control of their own learning (self-regulated learning).

In the training field, formative assessment is described as assessing the formation of the student. Facilitators do this by observing students as they:

- Respond to questions
- Ask questions
- Interact with other students during activities, etc.

This enables the facilitator to evaluate own delivery, fog index and relevance of content.

Michael Scriven (1967) coined the terms formative and summative evaluation and emphasized their differences both in terms of the goals of the information they seek and how the information is used. Benjamin Bloom (1968) just a year later made formative assessments a keystone of Learning for Mastery. He, along with Thomas Hasting and George Madaus (1971) produced the Handbook of Formative and Summative Evaluation and showed how formative assessments could be linked to instructional units in a variety of content areas. Almost 20 years ago, the Kentucky high-stakes assessment (Kifer, 1994) initially included a major emphasis on instructionally embedded tests; i.e., formative assessments.

Formative assessment has a long history. Formative assessments have evolved as a means to adapt to student needs. Historically formative assessments were of instructional units and diagnostic assessments were used for placement purposes. Formative assessments are part of instruction designed to provide crucial feedback for teachers and students. Assessment results inform the teacher of what has been taught well and not so well. They inform students of what they have learned well and not learned so well. As opposed to a summative assessment designed to make judgments about student performance and produce grades, the role of a formative assessment is to improve learning. As opposed to benchmark tests that are used to predict student performance on other tests (most often state assessments), formative assessments are intimately connected to instruction.

Formative assessments are:

- **For Learning** – The purpose of formative assessment is to enhance learning not to allocate grades. Summative assessments are designed to allocate grades. The goal of formative assessment is to improve; summative assessment to prove.
- **Embedded in Instruction** - Formative assessments are considered a part of instruction and the instructional sequence. What students are taught is reflected in what they are assessed.

They produce:

- **Non-threatening Results** - Formative assessments are scored but not graded. Students mark their own work and are encouraged to raise questions about the assessment and the material covered by the assessment.
- **Direct and Immediate Feedback-** Results of formative assessments are produced "on the spot;" teachers and students get them immediately. Teachers get a view of both individual and class performances while students learn how well they have done.
- **Structured Information** - Teachers can judge success and plan improvements based on the formative results. Students can see progress and experience success. Both teachers and students learn from the assessment results.
- **Ways to Improve** - Summarized formative results provide a basis for the teacher to re-visit topics in the unit if necessary. Individual student responses provide a basis for giving students additional experiences in areas where they performed less well.

Formative v. Summative

In 1967, Michael Scriven identified the differences between formative and summative assessments (as cited by many people, including Marzano 2006). The difference between the two types of assessments is that classroom formative assessments occur while content is being taught and learned and should continue throughout the period of learning and are not meant to assign grades, thus its primary objective is to inform the teacher of what his or her students know or do not know. More importantly, classroom formative assessments allow teachers to make decisions and monitor their instruction based on student performance, while summative assessment occurs at the end of a learning unit and determines if the content being taught was retained Ainsworth p. 23 (2006). A common formative assessment is slightly different in that it is designed by a group of teachers who teach the same content areas or grades, and it is directly aligned to the prioritized content standards. In addition, a common formative assessment includes both a pre- and a post-unit assessment. Again, teachers are given the opportunity to determine what students need to know and at the end, what they have learned from the learning unit Ainsworth pp. 23–24 (2006). Marzano states:

"Recall the finding from Black and Wiliam's (1998) synthesis of more than 250 studies that formative assessments, as opposed to summative ones, produce the more powerful effect on student learning. In his review of the research, Terrance Crooks (1988) reports that effects sizes for summative assessments are consistently lower than effect sizes for formative assessments. In short, it is formative assessment that has a strong research base supporting its impact on learning." (Marzano, 2006, p. 9)

Researchers have concluded that standards-based assessments are an effective way to "prescribe instruction and to ensure that no child is left behind" (Marzano, 2006 p. 13). Because the administration of formative assessments is ongoing the outcome is that standard-based assessments should be given frequently.

Evaluation done to improve or change a program while it is in progress is termed 'formative evaluation'. When evaluation focuses on the results or outcomes of a program, it is called 'summative evaluation'.

Formative Assessment in K-12

Formative assessment is more valuable for day-to-day teaching when it is used to adapt the teaching to meet students' needs. Formative assessment helps teachers to monitor their students' progress and to modify the instruction accordingly. It also helps students to monitor their own progress as they get feedback from their peers and the teacher. Students also find opportunity to revise and refine their thinking by means of formative assessment. Formative assessment is also called as educative assessment and classroom assessment.

Methods of Formative Assessment: There are many ways to integrate formative assessment into K-12 classrooms. Although the key concepts of formative assessment such as constant feedback, modifying the instruction, and information about students' progress do not vary among different disciplines or levels, the methods or strategies may differ.

For example, researchers developed generative activities (Stroup et al., 2004) and model-eliciting activities (Lesh et al., 2000) that can be used as formative assessment tools in mathematics and science classrooms. Others developed strategies computer-supported collaborative learning environments (Wang et al., 2004b). More information about implication of formative assessment in specific areas is given below.

Purpose of Formative Assessment: The following are examples of application of formative assessment to content areas:

Formative Assessment in Math Education:

In math education, it is really important for teachers to see how their students approach the problems and how much mathematical knowledge and at what level students use when solving the problems. That is, knowing how students think in the process of learning or problem solving makes it possible for teachers to help their students overcome conceptual difficulties and, in turn, improve learning. In that sense, formative assessment is diagnostic.

To employ formative assessment in the classrooms, a teacher has to make sure that each student participates in the learning process by expressing their ideas; there is a trustful environment -in which students can provide each other with feedback; s/he (the teacher) provides students with feedback; and the instruction is modified according to students' needs. In math classes, thought revealing activities such as model-eliciting activities (MEAs) and generative activities provide good opportunities for covering these aspects of formative assessment.

Formative assessment in Second/ Foreign Language Education:

As an ongoing assessment it focuses on the process, it helps teachers to check the current status of their students' language ability, that is, they can know what the students know and what the students do not know. It also gives chances to students to participate in modifying or replanning the upcoming classes (Bachman & Palmer, 1996).

Participation in their learning grows students' motivation to learn the target language. It also raises students' awareness on their target languages, which results in resetting their own goals. In consequence, it helps students to achieve their goals successfully as well as teachers be the facilitators to foster students' target language ability.

In classroom, short quizzes, reflectional journals, or portfolios could be used as a formative assessment (Cohen, 1994).

Formative Assessment in Elementary Education:

In primary schools is used to inform the next steps of learning. Teacher and students both use Formative Assessments as a tool to make decisions based on data. Formative assessment occurs when teachers feed information back to students in ways that enable the student to learn better, or when students can engage in a similar, self- reflective process. The evidence shows that high quality formative assessment does have a powerful impact on student learning.

Black and Wiliam (1998) report that studies of formative assessment show an effect size on Standardized Tests of between 0.4 and 0.7, larger than most known educational interventions. (The effect size is the ratio of the average improvement in test scores in the innovation to the range of scores of typical groups of pupils on the same tests; Black and Wiliam recognize that standardized tests are very limited measures of learning.) Formative assessment is particularly effective for students who have not done well in school, thus narrowing the gap between low and high achievers while raising overall achievement. Research examined by Black and

Wiliam supports the conclusion that summative assessments tend to have a negative effect on student learning.

Example of Formative Assessment in an Elementary Classroom

Model-eliciting Activities (MEAs): Model-eliciting activities are based on real-life situations where students, working in small groups, present a mathematical model as a solution to a client's need (Zawojewski & Carmona, 2001). The problem design enable students to evaluate their solutions according to the needs of a client identified in the problem situation and sustain themselves in productive, progressively effective cycles of conceptualizing and problem solving.

Model-eliciting activities (MEAs) are ideally structured to help students build their real-world sense of problem solving towards increasingly powerful mathematical constructs. What is especially useful for mathematics educators and researchers is the capacity of MEAs to make students' thinking visible through their models and modeling cycles.

Teachers do not prompt the use of particular mathematical concepts or their representational counterparts when presenting the problems. Instead, they choose activities that maximize the potential for students to develop the concepts that are the focal point in the curriculum by building on their early and intuitive ideas. The mathematical models emerge from the students' interactions with the problem situation and learning is assessed via these emergent behaviors.

Generative Activities: In a generative activity, students are asked to come up with outcomes that are mathematically same. Students can arrive at the responses or build responses from this sameness in a wide range of ways. The sameness gives coherence to the task and allows it to be an "organizational unit for performing a specific function." (Stroup et al., 2004)

Other activities can also be used as the means of formative assessment as long as they ensure the participation of every student, make students' thoughts visible to each other and to the teacher, promote feedback to revise and refine thinking. In addition, as a complementary to all of these is to modify and adapt instruction through the information gathered by those activities.

Formative Assessment in Computer Supported Learning

Six Strategies for web-based Formative Assessment

Many academics are seeking to diversify assessment tasks, broaden the range of skills assessed and provide students with more timely and informative feedback on their progress. Others are wishing to meet student expectations for more flexible delivery and to generate efficiencies in assessment that can ease academic staff workloads. The move to on-line and computer based assessment is a natural outcome of the increasing use of information and communication technologies to enhance learning. As more students seek flexibility in their courses, it seems inevitable there will be growing expectations for flexible assessment as well.

Wang et al. (2004b), developed the Formative Assessment Module of the Web-based Assessment and Test Analysis System (FAM-WATA), to help address this problem. This research not only applied FAM-WATA to assist teachers in giving feedback and interacting with students in an e-learning environment but also explored the effectiveness of FAM-WATA in facilitating student e-learning effectiveness. FAM-WATA offers six main strategies:

Strategy 1–3: 'Repeat the test', 'correct answers are not given', and 'ask questions' strategies.

The combination of two strategies, 'repeat the test' and 'correct answers are not given', in web-based formative assessment will increase e-learning effectiveness (Buchanan, 2000). The major purpose of these strategies is to provide students with opportunities to revise the mistakes they have made. In addition to these two strategies, the FAM-WATA tries to stimulate student interest and desire for new challenges through the design of the Web environment, as explained next.

When learners log in and perform a self-assessment, FAM-WATA will automatically choose some questions randomly from the database. The order of questions and options are randomly arranged. This is to prevent learner boredom with repeated tests. A given test item will not show up on the following test if a learner correctly answers the test item three times consecutively. Thus, the number of test items gradually decreases with each iteration of the test. At some point, all questions will be answered correctly, and the system will tag the successful learner with a 'pass the test' mark.

By the same token, if learners cannot answer the test item correctly three times consecutively, then the answer count will be reset to zero and begun again. Answering a test item correctly three times consecutively is necessary because the system judges that the learners may answer the question correctly simply by guessing. The purpose of this design is for learners to actively take on the challenge of learning, not passively guess their way through.

In the above design, 'timely feedback' is combined to form the strategy of 'correct answers are not given'. After learners submit their test papers, FAM-WATA will immediately give scores and present references to learners without directly giving the correct answers of the questions. Meanwhile, learners may also asynchronously interact with teachers by asking questions online. As for the function of 'timely feedback', the system offers learners reference materials to help them find correct answers.

Strategy 4: 'Monitor answering history' strategy

FAM-WATA provides an interface to check the answering history of the user and others who have taken the test, available to learners after they pass the test. Through understanding their own progress, learners are expected to take the initiative in monitoring their learning.

Strategy 5: 'Query scores' strategy

FAM-WATA provides an interface for learners to look up peer scores and see the progress of others, to encourage the learner to learn from peers, and motivate learning. Students may find out whether others have passed the test and how many tries are required for others to answer and to pass the test. Students can query the answering history of other students. The main purpose of these designs is to add the stimulus of competition. Those who perform well or pass the test will be marked by special signs, increasing their sense of achievement. The special signs can also be regarded as a form of encouragement.

Strategy 6: 'All pass and then reward' strategy

FAM-WATA will generate a flash (Adobe Systems Inc., CA, USA) animation to congratulate learners on passing the test. Animation effects can stimulate learner interest (Mayer & Moreno, 2002). This type of positive feedback can provide encouragement for learners who pass a task, creating a sense of achievement.

Formative Assessment in UK Education

In the UK education system, formative assessment (or assessment for learning) has been a key aspect of the agenda for personalised learning. The Working Group on 14–19 Reform led by Sir Mike Tomlinson, recommended that assessment of learners be refocused to be more teacher-led and less reliant on external assessment, putting learners at the heart of the assessment process.

The UK government has stated that personalised learning depends on teachers knowing the strengths and weaknesses of individual learners, and that a key means of achieving this is through formative assessment, involving high quality feedback to learners included within every teaching session.

The Assessment Reform Group has set out 10 principles for formative assessment. These are that assessment for learning should:

- be part of effective planning of teaching and learning
- focus on how students learn
- be recognised as central to classroom practice
- be regarded as a key professional skill for teachers
- be sensitive and constructive because any assessment has an emotional impact
- take account of the importance of learner motivation
- promote commitment to learning goals and a shared understanding of the criteria by which they are assessed
- enable learners to receive constructive guidance about how to improve
- develop learners' capacity for self-assessment so that they can become reflective and self-managing
- recognise the full range of achievements of all learners

Benefits of Formative Assessments for Teachers (Boston, 2002)

- Teachers are able to determine what standards students already know and to what degree.
- Teachers can decide what minor modifications or major changes in instruction they need to makes so that all students can succeed in upcoming instruction and on subsequent assessments.
- Teachers can create appropriate lessons and activities for groups of learners or individual students.
- Teachers can inform students about their current progress in order to help them set goals for improvement.
- In 2008, Katy Bainbridge began work on Align Assess Achieve, a method of teaching formative assessment to administrators and teachers.

Benefits of Formative Assessments for Students

- Students are more motivated to learn.
- Students take responsibility for their own learning.
- Students can become users of assessment alongside the teacher.
- Students learn valuable lifelong skills such as self-evaluation, self-assessment, and goal setting.
- Student achievement can improve from 21-41 percentile points.

Computer Aided Assessment

It is a term that covers all forms of assessment, whether Summative (i.e. tests that will contribute to formal qualifications) or Formative (i.e. tests that promote learning but are not part of a course's marking), delivered with the help of computers. This covers both assessments delivered on computer, either online or on a local network, and those that are marked with the aid of computers, such as those using Optical Mark Reading (OMR). There are number of open source online tools to handle exams conducted on OMR sheets.

Computer Aided Assessment can be viewed in a few different ways. Technically, assignments that are written on a computer and researched online are computer aided assessments. One of the most common forms of computer aided assessment (in terms of eLearning) is online quizzes or exams. These can be implemented online, and also marked by the computer by putting the answers in. Many Content Management Systems will have easy to setup and use systems for online exams.

It is also envisaged that computer-based formative assessment, in particular, will play an increasingly important role in learning, with the increased use of banks of question items for the construction and delivery of dynamic, on-demand assessments. This can be witnessed by current pioneering projects such as the SQA's SOLAR Project.

6

Curriculum in Education

In formal education, a curriculum is the set of courses, and their content, offered at a school or university. As an idea, curriculum stems from the Latin word for race course, referring to the course of deeds and experiences through which children grow to become mature adults. A curriculum is prescriptive, and is based on a more general syllabus which merely specifies what topics must be understood and to what level to achieve a particular grade or standard-

HISTORY OF CURRICULUM

In The Curriculum, the first textbook published on the subject, in 1918, John Franklin Bobbitt said that curriculum, as an idea, has its roots in the Latin word for race-course, explaining the curriculum as the course of deeds and experiences through which children become the adults they should be, for success in adult society. Furthermore, the curriculum encompasses the entire scope of formative deed and experience occurring in and out of school, and not only experiences occurring in school; experiences that are unplanned and undirected, and experiences intentionally directed for the purposeful formation of adult members of society. (cf. image at right.)

To Bobbitt, the curriculum is a social engineering arena. Per his cultural presumptions and social definitions, his curricular formulation has two notable features: (i) that scientific experts would best be qualified to and justified in designing curricula based upon their expert knowledge of what qualities are desirable in adult members of society, and which experiences would generate said qualities; and (ii) curriculum defined as the deeds-experiences the student ought to have to become the adult he or she ought to become.

Hence, he defined the curriculum as an ideal, rather than as the concrete reality of the deeds and experiences that form people to who and what they are.

Contemporary views of curriculum reject these features of Bobbitt's postulates, but retain the basis of curriculum as the course of experience(s) that forms human beings into persons. Personal formation via curricula is studied at the personal level and at the group level, i.e. cultures and societies (e.g. professional formation, academic discipline via historical experience). The formation of a group is reciprocal, with the formation of its individual participants.

Although it formally appeared in Bobbitt's definition, curriculum is a course of formative experience also pervades John Dewey's work (who disagreed with Bobbitt on important matters). Although Bobbitt's and Dewey's idealistic understanding of "curriculum" is different from current, restricted uses of the word, curriculum writers and researchers generally share it as common, substantive understanding of curriculum.

TYPES OF CURRICULUM

An essential feature of curriculum design, seen in every college catalog and at every other level of schooling, is the identification of prerequisites for each course. These prerequisites can be satisfied by taking particular courses, and in some cases by examination, or by other means, such as work experience. In general, more advanced courses in any subject require some foundation in basic courses, but some coursework requires study in other departments, as in the sequence of math classes required for a physics major, or the language requirements for students preparing in literature, music, or scientific research. A more detailed curriculum design must deal with prerequisites within a course for each topic taken up. This in turn leads to the problems of course organization and scheduling once the dependencies between topics are known.

Core curriculum

In education, a core curriculum is a curriculum, or course of study, which is deemed central and usually made mandatory for all students of a school or school system. However, this is not always the case. For example, a school might mandate a music appreciation class, but students may opt out if they take a performing musical class, such as orchestra, band, chorus, etc. Core curricula are often instituted, at the primary and secondary levels, by school boards, Departments of Education, or other administrative agencies charged with overseeing education. At the undergraduate level, individual college and university administrations and faculties sometimes mandate core curricula, especially in the liberal arts. But because of increasing specialization and depth in the student's major field of study, a typical core curriculum in higher education mandates a far smaller proportion of a student's course work than a high school or elementary school core curriculum prescribes.

Amongst the best known and most expansive core curricula programs at leading American colleges are that of Columbia College at Columbia University, as well as the University of Chicago's. Both can take up to two years to complete without advanced standing, and are designed to foster critical skills in a broad range of academic disciplines, including: the social sciences, humanities, physical and biological sciences, mathematics, writing and foreign languages.

In 1999, the University of Chicago announced plans to reduce and modify the content of its core curriculum, including lowering the number of required courses from 21 to 15 and offering a wider range of content. When The New York Times, The Economist, and other major news outlets picked up this story, the University became the focal point of a national debate on education. The National Association of Scholars released a statement saying, "It is truly depressing to observe a steady abandonment of the University of Chicago's once imposing undergraduate core curriculum, which for so long stood as the benchmark of content and rigor among American academic institutions." Simultaneously, however, a set of university administrators, notably then-President Hugo Sonnenschein, argued that reducing the core curriculum had become both a financial and educational imperative, as the university was struggling to attract a commensurate volume of applicants to its undergraduate division compared to peer schools as a result of what was perceived by the pro-change camp as a reaction by "the average eighteen year old" to the expanse of the collegiate core.

Further, as core curricula began to be diminished over the course of the twentieth century at many American schools, several smaller institutions became famous for embracing a core curriculum that covers nearly the student's entire undergraduate education, often utilizing classic texts of the western canon to teach all subjects including science. St. John's College in the United States is one example of this approach.

Distribution requirements

Some colleges opt for the middle ground of the continuum between specified and unspecified curricula by using a system of distribution requirements. In such a system, students are required to take courses in particular categories, but are free to choose within these categories.

Open curriculum

Other institutions have largely done away with core requirements in their entirety, as in the student-driven course selections of Brown University and Cornell University. Amherst College requires that students take one of a list of first-year seminars, but has no required classes or distribution requirements.

CURRICULUM IN FORMAL SCHOOLING

In formal education or schooling (cf. education), a curriculum is the set of courses, course work, and content offered at a school or university. A curriculum may be partly or entirely determined by an external, authoritative body (i.e. the National Curriculum for England in English schools). In the U.S., each state, with the individual school districts, establishes the curricula taught. Each state, however, builds its curriculum with great participation of national academic subject groups selected by the United States Department of Education, e.g. National Council of Teachers of Mathematics (NCTM) for mathematical instruction. In Australia each state's Education Department establishes curricula with plans for a National Curriculum in 2011. UNESCO's International Bureau of Education has the primary mission of studying curricula and their implementation worldwide.

Curriculum means two things: (i) the range of courses from which students choose what subject matters to study, and (ii) a specific learning program. In the latter case, the curriculum collectively describes the teaching, learning, and assessment materials available for a given course of study.

Currently, a spiral curriculum (or tycoil curriculum) is promoted as allowing students to revisit a subject matter's content at the different levels of development of the subject matter being studied. The constructivist approach, of the tycoil curriculum, proposes that children learn best via active engagement with the educational environment, i.e. Discovery learning. Crucial to the curriculum is the definition of the course objectives that usually are expressed as learning outcomes' and normally include the program's assessment strategy. These outcomes and assessments are grouped as units (or modules), and, therefore, the curriculum comprises a collection of such units, each, in turn, comprising a specialised, specific part of the curriculum. So, a typical curriculum includes communications, numeracy, information technology, and social skills units, with specific, specialized teaching of each.

IN THE FORM OF COURSE CATALOG (EDUCATION)

A course catalog or calendar is an organized, detailed, descriptive list of course offerings at a college, university or other educational outlet. Educational organizations usually publish a course catalog with additional information covering academic and administrative policies and procedures.

IN THE FORM OF LEARNSCAPES

Learnscapes are defined as "places where a learning program has been designed to permit users to interact with the environment". Their purpose is to promote and extend environmental awareness, by presenting biodiversity as the basis for environmental conservation and ecologically sustainable development. This is achieved through developing school based curricula that engage students interactively with their surrounding environment. Ideally, learnscapes incorporate educational, environmental and social outcomes that reflect the character of the community as well as the school site.

"A Learnscape feature, whether it be an outdoor classroom, worm farm, bush regeneration, recycling area, frog pond or herb garden, is not a Learnscape itself. It is the collaborative process within which the feature is created and plans for how it will be maintained and used for learning once it is created that make the feature a Learnscape".

Founding member and Program Director of the School Learnscapes Trust, Helen Tyas Tunggal emphasises that "Essential to all learnscape development is the active involvement and contribution of students, teachers, parents and other groups within the school community during the planning, preparation and implementation of a design." Helen was awarded the Gold Banksia Environmental Award in 1999. Her efforts were described by the awards' organisers as depicting "the importance of empowering future generations to become competent and involved caretakers of the planet for the next millennium."

Learncape programs also have a "calming effect" on classes, by invoking deeper relationships between students and their teachers.

IN THE FORM OF COURSE EQUIVALENCY

Course equivalency is the term used in higher education describing how a course offered by one college or university relates to a course offered by another. If a course is viewed as equal or better than the course offered by the receiving college or university, the course can be noted as an equivalent course. A course equivalency can be unilateral, meaning it is deemed equivalent by the receiver. Or, it could be bilateral, meaning both sender and receiver acknowledge their acceptance of each other's course as equivalent. The methods and measures used to determine course equivalency vary by institution, state, region and country.

History of Course Equivalency

College transfer often requires the determination and evaluation of prior course learning. Receiving institutions usually maintain course equivalency tables listing how courses equate by sender institution. Unless the receiving institution maintains an online public reference to the course equivalency tables, sending institutions often have difficulty projecting transferability of their course offerings. As a result, student transitions from sender to receiver, if outside the normal path, can be very problematic. This has led many states to legislate reforms, regulations and mandates to augment the tracking of course equivalencies in recent years. On the federal level, Congress and the Department of Education have been debating the issues well documented in the GAO report to Congress, October 2005.

Colleges and universities historically have utilized standalone electronic tools to track course equivalencies and facilitate the course evaluation process. Institutions, led by state education agencies are shifting to collaborative tracking tools and shared repositories like the National Course Atlas to facilitate how they propose, evaluate and manage course equivalency decisions online in a proactive manner. Further, utilizing shared collaborative tools enables institutions to ensure systematic procedures applied quickly, accurately, and equally by reducing the duplication of effort and the lack of transparency across institutional curricula since both sender and receiver see the results when sharing a common repository.

The most common course attributes evaluated to determine course equivalency are description, academic credits, accreditation, type of instructor, method of instruction, length of the course, number of meetings, total class time, level of rigor, level of instruction, learning outcomes, grade scale, pre-requisites, co-requisites and textbook. This is not an exclusive list of course attributes. Generally, faculty perform the determination of course equivalencies. Course equivalency decisions can be appealed by presenting evidence to an academic department.

AS NATIONAL COURSE ATLAS

The National Course Atlas is an online free repository of 3.5 million credit and noncredit educational courses offered by regionally and nationally accredited colleges and universities in the United States. Each course (education) is sourced from current postsecondary education providers in the United States offering the courses to the public or to private constituents.

Background

The National Course Atlas was launched in 2006 by AcademyOne, Inc. aggregates thousands of separate college course catalogs or what is also published as annual course listings making it simpler to search and compare courses across independent educational providers spread out throughout the United States or online across thousands of separate web sites. The repository includes links to course equivalencies published by colleges and universities. It also includes an electronic request and reply lookup to allow determination of transferability by course extending the use the repository to other systems that desire to display transfer links. The repository also includes lists of assessment tests such as Advanced Placement (AP), College Level Examination Program (CLEP) and course credit recommendation exhibits produced by American Council on Education (ACE).

The National Course Atlas is refreshed annually by collecting the college catalogs and course offerings from over 4,100 distinct educational providers including every two year (community college) and four year institution in the United States. AcademyOne collects and parses 18,000 files each year to produce the annual updates. The online repository indexes the full course title and descriptions allowing any user to perform keyword and title searches to support a range of needs such as curriculum alignment, course evaluation, transfer evaluation, cross registration, dual enrollment, study abroad, online registration and course planning.

Historically, colleges, universities, career schools, adult education centers, corporate university and other educational providers annually revise and publish course catalogs and listings in a variety of formats. The National Course Atlas combines these separate course listings from individual providers into a single, searchable and maintainable electronic repository abstracting the differences in format to make it easier to search and compare course attributes which include prerequisites and co-requisites.

Educational providers also advertise their course offerings online through a variety of formats and systems. The National Course Atlas allows students, faculty, advisors and other interested parties to search the repository to find courses they may enroll in satisfying program requirements or interests. The course equivalencies can be revealed if available to determine transferability between educational providers. The National Course Atlas also enables educational providers to add course objectives, syllabi, learning outcomes, expected competencies and attributes defining the course, such as title, cost, location, method of instruction, length of instruction, meeting times, prerequisites, co-requisites, number of credits to be awarded and other descriptive elements.

The National Course Atlas, published by AcademyOne is one of the first examples of an aggregated course repository established in the United States used to support course planning spanning multiple educational providers. The National Course Atlas is used by government agencies, research centers, higher education, institutions, employers, workforce development organizations and academic advisors in a range of capacities to help facilitate student enrollment and course planning that may or may not lead to a formal credential.

As Course Atlas for Education

A course atlas is an online repository created to address the need to aggregate and share a database of credit and noncredit courses offered by one to many educational providers across a State (administrative division), region, country or around the world to facilitate course planning and other learning activities. Courses listed in the course atlas reflect the availability of what educational providers offer the public or to their private constituents.

History

The term course atlas was coined by AcademyOne, Inc. as a means to describe an online repository built to aggregate, store and enable online searches to support a range of needs such as curriculum alignment, transfer evaluation, cross registration, dual enrollment, study abroad, online registration and course planning.

Historically, colleges, universities, career schools, adult education centers, corporate universities and other educational providers publish course catalogs and listings in a variety of formats. The course atlas combines course listings from individual providers into a single, searchable and maintainable electronic repository abstracting the differences in format to make it easier to search and compare course attributes.

Educational providers also advertise their course offerings online through a variety of formats and systems. A course atlas allows students, faculty, advisors and other interested parties to search the course atlas repository to find courses they may enroll in satisfying program requirements or interests. The course atlas also enables educational providers to denote course objectives, syllabi, learning outcomes, expected competencies and attributes defining the course, such as title, cost, location, method of instruction, length of instruction, meeting times, pre-requisities, co-requisites, number of credits to be awarded and other descriptive elements.

The National Course Atlas, published by AcademyOne is one of the first examples of an aggregated course repository established in the United States used to support course planning spanning multiple educational providers. The National Course Atlas is used by government agencies, research centers, higher education, institutions, employers, workforce development organizations and academic advisors in a range of capacities to help facilitate student enrollment and course planning that may or may not lead to a formal credential.

Block Scheduling

Block scheduling is a type of academic scheduling in which each student has fewer classes per day for a longer period of time. This is intended to result in more time for teaching due to less class switching and preparation. It also allows for a student to take four electives, rather than two, or three.

In some cases, such as in medical school or other intensive university program, a block schedule means taking one class at a time, all day, every day, until all of the material is covered. A normal university course might then be completed in three or four weeks of focused effort on a single topic. When used as a supplement to a normal academic term, instead of the normal schedule, this approach is sometimes called a mini-mester.

Conversion to block scheduling became a widespread trend in American middle schools and high schools in the 1990s. Prior to that, many schools scheduled classes such that a student saw every one of their teachers each day. Classes were approximately 40-60 minutes long, but under block scheduling, they became approximately 90 minutes long.

However, many American high schools still use the traditional eight- or nine-period day, and consider block scheduling to be one of many ill-considered education reform schemes.

Part of the motivation for block scheduling is to prepare students for taking end-of-grade/end-of-course standardized tests used to measure student achievement (and in some school districts, teacher pay and school funding). Another is social-to foster cooperation among students. This is done by having students work in groups (called "cooperative learning") to help them learn from each other, rather than have classes that focus on teacher-delivered content, as some experts believe that students learn better from peers than from professionals.

ARTS INTEGRATION

Arts integration is a term applied to an approach to teaching and learning that uses the fine and performing arts as primary pathways to learning. Arts integration differs from traditional arts education by its inclusion of both an arts discipline and a traditional subject as part of learning (e.g. using improvisational drama skills to learn about conflict in writing.) The goal of arts integration is to increase knowledge of a general subject area while concurrently fostering a greater understanding and appreciation of the fine and performing arts.

History of Arts Education and Arts Integration

Arts integration is related to arts education in schools. Arts education, while existing in different forms during the 19th century, gained popularity as part of John Dewey's Progressive Education Theory. The first publication that describes a seamless interplay between the arts and other subjects (arts integration) taught in American schools was Leon Winslow's The Integrated School Art Program (1939). For the remainder of the 20th century, arts education's role in public schools ebbed and flowed with the country's political leanings and financial well-being.

According to Liora Bresler, during the 1970s and 1980s, two advocates for arts integration emerged: Harry Broudy and Elliot Eisner. Broudy advocated for the arts on the basis of strengthening the imagination. Broudy viewed imagination as an essential component of learning that should be cultivated in schools, and he advocated for the integration of aesthetic education into all subject matters in his work, Enlightened Cherishing. Eisner followed Broudy, citing that the arts were important to varying types of cognition. He believed that arts brought about a deeper understanding of the world due to their interactivity-the arts move learning beyond what is written or read.

Currently, No Child Left Behind legislation describes arts education as "essential to every child's education," and include it as one of the Core Subjects.. No Child Left Behind legislation also emphasizes accountability through assessment (often taking the form of the standardized test.) While no standardized assessment has been mandated in any of the arts, the need for academic accountability in the arts, as well as in other academic subject areas, has led to increased research on and advocacy of arts integration and its impact on student learning.

Research and Advocacy in Arts Integration

The impetus for arts integration is a growing body of research that demonstrates how learners experience success when taught why and how to use music, visual art, drama/dance, theatre and the literary arts to both express and understand ideas, thoughts and feelings. Critical Links, a compendium published by the Arts Education Partnership (AEP), includes 62 studies which examine the relationship between arts learning, academic achievement, and social development of students. Highlights include studies which explore the use of drama to increase students' reading comprehension and studies which examine the relationship between music and math concepts. The Arts Education Partnership has also published The Third Space, which profiles ten arts-integrated schools across the United States.

Another American organization conducting research in arts integration is the Chicago Arts Partnerships in Education. It has published, through Lawrence Erlbaum Associates, Renaissance in the Classroom: Arts Integration and Meaningful Learning The book, edited by Gail Burnaford, Ph.D, former professor at Northwestern

University and current professor at Florida Atlantic University; Cynthia Weiss, teaching artist and former CAPE associate (2000 to 2002); and Arnold Aprill, CAPE's Founding & Creative Director, combines the contributions of two-hundred seventy-two participants in CAPE's arts integration partnerships. James Catterall, arts education researcher and professor at University of California, Los Angeles's Graduate School of Education and Information Studies, has collaborated with CAPE on publications.

Harvard University's Graduate School of Education supports Project Zero, an educational research group founded in 1967 by Nelson Goodman, which investigates learning in the arts. Former directors of Project Zero include David Perkins and Howard Gardner. Currently, it is directed by Steve Seidel, and has expanded its research in arts learning to include other branches of education. Howard Gardner's Theory of multiple intelligences has been used as part of the rationale for the use of integrated arts models in teaching and learning.

The Kennedy Center Partners in Education, headquartered in Washington, DC, is an organization that has promoted arts integration for over two decades. While The Kennedy Center does conduct research in arts learning, they also provide networking opportunities for arts education programs nation-wide through The Kennedy Center Alliance for Arts Education Network KCAAEN. This organization advocates for arts education, fosters collaboration between artists and schools to support arts learning, develops and conducts professional development in arts education for teachers, and recognizes achievement in the arts.

Academic Transfer

College transfer is the movement of students from one higher education institution to another and the process by which academic credits are accepted or not accepted by a receiving institution.

History

College transfer and articulation involve planned and unplanned movement of students among institutions of higher education. Planned transfers may be facilitated by carefully negotiated articulation agreements between institutions, and enable students to start an academic program at one institution with the knowledge that they will continue their program and obtain their academic credential at another institution. It is important to note that not all planned transfers are based on such prior institutional arrangements, and that students may independently plan to transfer from one institution to another without having complete knowledge of the credit-acceptance policies of the institution to which they intend to transfer.

Unanticipated factors and the general mobility of our society create numerous circumstances under which students must move from one institution to another without prior planning. Reasons for such movements can range from mismatches between students and institutions, employment, military movement, to geographic relocations by the families. The fundamental challenge with college transfer, whether planned or unplanned, is to aggregate coursework conducted at different institutions with different academic policies, different curricula, and different levels of expected rigor into an academic credential that the issuing institution can stand behind. College transfer is complex, because disparate and sometimes non-comparable coursework is brought together, often without prior involvement of the institutions from which the student enrolls and expects to graduate.

According to the National Center for Education Statistics (NCES), in 2005 nearly 60% of college graduates in the United States who completed undergraduate degrees had attended two or more institutions prior to graduation. Roughly 2.5 million students transfer every year. Student mobility spans institutional structures, differing policies and practices often extending college degree completion by an average of one semester according to the GAO in a report to Congress in October 2005.

In The Form of Active Learning

Active learning is an umbrella term that refers to several models of instruction that focus the responsibility of learning on learners. Bonwell and Eison (1991) popularized this approach to instruction. This "buzz word" of the 1980s became their 1990s report to the Association for the Study of Higher Education (ASHE). In this report they discuss a variety of methodologies for promoting "active learning." However according to Mayer (2004) strategies like "active learning" developed out of the work of an earlier group of theorists - those promoting discovery learning. Practice after initial learning, is of vital importance in one's education/career, and is important for cognitive development, but is practice required during learning?

It has been suggested that students who actively engage with the material are more likely to recall information (Bruner 1961), but several well known authors have argued this claim is not well supported by the literature. Rather than being behaviorally active during learning, Mayer (2004) suggests learners should be cognitively active.

Role of Articulation in Education

In Australia and the United States education, articulation or more specifically course articulation, refers to the process of comparing the content of courses that are transferred between postsecondary institutions such as TAFE institutes, colleges or universities. In other words, course articulation is the process by which one institution matches its courses or requirements to course work completed at another institution. Students use course articulation to assure that the courses they complete will not have to be repeated at the institution to which they are transferring.

Course articulation is distinct from the process of acceptance by one institution of earned credit, from another institution, as applicable towards its degree requirements, i.e. "transferring credit".

Course articulation may be done on an ad hoc basis when a student actually wishes to transfer. It may also be done pursuant to existing course-to-course comparison data, or based on formal articulation agreements. In the last case, representatives of each institution compare their respective course curricula, to determine which courses are comparable and which are not. Their consensus is then formalized in a written agreement which is used by students and advisors and is regularly updated according to a mutual schedule.

Although Credit Transfer can be conducted between education bodies in separate countries, the process of articulation can become very complicated when students transfer courses earned at multiple and international campuses, more than 5-10 years ago, or have alternative credit experiences such as exam or military credit.

Career Clusters

Career Clusters provide students with a context for studying traditional academics and learning the skills specific to a career, and provide U.S. schools with a structure for organizing or restructuring curriculum offerings and focusing class make-up by a common theme such as interest.

In the U.S. Department of Education model, 16 Career Clusters link to 70+ more specific Career Pathways - each have their own knowledge and skills requirements. Within the 70+ career pathways, 1800 Career Specialties are defined. The structure has evolved over time and may vary by state. The U.S. DOE Career Clusters framework is useful for connecting students with courses of study and careers via Career Assessments, and allows them to learn general, more transferable skills at the cluster level, with more specific skills and knowledge acquired at the career pathways and speciality levels. The nonprofit Vocational Research Institute adapted an interest and aptitude assessment, Careerscope, to help students choose curriculum and careers for which they have both interest and aptitude - at the cluster, pathway and career specialty levels. A concept related to Career Clusters, Small Learning Community is primarily concerned with restructuring secondary schools, in many cases using a career clusters framework.

Co-operative Learning

Cooperative learning is an approach to organizing classroom activities into academic and social learning experiences. Students must work in groups to complete the two sets of tasks collectively. Everyone succeeds when the group succeeds.

Cooperative Learning has 5 basic elements:

- Positive Interdependence requires that group members feel connected to each other in the process of accomplishing the goal.
- Positive Interdependence encompasses 9 subcategories:
    - goal - the expected outcome of the activity
    - incentive; the reason the group wishes to complete the task
    - resource; the tools needed to complete the task

- o role; roles assigned to students to ensure each person contributes
- o sequence; steps to completing the task
- o simulation; the alternative mindset needed to complete the goal
- o outside force; something limiting the time or used as a driving force
- o environmental; that every group member is in close proximity to one another
- o identity; that the group feels connected in one team.

Individual Accountability means that every group member is responsible for being able to demonstrate understanding and comprehension of the learned academic expectations and social goals.

Face to Face Interaction suggests that the group must participate by communicating and discussing the goal.

Social Skills include listening, body language, sharing, accepting ideas and differences, etc. These are the skills needed prior to or being developed during the group work.

Processing is when the students assess their efforts as a group and can pin point areas of improvement in their social skills.

When doing activities in Cooperative Learning it is important to do a Contact Activity to ensure that the group has a basis for comfortable communication and feel open to one another.

Benefits include: higher self esteem, achievement and retention of academic information

- social support
- positive school attitude
- positive attitude towards educators and classmates

ON-TASK BEHAVIOUR

- collaborative skills
- increase in level of reasoning

Considerations include:

- sometimes manipulation of groups may be necessary
- some students may not respond well in forced group situations
- time consuming
- it is important to be alert and promoting success

CONTINUING EDUCATION UNIT

A Continuing Education Unit (CEU) is a measure used in continuing education programs, particularly those required in a licensed profession in order for the professional to maintain the license. Examples of people who need CEUs include architects, engineers, educators, nurses, mental health professionals, and social workers. Generally, a CEU is defined as ten hours of participation in a recognized continuing education program, with qualified instruction and sponsorship. CEU records are widely used to provide evidence of completion of continuing education requirements mandated by certification bodies, professional societies, or governmental licensing boards. The records also provide employers with information on training pertinent to particular occupations.

The term CEU is in the public domain. Any organization may award a traditional CEU without requiring any accreditation. With a traditional CEU an employer or other organization must decide on an individual basis whether to honor the CEU from a training provider.

Due to certain CEU providers not adhering to high standards, and the lack of standards for specific fields, there is sometimes a distrust of the value of a CEU, and accrediting organizations have been created to standardize what a CEU means. The International Association for Continuing Education & Training (IACET) offers the most industry wide accreditation of CEUs. Specific industries, such as nursing, health, etc., have their own accrediting processes for CEUs. Any accredited CEU generally has a preface of the accrediting body. For instance training institutions accredited by the IACET can offer IACET CEUs.

CONTRACT GRADING

Contract Grading is a form of grading which results from an instructor to student cooperation, and entails contracted number of assignments of specified quality that correspond to specific letter grades. Contract grading may be contrasted with other grading methods, such as grading on a curve or percentile systems.

COURSE (EDUCATION)

In U.S. and Canadian education, a course is a unit of teaching that typically lasts one academic term, is led by one or more instructors (teachers or professors), has a fixed roster of students, and gives each student a grade and academic credit.

The original meaning-a course of instruction, the unit of instruction embodied by a course-is also used, so textbooks may be entitled, e.g., A Course in Modern Physics.

In Australia, however, the term "course" refers to the entire programme of studies required to complete a university degree, and the word "unit" would be used to refer to an academic course in the North American sense.

CULTURALLY RELEVANT TEACHING

"Culturally Relevant Teaching is a pedagogy that empowers students intellectually, socially, emotionally, and politically by using cultural referents to impart knowledge, skills, and attitudes."

First introduced by Dr.Gloria Ladson-Billings in 1992 as "culturally relevant teaching", the term is now widely known and accepted in the education field. Many leading scholars have added to the quality research and study Dr. Ladson-Billings originally published. According to John Uzo Ogbu, "A culturally relevant pedagogy must provide a way for students to maintain their cultural identity while succeeding academically".

INSTRUCTIONAL DESIGN

Instructional Design (also called Instructional Systems Design (ISD)) is the practice of maximizing the effectiveness, efficiency and appeal of instruction and other learning experiences. The process consists broadly of determining the current state and needs of the learner, defining the end goal of instruction, and creating some "intervention" to assist in the transition. Ideally the process is informed by pedagogically and and ragogically (adult learning) tested theories of learning and may take place in student-only, teacher-led or community-based settings. The outcome of this instruction may be directly observable and scientifically measured or completely hidden and assumed. There are many instructional design models but many are based on the ADDIE model with the phases analysis, design, development, implementation, and evaluation. As a field, instructional design is historically and traditionally rooted in cognitive and behavioral psychology.

EMERGENT CURRICULUM

Emergent curriculum is a way of planning curriculum based on the student's interest and passions as well as the teacher's. To plan an emergent curriculum requires observation, documentation, creative brainstorming, flexibility and patience. Rather than starting with a lesson plan which requires a "hook" to get the children interested, emergent curriculum starts with the children's interests. This is not to say that the teacher has no input, in fact teachers may well have a general topic they think is important for children to study and they may purposely include certain materials or experiences related to it as jumping off points. Elizabeth Jones points out:

We are the stage directors; curriculum is teacher's responsibility, not children's. People who hear the words emergent curriculum may wrongly assume that everything simply emerges from the children. The children's ideas are an important source of curriculum but only one of many possible sources that reflect the complex ecology of their lives.

This process requires a great deal of flexibility and creativity on the part of the teacher. Carolyn Edwards notes: "The teachers honestly do not know where the group will end up. Although this openness adds a dimension of difficulty to their work, it also makes it more exciting."

Once teachers see an interest "emerging" they brainstorm ways to study the topic in depth. Webbing is often used because of its playful and flexible nature. A web doesn't show everything that will be learned, it shows many things that could be learned. However it is important to use the webbing as a tool to open the teacher to possibilities not a "plan." Teachers brainstorm many possibilities for study sparked from the particular interest, not as a plan but more as a 'road map' as one teacher put it: To get a plan, we chose an idea and brainstormed ways that children could play it - hands-on activities we could provide. Putting all the activities on a web gives you a road map full of possible journeys.

TRADITIONAL EDUCATION

Traditional education or back-to-basics refers to long-established customs found in schools that society has traditionally deemed appropriate. Some forms of education reform promote the adoption of progressive education practices, a more holistic approach which focuses on individual students' needs and self-expression. In the eyes of reformers, traditional teacher-centered methods focused on rote learning and memorization must be abandoned in favor of student-centered and task-based approaches to learning. However, many parents and conservative citizens are concerned with the maintenance of objective educational standards based on testing, which favors a more traditional approach.

Depending on the context, the opposite of traditional education may be progressive education, modern education (the education approaches based on developmental psychology), or alternative education. The definition of traditional education varies greatly with geography and by historical period.

The chief business of traditional education is to transmit to a next generation those skills, facts, and standards of moral and social conduct that adults deem to be necessary for the next generation's material and social success. As beneficiaries of this scheme, which educational progressivist John Dewey described as being "imposed from above and from outside", the students are expected to docilely and obediently receive and believe these fixed answers. Teachers are the instruments by which this knowledge is communicated and these standards of behavior are enforced.

Historically, the primary educational technique of traditional education was simple oral recitation: In a typical approach, students sat quietly at their places and listened to one individual after another recite his or her lesson, until each had been called upon. The teacher's primary activity was assigning and listening to these recitations; students studied at home. A test might be given at the end of a unit, and the process, which was called "assignment-study-recitation-test", was repeated. In addition to its overemphasis on verbal answers, reliance on rote memorization (mindless memorization with no effort at understanding the meaning), and disconnected, unrelated assignments, it was also an extremely inefficient use of students' and teachers' time. It also insisted that all students be taught the same materials at the same point; students that did not learn quickly enough failed, rather than being allowed to succeed at their natural speeds. This approach, which had been imported from Europe, dominated American education until the end of the 19th century, when the reform movement imported progressive education techniques from Europe.

Traditional education is associated with much stronger elements of coercion than seems acceptable now in most cultures. It has sometimes included: the use of corporal punishment to maintain classroom discipline or punish errors; inculcating the dominant religion and language; separating students according to gender, race, and social class, as well as teaching different subjects to girls and boys. In terms of curriculum there was and still is a high level of attention paid to time-honoured academic knowledge.

In the present it varies enormously from culture to culture, but still tends to be characterised by a much higher level of coercion than alternative education. Traditional schooling in Britain and its possessions and former colonies tends to follow the English Public School style of strictly enforced uniforms and a militaristic style of discipline. This can be contrasted with South African, USA and Australian schools, which can have a much higher tolerance for spontaneous student-to-teacher communication.

HIDDEN CURRICULUM

Hidden curriculum, in the most general terms, is "some of the outcomes or by-products of schools or of non-school settings, particularly those states which are learned but not openly intended." However, a variety of definitions have been developed based on the broad range of perspectives of those who study this phenomenon. Any setting, including traditionally recreational and social activities, may teach unintended lessons since it is tied not necessarily to schools but rather to learning experiences. But most often, hidden curriculum refers to various types of knowledge gained in primary and secondary school settings, usually with a negative connotation referring to inequalities suffered as a result of its presence. This attitude stems from the commitment of the school system of the United States to promote democracy and ensure equal intellectual development, goals that are hindered by these intangible lessons. In this context, hidden curriculum is said to reinforce existing social inequalities by educating students in various matters and behaviors according to their class and social status. In the same way that there is an unequal distribution of cultural capital in this society, there is a corresponding distribution of knowledge amongst its students. The hidden curriculum can also refer to the transmission of norms, values, and beliefs conveyed in both the formal educational content and the social interactions within these schools. Hidden curriculum is difficult to explicitly define because it varies among its students and their experiences and because is it constantly changing as the knowledge and beliefs of a society evolve.

The concept that the hidden curriculum expresses is the idea that schools do more than simply transmit knowledge, as laid down in the official curricula. Behind it lies criticism of the social implications, political underpinnings, and cultural outcomes of modern educative activities. While early examinations were concerned with identifying the anti-democratic nature of schooling, later studies have taken various tones, including those concerned with socialism, capitalism, and anarchism in education.

FLEXIBLE MODULAR SCHEDULING

Flexible modular scheduling is a type of academic scheduling where a day is broken into many 10-20 minute modules or "mods". The technique resembles some common college scheduling schemes.

One such example of high school modular scheduling is utilized at the Bergen County Academies in New Jersey. At this school, the day is broken down into 27 separate 18 minute modules. Classes vary in size, from a small class of 2 mods to a larger class of 3 mods. Labs, projects, and certain electives can even run for as long as 9 mods. Student schedules often change between different weekdays (i.e. one could have Literature one day for 3 mods, then 2 mods on the next day - or not at all). This type of scheduling allows for many free periods during the day as well as the possibility for more classes. These "free mods" can go to as long as 180 minutes of continuous free time without classes. This time could be utilized for lunch, study, or socializing. Due to the latter, students are advised to spend most of their free time in study halls so that such time is not misused. An additional bonus is the ability for students to have more than 2 elective classes (according to free time), whereas in the traditional period scheduling, students are limited to 1-2 electives.

E-SYLLABUS

An eSyllabus- also known as an electronic syllabus, online syllabus, or course homepage, provides the information of a traditional syllabus but can also link to online materials used in a course. Typically the eSyllabus is written in HTML and posted on the.

The advantages of the eSyllabus lies in its inexpensiveness and ease of distribution, its visibility beyond the course participants, and the inexpensive, effective and well-organized distribution of class materials such as lecture notes or overheads.

Curriculum Theory and Practice

The organization of schooling and further education has long been associated with the idea of curriculum. But what actually is curriculum, and how might it be conceptualized? We explore curriculum theory and practice and its relation to informal education.

contents: introduction o curriculum as transmission o curriculum as product o curriculum as process o curriculum as praxis o curriculum and context o curriculum and informal education o

The idea of curriculum is hardly new - but the way we understand and theorize it has altered over the years - and there remains considerable dispute as to meaning.

It has its origins in the running/chariot tracks of Greece. It was, literally, a course. In Latin curriculum was a racing chariot; currere was to run.

A useful starting point for us here might be the definition offered by John Kerr and taken up by Vic Kelly in his standard work on the subject. Kerr defines curriculum as, 'All the learning which is planned and guided by the school, whether it is carried on in groups or individually, inside or outside the school. This gives us some basis to move on - and for the moment all we need to do is highlight two of the key features:

Learning is planned and guided. We have to specify in advance what we are seeking to achieve and how we are to go about it. The definition refers to schooling. We should recognize that our current appreciation of curriculum theory and practice emerged in the school and in relation to other schooling ideas such as subject and lesson.

In what follows we are going to look at four ways of approaching curriculum theory and practice:

1. Curriculum as a body of knowledge to be transmitted.
2. Curriculum as an attempt to achieve certain ends in students - product.
3. Curriculum as process.
4. Curriculum as praxis.

It is helpful to consider these ways of approaching curriculum theory and practice in the light of Aristotle's influential categorization of knowledge into three disciplines: the theoretical, the productive and the practical.

Here we can see some clear links - the body of knowledge to be transmitted in the first is that classically valued as 'the canon'; the process and praxis models come close to practical deliberation; and the technical concerns of the outcome or product model mirror elements of Aristotle's characterization of the productive. More this will be revealed as we examine the theory underpinning individual models.

CURRICULUM AS PROCESS

We have seen that the curriculum as product model is heavily dependent on the setting of behavioural objectives. The curriculum, essentially, is a set of documents for implementation. Another way of looking at curriculum theory and practice is via process. In this sense curriculum is not a physical thing, but rather the interaction of teachers, students and knowledge. In other words, curriculum is what actually happens in the classroom and what people do to prepare and evaluate. What we have in this model is a number of elements in constant interaction. It is an active process and links with the practical form of reasoning set out by Aristotle.

Teachers enter particular schooling and situations with an ability to think critically, -in-action an understanding of their role and the expectations others have of them, and a proposal for action which sets out essential principles and features of the educational encounter. Guided by these, they encourage conversations between, and with, people in the situation out of which may come thinking and action. They continually evaluate the process and what they can see of outcomes.

Perhaps the two major things that set this apart from the model for informal education are first, the context in which the process occurs ('particular schooling situations'); and second, the fact that teachers enter the classroom or any other formal educational setting with a more fully worked-through idea of what is about to happen. Here I have described that as entering the situation with 'a proposal for action which sets out essential principles and features of the educational encounter'.

This form of words echoes those of Lawrence Stenhouse (1975) who produced one of the best-known explorations of a process model of curriculum theory and practice. He defined curriculum tentatively: 'A curriculum is an attempt to communicate the essential principles and features of an educational proposal in such a form that it is open to critical scrutiny and capable of effective translation into practice'. He suggests that a curriculum is rather like a recipe in cookery.

It can be criticized on nutritional or gastronomic grounds - does it nourish the students and does it taste good? - and it can be criticized on the grounds of practicality - we can't get hold of six dozen larks' tongues and the grocer can't find any ground unicorn horn! A curriculum, like the recipe for a dish, is first imagined as a possibility, then the subject of experiment. The recipe offered publicly is in a sense a report on the experiment. Similarly, a curriculum should be grounded in practice. It is an attempt to describe the work observed in classrooms that it is adequately communicated to teachers and others. Finally, within limits, a recipe can varied according to taste. So can a curriculum.

Stenhouse shifted the ground a little bit here. He was not saying that curriculum is the process, but rather the means by which the experience of attempting to put an educational proposal into practice is made available. The reason why he did this, I suspect, is that otherwise there is a danger of widening the meaning of the term so much that it embraces almost everything and hence means very little. For example, in a discussion of the so-called 'youth work curriculum' , the following definition was taken as a starting point: 'those processes which enhance or, if they go wrong, inhibit a person's learning'. This was then developed and a curriculum became: 'an organic process by which learning is offered, accepted and internalized'. The problem with this sort of definition, as Robin Barrow (1984) points out, is that what this does is to widen the meaning of the term to such an extent that it just about becomes interchangeable with 'education' itself. More specifically, if curriculum is process then the word curriculum is redundant because process would do very nicely!

The simple equation of curriculum with process is a very slap-happy basis on which to proceed.

We also need to reflect on why curriculum theory and practice came into use by educators (as against policy-makers). It was essentially as a way of helping them to think about their work before, during and after interventions; as a means of enabling educators to make judgments about the direction their work was taking. This is what Stenhouse was picking up on.

STENHOUSE ON CURRICULUM

As a minimum, a curriculum should provide a basis for planning a course, studying it empirically and considering the grounds of its justification. It should offer:

A. In planning:

1. Principle for the selection of content - what is to be learned and taught
2. Principles for the development of a teaching strategy - how it is to be learned and taught.
3. Principles for the making of decisions about sequence.
4. Principles on which to diagnose the strengths and weaknesses of individual students and differentiate the general principles 1, 2 and 3 above, to meet individual cases.

B. In empirical study:

1. Principles on which to study and evaluate the progress of students.
2. Principles on which to study and evaluate the progress of teachers.
3. Guidance as to the feasibility of implementing the curriculum in varying school contexts, pupil contexts, environments and peer-group situations.
4. Information about the variability of effects in differing contexts and on different pupils and an understanding of the causes of the variation.

C. In relation to justification:

A formulation of the intention or aim of the curriculum which is accessible to critical scrutiny. Stenhouse 1975: 5

There are a number of contrasts in this model of curriculum theory and practice as compared with the product model. First, where the product model appeals to the workshop for a model, this process model looks to the world of experimentation. The idea is that of an educational science in which each classroom is a laboratory, each teacher a member of the scientific community... The crucial point is that the proposal is not to be regarded as an unqualified recommendation but rather as a provisional specification claiming no more than to be worth putting to the test of practice, Such proposals claim to be intelligent rather than correct.

Thus, in this sense, a curriculum is a particular form of specification about the practice of teaching. It is not a package of materials or a syllabus of ground to be covered. 'It is a way of translating any educational idea into a hypothesis testable in practice. It invites critical testing rather than acceptance'.

Second, and associated with the above, given the uniqueness of each classroom setting, it means that any proposal, even at school level, needs to be tested, and verified by each teacher in his/her classroom. It is not like a curriculum package which is designed to be delivered almost anywhere.

Third, outcomes are no longer the central and defining feature. Rather than tightly specifying behavioural objectives and methods in advance, what happens in this model of curriculum theory and practice is that content and means develop as teachers and students work together.

Fourth, the learners in this model are not objects to be acted upon. They have a clear voice in the way that the sessions evolve. The focus is on interactions. This can mean that attention shifts from teaching to learning. The product model, by having a pre-specified plan or programme, tends to direct attention to teaching. For example, how can this information be got over? A process approach to curriculum theory and practice, it is argued by writers like Grundy (1987), tends towards making the process of learning the central concern of the teacher. This is because this way of thinking emphasizes interpretation and meaning-making. As we have seen each classroom and each exchange is different and has to be made sense of.

However, when we come to think about this way of approaching curriculum in practice, a number of possible problems do arise. The first is a problem for those who want some greater degree of uniformity in what is taught. This approach to the theory of curriculum, because it places meaning-making and thinking at its core and treats learners as subjects rather than objects, can lead to very different means being employed in classrooms and a high degree of variety in content. As Stenhouse comments, the process model is essentially a critical model, not a marking model.

It can never be directed towards an examination as an objective without loss of quality, since the standards of the examination then override the standards immanent in the subject. This does not mean that students taught on the process model cannot be examined, but it does mean that the examinations must be taken in their stride as they pursue other aspirations. And if the examination is a by-product there is an implication that the quality the student shows in it must be an under-estimate of his real quality. It is hence rather difficult to get the weak student through an examination using a process model. Crammers cannot use it, since it depends upon a commitment to educational aims.

To some extent variation is limited by factors such as public examinations. The exchange between students and teachers does not float free of the context in which it arises. At the end of the day many students and their families place a high premium on exam or subject success and this inevitably enters into the classroom. This highlights a second problem with the model we have just outlined - that it may not pay enough attention to the context in which learning takes place (more of this later).

Third, there is the 'problem' of teachers. The major weakness and, indeed, strength of the process model is that it rests upon the quality of teachers. If they are not up to much then there is no safety net in the form of prescribed curriculum materials. The approach is dependent upon the cultivation of wisdom and meaning-making in the classroom. If the teacher is not up to this, then there will be severe limitations on what can happen educationally. There have been some attempts to overcome this problem by developing materials and curriculum packages which focus more closely on the 'process of discovery' or 'problem-solving', for example in science. But there is a danger in this approach. Processes become reduced to sets of skills - for example, how to light a bunsen burner. When students are able to demonstrate certain skills, they are deemed to have completed the process. As Grundy comments, the actions have become the ends; the processes have become the product. Whether or not students are able to apply the skills to make sense of the world around them is somehow overlooked.

Fourth, we need to look back at our process model of curriculum theory and practice and what we have subsequently discussed, and return to Aristotle and to Freire. The model we have looked at here does not fully reflect the process explored earlier. In particular, it does not make explicit the commitments associated with phronesis. And it is to that we will now turn.

Curriculum as a Syllabus to be Transmitted

Many people still equate a curriculum with a syllabus. Syllabus, naturally, originates from the Greek (although there was some confusion in its usage due to early misprints). Basically it means a concise statement or table of the heads of a discourse, the contents of a treatise, the subjects of a series of lectures. In the form that many of us will have been familiar with it is connected with courses leading to examinations - teachers talk of the syllabus associated with, say, the Cambridge Board French GCSE exam. What we can see in such documents is a series of headings with some additional notes which set out the areas that may be examined.

A syllabus will not generally indicate the relative importance of its topics or the order in which they are to be studied. In some cases as Curzon (1985) points out, those who compile a syllabus tend to follow the traditional textbook approach of an 'order of contents', or a pattern prescribed by a 'logical' approach to the subject, or - consciously or unconsciously - a the shape of a university course in which they may have participated. Thus, an approach to curriculum theory and practice which focuses on syllabus is only really concerned with content. Curriculum is a body of knowledge-content and/or subjects. Education in this sense, is the process by which these are transmitted or 'delivered' to students by the most effective methods that can be devised (Blenkin et al. 1992: 23).

Where people still equate curriculum with a syllabus they are likely to limit their planning to a consideration of the content or the body of knowledge that they wish to transmit. 'It is also because this view of curriculum has been adopted that many teachers in primary schools', Kelly (1985: 7) claims, 'have regarded issues of curriculum as of no concern to them, since they have not regarded their task as being to transmit bodies of knowledge in this manner'.

CURRICULUM IN CONTEXT

To round off this discussion of curriculum we do need to pay further attention to the social context in which it is created. One criticism that has been made of the praxis model is that it does not place a strong enough emphasis upon context. This is a criticism that can also be laid at the door of the other approaches. In this respect the work of Catherine Cornbleth (1990) is of some use.

She sees curriculum as a particular type of process. Curriculum for her is what actually happens in classrooms, that is, "an ongoing social process comprised of the interactions of students, teachers, knowledge and milieu" (1990: 5). In contrast,

Stenhouse defines curriculum as the attempt to describe what happens in classrooms rather than what actually occurs. Cornbleth further contends that curriculum as practice cannot be understood adequately or changed substantially without attention to its setting or context. Curriculum is contextually shaped. While I may quibble about the simple equation of curriculum with process, what Cornbleth does by focusing on the interaction is to bring out the significance of context.

First, by introducing the notion of milieu into the discussion of curriculum she again draws attention to the impact of some factors that we have already noted. Of especial significance here are examinations and the social relationships of the school - the nature of the teacher-student relationship, the organization of classes, streaming and so on. These elements are what are sometimes known as the hidden curriculum. This was a term credited to Philip W. Jackson (1968) but it had been present as an acknowledged element in education for some time before. For example, John Dewey in Experience and Education referred to the 'collateral learning' of attitudes that occur in schools, and that may well be of more long-range importance than the explicit school curriculum (1938: 48). A fairly standard (product) definition of the 'hidden curriculum' is given by Vic Kelly. He argues it is those things which students learn, 'because of the way in which the work of the school is planned and organized but which are not in themselves overtly included in the planning or even in the consciousness of those responsible for the school arrangements (1988: 8). The learning associated with the 'hidden curriculum' is most often treated in a negative way. It is learning that is smuggled in and serves the interests of the status quo. The emphasis on regimentation, on bells and time management, and on streaming are sometimes seen as preparing young people for the world of capitalist production. What we do need to recognize is that such 'hidden' learning is not all negative and can be potentially liberating. 'In so far as they enable students to develop socially valued knowledge and skills... or to form their own peer groups and subcultures, they may contribute to personal and collective autonomy and to possible critique and challenge of existing norms and institutions' What we also need to recognize is that by treating curriculum as a contextualized social process, the notion of hidden curriculum becomes rather redundant. If we need to stay in touch with milieu as we build curriculum then it is not hidden but becomes a central part of our processes.

Second, by paying attention to milieu, we can begin to get a better grasp of the impact of structural and socio-cultural process on teachers and students. As Cornbleth argues, economic and gender relations, for example, do not simply bypass the systemic or structural context of curriculum and enter directly into classroom practice. They are mediated by intervening layers of the education system. Thus, the impact of these factors may be quite different to that expected.

Third, if curriculum theory and practice is inextricably linked to milieu then it becomes clear why there have been problems about introducing it into non-schooling contexts like youth work; and it is to this area which we will now turn.

CURRICULUM AS PRODUCT

The dominant modes of describing and managing education are today couched in the productive form. Education is most often seen as a technical exercise. Objectives are set, a plan drawn up, then applied, and the outcomes (products) measured. It is a way of thinking about education that has grown in influence in the United Kingdom since the late 1970s with the rise of vocationalism and the concern with competencies. Thus, in the late 1980s and the 1990s many of the debates about the National Curriculum for schools did not so much concern how the curriculum was thought about as to what its objectives and content might be.

It is the work of two American writers Franklin Bobbitt (1918; 1928) and Ralph W. Tyler (1949) that dominate theory and practice within this tradition. In The Curriculum Bobbitt writes as follows:

The central theory [of curriculum] is simple. Human life, however varied, consists in the performance of specific activities. Education that prepares for life is one that prepares definitely and adequately for these specific activities. However numerous and diverse they may be for any social class they can be discovered. This requires only that one go out into the world of affairs and discover the particulars of which their affairs consist. These will show the abilities, attitudes, habits, appreciations and forms of knowledge that men need. These will be the objectives of the curriculum. They will be numerous, definite and particularized. The curriculum will then be that series of experiences which children and youth must have by way of obtaining those objectives. (1918: 42)

This way of thinking about curriculum theory and practice was heavily influenced by the development of management thinking and practice. The rise of 'scientific management' is often associated with the name of its main advocate F. W. Taylor. Basically what he proposed was greater division of labour with jobs being simplified; an extension of managerial control over all elements of the workplace; and cost accounting based on systematic time-and-motion study. All three elements were involved in this conception of curriculum theory and practice. For example, one of the attractions of this approach to curriculum theory was that it involved detailed attention to what people needed to know in order to work, live their lives and so on. A familiar, and more restricted, example of this approach can be found in many training programmes, where particular tasks or jobs have been analyzed - broken down into their component elements - and lists of competencies drawn up. In other words, the curriculum was not to be the result of 'armchair speculation' but the product of systematic study. Bobbitt's work and theory met with mixed responses. One telling criticism that was made, and can continue to be made, of such approaches is that there is no social vision or programmed to guide the process of curriculum construction. As it stands it is a technical exercise. However, it wasn't criticisms such as this which initially limited the impact of such curriculum theory in the late 1920s and 1930s. Rather, the growing influence of 'progressive', child-centred approaches shifted the ground to more romantic notions of education.

Bobbitt's long lists of objectives and his emphasis on order and structure hardly sat comfortably with such forms.

The Progressive movement lost much of its momentum in the late 1940s in the United States and from that period the work of Ralph W. Tyler, in particular, has made a lasting impression on curriculum theory and practice. He shared Bobbitt's emphasis on rationality and relative simplicity. His theory was based on four fundamental questions:

1. What educational purposes should the school seek to attain?
2. What educational experiences can be provided that are likely to attain these purposes?
3. How can these educational experiences be effectively organized?
4. How can we determine whether these purposes are being attained? (Tyler 1949: 1)

Like Bobbitt he also placed an emphasis on the formulation of behavioral objectives. Since the real purpose of education is not to have the instructor perform certain activities but to bring about significant changes in the students' pattern of behavior, it becomes important to recognize that any statements of objectives of the school should be a statement of changes to take place in the students. (Tyler 1949: 44)

We can see how these concerns translate into a nicely-ordered procedure: one that is very similar to the technical or productive thinking set out below.

Step 1: Diagnosis of need

Step 2: Formulation of objectives

Step 3: Selection of content

Step 4: Organization of content

Step 5: Selection of learning experiences

Step 6: Organization of learning experiences

Step 7: Determination of what to evaluate and of the ways and means of doing it.

The attraction of this way of approaching curriculum theory and practice is that it is systematic and has considerable organizing power. Central to the approach is the formulation of behavioural objectives - providing a clear notion of outcome so that content and method may be organized and the results evaluated.

There are a number of issues with this approach to curriculum theory and practice. The first is that the plan or programme assumes great importance. For example, we might look at a more recent definition of curriculum as: 'A programme of activities (by teachers and pupils) designed so that pupils will attain so far as possible certain educational and other schooling ends or objectives. The problem here is that such programmes inevitably exist prior to and outside the learning experiences. This takes much away from learners. They can end up with little or no voice. They are told what they must learn and how they will do it. The success or failure of both the programme and the individual learners is judged on the basis of whether pre-specified changes occur in the behaviour and person of the learner (the meeting of behavioural objectives). If the plan is tightly adhered to, there can only be limited opportunity for educators to make use of the interactions that occur. It also can deskill educators in another way. For example, a number of curriculum programmes, particularly in the USA, have attempted to make the student experience 'teacher proof'. The logic of this approach is for the curriculum to be designed outside of the classroom or school, as is the case with the National Curriculum in the UK. Educators then apply programmes and are judged by the products of their actions. It turns educators into technicians.

Second, there are questions around the nature of objectives. This model is hot on measurability. It implies that behaviour can be objectively, mechanistically measured. There are obvious dangers here - there always has to be some uncertainty about what is being measured. We only have to reflect on questions of success in our work. It is often very difficult to judge what the impact of particular experiences has been. Sometimes it is years after the event that we come to appreciate something of what has happened. For example, most informal educators who have been around a few years will have had the experience of an ex-participant telling them in great detail about how some forgotten event (forgotten to the worker that is) brought about some fundamental change. Yet there is something more.

In order to measure, things have to be broken down into smaller and smaller units. The result, as many of you will have experienced, can be long lists of often trivial skills or competencies. This can lead to a focus in this approach to curriculum theory and practice on the parts rather than the whole; on the trivial, rather than the significant. It can lead to an approach to education and assessment which resembles a shopping list. When all the items are ticked, the person has passed the course or has learnt something. The role of overall judgment is somehow sidelined.

Third, there is a real problem when we come to examine what educators actually do in the classroom, for example. Much of the research concerning teacher thinking and classroom interaction, and curriculum innovation has pointed to the lack of impact on actual pedagogic practice of objectives One way of viewing this is that teachers simply get it wrong - they ought to work with objectives. I think we need to take this problem very seriously and not dismiss it in this way. The difficulties that educators experience with objectives in the classroom may point to something inherently wrong with the approach - that it is not grounded in the study of educational exchanges. It is a model of curriculum theory and practice largely imported from technological and industrial settings.

Fourth, there is the problem of unanticipated results. The focus on pre-specified goals may lead both educators and learners to overlook learning that is occurring as a result of their interactions, but which is not listed as an objective.

The apparent simplicity and rationality of this approach to curriculum theory and practice, and the way in which it mimics industrial management have been powerful factors in its success. A further appeal has been the ability of academics to use the model to attack teachers:

I believe there is a tendency, recurrent enough to suggest that it may be endemic in the approach, for academics in education to use the objectives model as a stick with which to beat teachers. 'What are your objectives?' is more often asked in a tone of challenge than one of interested and helpful inquiry. The demand for objectives is a demand for justification rather than a description of ends... It is not about curriculum design, but rather an expression of irritation in the problems of accountability in education.

CURRICULUM AS PRAXIS

Curriculum as praxis is, in many respects, a development of the process model. While the process model is driven by general principles and places an emphasis on judgment and meaning making, it does not make explicit statements about the interests it serves. It may, for example, be used in such a way that does not make continual reference to collective human well-being and to the emancipation of the human spirit. The praxis model of curriculum theory and practice brings these to the centre of the process and makes an explicit commitment to emancipation. Thus action is not simply informed, it is also committed. It is praxis.

Critical pedagogy goes beyond situating the learning experience within the experience of the learner: it is a process which takes the experiences of both the learner and the teacher and, through dialogue and negotiation, recognizes them both as problematic... [It] allows, indeed encourages, students and teachers together to confront the real problems of their existence and relationships... When students confront the real problems of their existence they will soon also be faced with their own oppression.

We can amend our 'curriculum as process' model to take account of these concerns.

Teachers enter particular schooling and situations with a personal, but shared idea of the good and a commitment to human emancipation, an ability to think critically, -in-action an understanding of their role and the expectations others have of them, and a proposal for action which sets out essential principles and features of the educational encounter.

Guided by these, they encourage conversations between, and with, people in the situation out of which may come informed and committed action. They continually evaluate the process and what they can see of outcomes.

In this approach the curriculum itself develops through the dynamic interaction of action and reflection. 'That is, the curriculum is not simply a set of plans to be implemented, but rather is constituted through an active process in which planning, acting and evaluating are all reciprocally related and integrated into the process' . At its centre is praxis: informed, committed action.

How might we recognize this? First, I think we should be looking for practice which does not focus exclusively on individuals, but pays careful attention to collective understandings and practices and to structural questions. For example, in sessions which seek to explore the experiences of different cultural and racial groups in society, we could be looking to see whether the direction of the work took people beyond a focus on individual attitudes. Are participants confronting the material conditions through which those attitudes are constituted, for example?

Second, we could be looking for a commitment expressed in action to the exploration of educators' values and their practice. Are they, for example, able to say in a coherent way what they think makes for human well-being and link this with their practice? We could also be looking for certain values - especially an emphasis on human emancipation.

Third, we could expect practitioners committed to praxis to be exploring their practice with their peers. They would be able to say how their actions with respect to particular interventions reflected their ideas about what makes for the good, and to say what theories were involved.

CONCLUSION OF CURRICULUM

We have explored four different approaches to curriculum theory and practice:

- Curriculum as a body of knowledge to be transmitted.
- Curriculum as an attempt to achieve certain ends in students - product.
- Curriculum as process.
- Curriculum as praxis.

In a number of respects these different bodies of curriculum theory and practice link to the four main forces in North American curriculum-making in the twentieth century: the liberal educators; the scientific curriculum makers; the developmental/person-centred; and the social meliorists (those that sought more radical social change).

CURRICULUM MAPPING

Curriculum Mapping is a procedure for reviewing the operational curriculum as it is entered into an electronic database at any education setting. It is based largely on the work of Heidi Hayes Jacobs in Mapping the Big Picture: Integrating Curriculum and Assessment K-12 (ASCD, 1997) and Getting Results with Curriculum Mapping (2004, ASCD). Schools are using curriculum templates that display key components of the curriculum: content, skills, assessments, and essential questions.

Key to the approach is that each teacher enters what is actually taught in real-time during the school year, in contrast to having an outside or separate committee determine decisions. The entries by teachers are not left alone, however; in fact, because the work is displayed via internet-based programs, it is open to view by all personnel in a school or district. This allows educators to view both K-12 and across grade levels and subjects what is transpiring in order to be informed and to revise their work.

The curriculum mapping model has seven specific steps that schools use to thoroughly examine and then revise their curriculum. There are both commercial companies and not-for-profit groups that have generated curriculum mapping software used around the world. Related to mapping, but separate from it, is the concept of a curriculum audit, described by Fenwick W. English. in "Deciding What to Teach and Test: Developing, Auditing, and Aligning the Curriculum" (1999, Sage).

Curriculum mapping is not limited to United States public schools. A number of independent schools have adopted the curriculum mapping process to review and revise their curriculum. The bulk of schools using curriculum mapping outside the US tend to be independent schools that follow an international curriculum (such as IB, AERO, or IGCSE) or public schools located in Anglo-Saxon countries.

Curriculum mapping requires a cultural shift in certain schools. The curriculum needs to be perceived as a 'work-in-progress', a 'living and breathing' document, whose ultimate owners are students. Curriculum mapping is a 'process', not a one-time initiative. Curriculum mapping software are just tools available to make the review process easier.

OPEN SOURCE CURRICULUM

An open source curriculum (OSC) is an online instructional resource that can be freely used, distributed and modified. OSC is based on the open source practice of creating products or software that opens up access to source materials or codes. Applied to education, this process invites feedback and participation from developers, educators, government officials, students and parents and empowers them to exchange ideas, improve best practices and create world-class curricula. These "development" communities can form ad-hoc, within the same subject area or around a common student need, and allow for a variety of editing and workflow structures.

OUTCOME-BASED EDUCATION

Outcome-based education (OBE) is a recurring education reform model. It is a student-centered learning philosophy that focuses on empirically measuring student performance, which are called outcomes. OBE contrasts with traditional education, which primarily focuses on the resources that are available to the student, which are called inputs.

While OBE implementations often incorporate a host of many progressive pedagogical models and ideas, such as reform mathematics, block scheduling, project-based learning and whole language reading, OBE in itself does not specify or require any particular style of teaching or learning. Instead, it requires that students demonstrate that they have learned the required skills and content. However in practice, OBE generally promotes curricula and assessment based on constructivist methods and discourages traditional education approaches based on direct instruction of facts and standard methods. Though it is claimed the focus is not on "inputs", OBE generally is used to justify increased funding requirements, increased graduation and testing requirements, and additional preparation, homework, and continuing education time spent by students, parents and teachers in supporting learning.

Each independent education agency specifies its own outcomes and its own methods of measuring student achievement according to those outcomes. The results of these measurements can be used for different purposes. For example, one agency may use the information to determine how well the overall education system is performing, and another may use its assessments to determine whether an individual student has learned required material.

Outcome-based methods have been adopted in significant ways in the United States, Australia, South Africa, Hong Kong, and other countries. On a smaller scale, some OBE practices, such as not passing a student who does not know the required material, have been used by individual teachers around the world for centuries.

Small Learning Community

A Small Learning Community (SLC), also referred to as a School-Within-A-School, is a form of school structure that is increasingly common in secondary schools to subdivide large school populations into smaller, autonomous groups of students and teachers.

The primary purpose of restructuring secondary schools into SLCs is to create a more personalized learning environment to better meet the needs of students. Each community will often share the same teachers and student members from grade to grade.

As A Syllabus

A syllabus (from Latin syllabus "list" probably of Greek origin), is an outline and summary of topics to be covered in an education or training course. It is descriptive (unlike the prescriptive or specific curriculum). A syllabus (plural syllabi, or syllabuses) often either set out by an exam board, or prepared by the professor who supervises or controls the course quality.

Both syllabus and curriculum are often fused, and usually given to each student during the first class session so that the objectives and the means of obtaining them are clear. A syllabus usually contains specific information about the course, such as information on how, where and when to contact the lecturer and teaching assistants; an outline of what will be covered in the course; a schedule of test dates and the due dates for assignments; the grading policy for the course; specific classroom rules; etc.

Within many courses concluding in an exam, syllabi are used to ensure consistency between schools and that all teachers know what must be taught and what is not required (extraneous). Exams can only test knowledge based on information included in the syllabus.

Uses of Syllabus

The syllabus serves many purposes for the students and the teacher such as ensuring a fair and impartial understanding between the instructor and students such that there is minimal confusion on policies relating to the course, setting clear expectations of material to be learned, behavior in the classroom, and effort on student's behalf to be put into the course, providing a roadmap of course organization/ direction relaying the instructor's teaching philosophy to the students, and providing a marketing angle of the course such that students may choose early in the course whether the subject material is attractive.

Many generalized items of a syllabus can be amplified in a specific curriculum to maximize efficient learning by clarifying student understanding of specified material such as grading policy, locations and times, other contact information for instructor and teaching assistant such as phone or email, materials required and/ or recommended such as textbooks, assigned reading books, calculators (or other equipment), lab vouchers, etc, outside resources for subject material assistance (extracurricular books, tutor locations, resource centers, etc), important dates in course such as exams and paper due-dates, tips for succeeding in mastering course content such as study habits and expected time allotment, suggested problems if applicable, necessary pre-requisites or co-requisites to current course, safety rules if appropriate, and objectives of the course.

Student-centred Learning

Student-centered learning (also called child-centered learning) is an approach to education focusing on the needs of the students, rather than those of others involved in the educational process, such as teachers and administrators. This approach has many implications for the design of curriculum, course content, and interactivity of courses.

For instance, a student-centered course may address the needs of a particular student audience to learn how to solve some job-related problems using some aspects of mathematics. In contrast, a course focused on learning mathematics might choose areas of mathematics to cover and methods of teaching which would be considered irrelevant by the student.

Student-centered learning, that is, putting students first, is in stark contrast to existing establishment/teacher-centred lecturing and careerism. Student-centered learning is focused on the student's needs, abilities, interests, and learning styles with the teacher as a facilitator of learning. This classroom teaching method acknowledges student voice as central to the learning experience for every learner. Teacher-centered learning has the teacher at its centre in an active role and students in a passive, receptive role. Student-centered learning requires students to be active, responsible participants in their own learning.

7

E-LEARNING

E-learning is a wide-ranging phrase that's used to describe learning by the use of a computer that's typically linked to a network. E-learning can also be referred to as online learning or education, distance learning or education and technology, web or computer-based training.

Due its rise in popularity, numerous educational facilities, businesses and organizations now offer accredited classes, degrees and training through their e-learning programs

E-learning comprises all forms of electronically supported learning and teaching. The information and communication systems, whether networked learning or not, serve as specific media to implement the learning process. The term will still most likely be utilized to reference out-of-classroom and in-classroom educational experiences via technology, even as advances continue in regard to devices and curriculum.

E-learning is essentially the computer and network-enabled transfer of skills and knowledge. E-learning applications and processes include Web-based learning, computer-based learning, virtual education opportunities and digital collaboration. Content is delivered via the Internet, intranet/extranet, audio or video tape, satellite TV, and CD-ROM. It can be self-paced or instructor-led and includes media in the form of text, image, animation, streaming video and audio.

Abbreviations like CBT (Computer-Based Training), IBT (Internet-Based Training) or WBT (Web-Based Training) have been used as synonyms to e-learning. Today one can still find these terms being used, along with variations of e-learning such as e-learning, E-learning, and eLearning. The terms will be utilized throughout this article to indicate their validity under the broader terminology of E-learning.

Functions of E-Learning

Since e-learning make use of digital tools and content, resources and equipment such as the computer, Internet, various software programs, CD-ROMs and DVDs are often employed as learning materials.

Features of E-Learning

E-learning also incorporates different types of interactivity such as interactions between the students and the instructor; e-learners may correspond with their classmates via group discussion boards or online chats.

Significance of E-Learning

E-learning affords students the opportunity to learn and participate around a schedule that suits their lifestyle; completing coursework at their own pace, at a convenient location. The accessibility and flexibility are particularly beneficial to those who are working or cannot attend a traditional facility.

Potential of E-Learning

E-learning can enhance a student's computer skills and result in her understanding and proficiency regarding assorted new skills that are critical in today's environment.

Considerations of E-Learning

Note that there are both pros and cons that come with the e-learning experience and it may not be the most viable option for every individual. Students who lack the necessary time management skills and require face to face interactions may struggle with this method of learning.

History of E-Learning

In the early 1960s, Stanford University psychology professors Patrick Suppes and Richard C. Atkinson experimented with using computers to teach math and reading to young children in elementary schools in East Palo Alto, California. Stanford's Education Program for Gifted Youth is descended from those early experiments.

Early e-learning systems, based on Computer-Based Learning/Training often attempted to replicate autocratic teaching styles whereby the role of the e-learning system was assumed to be for transferring knowledge, as opposed to systems developed later based on Computer Supported Collaborative Learning (CSCL), which encouraged the shared development of knowledge.

As early as 1993, William D. Graziadei described an online computer-delivered lecture, tutorial and assessment project using electronic mail.

In 1997 Graziadei, W.D., et al., published an article entitled "Building Asynchronous and Synchronous Teaching-Learning Environments: Exploring a Course/Classroom Management System Solution". They described a process at the State University of New York (SUNY) of evaluating products and developing an overall strategy for technology-based course development and management in teaching-learning. The product(s) had to be easy to use and maintain, portable, replicable, scalable, and immediately affordable, and they had to have a high probability of success with long-term cost-effectiveness. Today many technologies can be, and are, used in e-learning, from blogs to collaborative software, ePortfolios, and virtual classrooms. Most eLearning situations use combinations of these techniques.

E-Learning 2.0

The term E-Learning 2.0 is a neologism for CSCL systems that came about during the emergence of Web 2.0 From an E-Learning 2.0 perspective, conventional e-learning systems were based on instructional packets, which were delivered to students using assignments. Assignments were evaluated by the teacher. In contrast, the new e-learning places increased emphasis on social learning and use of social software such as blogs, wikis, podcasts and virtual worlds such as Second Life. This phenomenon has also been referred to as Long Tail Learning

E-Learning 2.0, by contrast to e-learning systems not based on CSCL, assumes that knowledge (as meaning and understanding) is socially constructed. Learning takes place through conversations about content and grounded interaction about problems and actions. Advocates of social learning claim that one of the best ways to learn something is to teach it to others.

However, it should be noted that many early online courses, such as those developed by Murray Turoff and Starr Roxanne Hiltz in the 1970s and 80s at the New Jersey Institute of Technology, courses at the University of Guelph in Canada, the British Open University, and the online distance courses at the University of British Columbia (where Web CT, now incorporated into Blackboard Inc. was first developed), have always made heavy use of online discussion between students. Also, from the start, practitioners such as Harasim (1995) have put heavy emphasis on the use of learning networks for knowledge construction, long before the term e-learning, let alone e-learning 2.0, was even considered.

There is also an increased use of virtual classrooms (online presentations delivered live) as an online learning platform and classroom for a diverse set of education providers such as Minnesota State Colleges and Universities and Sachem School District.

In addition to virtual classroom environments, social networks have become an important part of E-learning 2.0. Social networks have been used to foster online learning communities around subjects as diverse as test preparation and language education. Mobile Assisted Language Learning (MALL) is a term used to describe using handheld computers or cell phones to assist in language learning. Some feel, however, that schools have not caught up with the social networking trends. Few traditional educators promote social networking unless they are communicating with their own colleagues.

ADVANTAGES AND DIS ADVANTAGES OF E-LEARNING

E-learning is a broad term that generally refers to any kind of learning done with a computer and Internet connection or CD-ROM. It is used by individuals, educational institutions and businesses. As with any type of learning, it works better for some than others. The quality of e-learning has improved in recent years, as teachers and students have become more comfortable with the technology

E-learning is an excellent option in education, particularly when there are hindrances to traditional learning situations. For example, some people wish to continue their educations but do not live within driving distance of a college or university and don't find it feasible to relocate. E-learning is a viable alternative for these students. Another hindrance to traditional learning, especially in grades K through 12, is the "one size fits all" mentality it embraces. Many students just do not learn well in a traditional learning environment, but thrive in a more flexible setting. To address this issue, parents are turning to e-learning opportunities for their children. Some choose full-time enrollment in a virtual school, while others use e-learning to supplement a home school curriculum. In the business world, e-learning provides a way for companies to train and instruct employees without requiring them to travel to a central location.

Advantages

Convenience is one of the major advantages of e-learning. It allows students to work and learn at their own pace without the unyielding time restrictions of traditional learning. Because e-learning provides access to learning materials at any time, students have the flexibility to schedule around families, jobs and other activities. Another major benefit of e-learning is the accessibility it provides. Students can learn from anywhere in the world. This is an especially important consideration for students who wish to study in a different country. In addition, because e-learning can be done from home, students have less clothing and driving expenses than with traditional learning.

Disadvantages

A major disadvantage to e-learning is the self-discipline it requires. While being able to work at your own pace can be an advantage, it can also be a disadvantage. This is especially true for students who have difficulty with time management and procrastination. These students tend to be more successful with the structure of traditional learning. Another disadvantage to e-learning is the technology involved. Some people do not have ready access to a computer and Internet connection. And some who do have the required equipment feel ill-equipped to use it. Lack of interaction between teacher and student is another drawback to e-learning. Some students need the immediate feedback that interaction provides.

Types

There are several types of e-learning situations. The most common include taking a single course online, full-time enrollment in an online high school or college, distance learning via satellite and learning from information on a CD-ROM. Many businesses and organizations offer training for their employees using various e-learning methods.

Warning

E-learning greatly increases the availability of educational opportunities. Unfortunately, it also increases the number of scams related to online education. Persons considering e-learning possibilities should be alert to such scams and thoroughly investigate any program before making a commitment.

Elements of Effective E-Learning Design

E-learning is a relatively new and exciting means of providing education and training, and more trainers are expected to provide successful academic and work related e-learning modules. Studies highlight the similarities and differences between e-learning and more traditional training methodologies. Henry L. Steen, an eLearning Specialist, states that e-learning requires a "blend of color, style, sound and video usage in a manner that educates while entertaining the student without distracting from the learning experience" in his article "Effective eLearning Design" published in MERLOT Journal of Online Learning and Teaching in December 2008

Interactivity

According to the theories of educational psychologist William Glasser, interactivity and learner involvement are key to retaining learning. Purely reading information only produces a 10 percent retention of information, hearing results in 20 percent retention. When the method of information transfer involves both hearing and seeing, seeing video, pictorial or graphical information, then retention raises to 50 percent. The use of multimedia that is available to creators of e-learning courses can be integral to making courses effective, but doing and experiencing something -- being actively involved -- raises the retention levels to 80 percent. Active experiential learning methods can provide the highest success rates in any form of education.

Usability

E-learning students need to be learning the substance of the training course, not how to work a program. Keeping the courseware simple and consistent is vital to keep focus on the subject matter. Keeping graphics and pictorial features simple provides a better chance of students understanding them. Overly complex systems of information transfer distract users, as they spend more time aware of the method as they figure out how to use it, rather than the subject matter.

Feedback

A positive aspect of e-learning is its ability to provide near instantaneous feedback. Using frequent quizzes with instant response can be a useful method to provide feedback. It raises motivation and provides both interaction and re-affirmation of given information. However Will Thalheimer, an e-learning researcher, suggest in Providing Learners Feedback (2008) that a short delay in receiving results can be even more effective, as it allows students time to consider their responses and internalize information before receiving feedback.

Relevance

Keeping the learner's attention focused has always been an accepted problem in teaching; keeping the attention of an e-learning recipient has been shown to be even more problematic, as there is no instructor or trainer present to notice inattention or distraction. A means of dissipating this effect is to maintain a level of relevance in the presentation of information. Keeping the data work and task related, using real-world examples, and personalizing information via storytelling are all viable ways of maintaining relevance.

Accessibility Concerns For E-Learning

Digital resources for learning, or e-learning tools, tend to use a wide variety of technologies, interfaces and educational styles. When designed without adequate attention to accessibility, an e-learning resource may inhibit the learning process for at least some users. However, when accessibility in made a priority, an e-learning tool may provide an educational experience that would not be possible through any other type of media. There are numerous accessibility concerns for e-learning tools when deployed through software or over the Internet.

Auditory Accessibility

Users who have total or partial hearing loss may encounter similar difficulty accessing certain e-learning materials, if those materials rely on auditory information. This is more of an issue for certain subjects, such as oral language learning and those with some relation to music. Information that is presented in audio form, such as spoken word textual content, will be difficult for users with hearing problems, unless that content also is presented in another way that is accessible to them.

Mobility

Mobility is another major accessibility issue. Many e-learning resources rely on the user's ability to use a keyboard, mouse and monitor, which cannot always be assumed. Tools for e-learning are typically interactive, making use of standard types of interface, which can enhance the educational process for most users but inhibit it for those with mobility issues. In some cases, specially designed hardware for interaction is available for disabled users, which can make such resources accessible again.

Cognition

Various cognitive issues can compromise the accessibility of an e-learning resource. If users have attention problems, linguistic difficulties, psychological impairments or disabilities related to learning or concentration, an e-learning tool may be out of reach to them. This is a particular issue if a tool relies heavily on textual content, requiring significant periods of focus. This issue can be addressed by using different media such as images, audio and video, as well as breaking the information into smaller sections.

Visual Accessibility

Visual impairments can pose a problem for accessing e-learning tools. Learners who are blind or partially sighted, or who have health conditions preventing them from being able to stare at a computer monitor for extended periods, may find accessibility for e-learning difficult. If a tool uses material that is presented only in visual form, or if the material is presented in a way that is unclear or difficult to focus on, then the tool has limited accessibility. Use of non-visual material can help to address these issues.

EVALUATION METHODS IN ELEARNING

Evaluating eLearning means assessing how well the online learning educational format teaches students course goals and objectives. It also allows educators to learn how to better teach the course. Students choosing this way to learn typically like the time and location flexibility eLearning offers. More than 65 percent of two- and four-year schools offer online learning, according to the National Center for Education Statistics.

Interviews

Assessing what students learn through interviews allows educators to get in-depth answers, finding out what they think of the course, how they learned and what they would do to make improvements. Interviewing gives the interviewer the chance to listen to the responses and ask follow-up questions. This process allows the interviewer to watch body language and how students answer questions, whether they hesitate, stutter or take a long time to answer questions. The tone of the voice also exposes how they feel and whether they seem generally excited about the material. Even if a course is online, Web conferencing software enables something that can mirror a face-to-face interview.

Learning Journals

Learning journals allow students to reflect on what they learn, giving educators insight into what and how they learn. Students can write in their learning journal once a week, after every class or once a day. Depending on the level of the course, teachers should give students questions to answer to start the process. In an online course, giving students the opportunity to start a blog lets them write about what they learn in the course and also concepts and methods they struggle with throughout the course. The blog also lets other students read what is on the mind of their fellow students, making the learning process a collaborative effort.

Surveys

Developing a checklist or rubric identifying the goals and objectives as set forth by the instructor launches a starting point for assessing online learning. Educators quickly learn what works and what doesn't by asking simple questions of students. The survey can ask questions about how to better organize the course, how to better state the objectives of the syllabus or if students think they can complete online assignments in a timely manner. It also addresses feedback, grades and interaction with the teacher. Surveys and questionnaires work in both an assigned or anonymous manner.

Testing

Developing a test and giving students a grade is by far the easiest way to assess learning in any course. Teachers giving true/false, short-answer and multiple-choice questions can figure out what concepts, methods and material students learned throughout a course. Assessment using testing also allows teachers to develop statistical data to find out how online classes score versus in-class students. In an online course with an online test, teachers learn a number of things including how long it takes students to answer questions, which questions they answer first and how they answer them.

HOW TO MANAGE E-LEARNING ENVIRONMENTS

As a teacher for electronic and distance learning environments, it's important to manage all aspects of the online learning community for your students. As a teacher, you must learn to set new types of boundaries for your classroom environment, both for yourself and your students. Whereas most live classrooms have a set time to meet, specific outline for each class and may rely heavily on lectures from the teacher, online and electronic environments are more flexible, do not necessarily have a specific meeting time and are driven more by assignment completion and student to student interaction.

" Make a plan for managing your online classes. Part of your plan should include when and how you are going to post your assignments for your students to view. Similar to handing out a syllabus on the first day of class, you may decide to post all assignments in advance so that students can be fully responsible for completing their work or they can choose to finish their work in advance. Also schedule specific times you want to dedicate toward replying to e-mails, forum posts or other components of your online class.

" Give your students regular feedback on their assignments. Since students are not able to see your non-verbal cues by watching your body language as you would in a normal class setting, written feedback should be explicit and clear so that there is no mistake about your thoughts concerning students' work.

" Plan for flexibility in your class. According to Learning to Teach Online, it's a given that your students will not be on the same time schedule or even in the same time zone. Effective management of your online class also means effective time management for you as a teacher. Tips include working in smaller, more fragmented blocks of time to follow-up on the continuous discussion that often accompanies online learning environments.

" Plan for open book tests by requiring critical thinking exercises rather than multiple choice tests. One of the advantages of online learning for the student is quick access to data for nearly every kind of question, ranging from who killed whom in Macbeth to being able to solve algebra problems with math calculators. As a result, unless you want to implement a closed-book honor code, offer essay and short answer questions that require students to examine and analyze the teaching material rather than spouting off answers that can be acquired through a search engine.

TECHNICAL BARRIERS IN E-LEARNING

E-Learning is a viable option for students that want to save money on courses, have classes revolve around their busy lives and experience a broader selection of classes. E-Learning is primarily used for post-secondary school and is popular with non-traditional students.

Distractions

Teachers may underestimate the time needed to invest in delivering E-Learning. As a result they may over schedule with research, writing and other unrelated activities while neglecting teaching responsibilities. The diminished communication and participation of the teacher can discourage some students from extending effort. Many students that are e-learning have numerous life distractions. Some have full-time jobs, children, deep relationships, which can lower the priority of school. E-Learning also make it easier for students to procrastinate. Students that are battling procrastination, attention deficit hyperactivity disorder and online addiction may find it difficult to focus.

Not Prepared

Teachers and students may not be prepared technologically, emotionally and academically to learn or teach through e-Learning. Teachers who are not given the necessary training may feel overwhelmed by the technological demands, lack of prestige and lack of face to face interaction with the students. The ability to convey an quality message through e-learning may be especially difficult for teachers. Students may not be mature, motivated or disciplined enough for e-learning. Some students are still novice to proper study techniques and require more assistance from the teacher. Therefore e-learning may be too autonomous for some students.

Less Interaction

While some personality types fare better working by themselves or in cyberspace, a person that enjoys working in groups is more likely to disengage from e-Learning. Classroom interactions can foster friendships, create a wholesome learning experience and hold each student accountable. However e-Learning can conjure feelings of alienation due to the lack of instant feedback from teachers and close interaction with students. E-learning also does not mimic a number of careers. For example, many jobs use personal training. Therefore solely takes classes by e-Learning puts a person at a disadvantage if she does not have adequate practice learning through social means.

Distractions

Teachers may underestimate the time needed to invest in delivering E-Learning. As a result they may over schedule with research, writing and other unrelated activities while neglecting teaching responsibilities. The diminished communication and participation of the teacher can discourage some students from extending effort. Many students that are e-learning have numerous life distractions. Some have full-time jobs, children, deep relationships, which can lower the priority of school. E-Learning also make it easier for students to procrastinate. Students that are battling procrastination, attention deficit hyperactivity disorder and online addiction may find it difficult to focus.

No Hands-On Practice

Primarily e-Learning also limits the opportunity to apply the lessons outside the classroom to social experiences. For example, it would beneficial for a student that is interested in counseling to take in-person classes to practice their lessons with others and mimic social interactions. Online labs may not as effective as being in a lab. Also by primarily e-learning the person misses out on joining student organizations and associations which could build skills, confidence and networks.

BARRIERS TO E-LEARNING

E-Learning has steadily grown since its inception in the 1990s. Many students have attested to the benefits of e-learning such as the convenience and accessibility to online learning resources and communities. However, the growth rate of e-learning has been slower than expected despite these benefits. Certain obstacles were underestimated during the inception of e-learning that has some students thinking twice about going through an e-learning program.

Cost

During the 1990s, online costs were relatively low as the Internet was rapidly growing in popularity and use. Based on this idea, universities thought that the e-learning business model was a highly distributable, low-cost option for distance learning. However, universities later found out that the upkeep of this technology was relatively higher than other online tools. Constant 24/7 support had to be given to students studying in different time zones, and buying research material for mass distribution to students was very expensive. Schools are now more hesitant to adopt e-learning courses because of these expenses.

Credibility

The issue of credibility is a psychosocial barrier in the minds of students and professors. Academia as an industry is traditionally hesitant in adopting frontier technologies such as e-learning; academics have questioned the dependability of these new methods and the accuracy of the people behind the content. Although there is a growing acceptance rate, instructors and students remain cautious toward schools that deliver rapid changes to their curriculum.

People

According to a study done in the United Kingdom in 2009, the most significant barrier to successful implementation of e-learning has been the overall reluctance of people to use the service. For professors, they are reluctant to pick up this technology because online-course professors are effectively quarantined in their own homes or offices as they teach. Courses tend to also be made for a mass audience that forces professors to broaden and generalize their content. Students indicated they preferred the traditional versions of classes due to the lack of adequate learning support online; there can still be a lack of one-on-one sessions with professors or customized materials for each course.

Technology

The technology for e-learning is not yet perfect. Certain e-learning suites have compatibility issues with some browsers. E-learning program access is also restricted in certain countries where networks are not as advanced or are highly privatized and monitored. Lastly, the IT structure of e-learning suites is not yet mainstreamed--the user interface is constantly upgraded and varies greatly across different suites, which makes a high learning curve for potential users.

ISSUES IN ELEARNING

Online education, or eLearning, is any type of learning that can be done online or with the help of online technology or computers. Teaching by this method is an example of how the Internet has democratized who can learn and become educated around the world, yet the this method also has its issues and disadvantages. Knowing what these disadvantages are can prepare those who are learning online to work around them before they occur.

Cheating

It is difficult to regulate if students cheat or not or actually learn the material within the eLearning environment, as when a test is given or a paper is written the Internet allows answers to be provided with an easy search, which doesn't force or encourage the student to actually learn the material on their own. While many online colleges and courses force students to come into actual classrooms in person to take tests, many satellite students who live hundreds if not thousand of miles away cannot do that, defeating the purpose of online learning. Much of the effectiveness of eLearning is based on the honor code in these circumstances and students who really want to learn rather then just pass the course.

Personal Interaction

When a teacher is present in person, students often respond and understand different lessons better then they do when they are reading it out of a textbook or learning a computerized lesson online. Online education doesn't necessarily have this personal touch as students study the different lessons in a course online. However, online colleges are trying to remedy this by creating hot lines that allow students to call and talk to professors or their teaching assistants, or even have video chat conferences or lectures with them via new forms of communication technology like Skype.

Student Interaction

Another downside of eLearning is that students who are taking online courses can't personally interact with other students and learn from them in their own ways. Seeing other students who have been going over a lesson plan ask questions and interact with the professor and each other in lessons or activities about the material teaches students in a more immersive way then any type of eLearning. While videos of the lesson plan can be presented to help teach students who are learning online, this student to student classroom interaction is more or less lost through the isolated eLearning environment.

APPROACHES TO E-LEARNING SERVICES

E-learning services have evolved since computers were first used in education. There is a trend to move towards blended learning services, where computer-based activities are integrated with practical or classroom-based situations.

Bates and Poole (2003) and the OECD (2005) suggest that different types or forms of e-learning can be considered as a continuum, from no e-learning, i.e. no use of computers and/or the Internet for teaching and learning, through classroom aids, such as making classroom lecture Powerpoint slides available to students through a course web site or learning management system, to laptop programs, where students are required to bring laptops to class and use them as part of a face-to-face class, to hybrid learning, where classroom time is reduced but not eliminated, with more time devoted to online learning, through to fully online learning, which is a form of distance education. This classification is somewhat similar to that of the Sloan Commission reports on the status of e-learning, which refer to web enhanced, web supplemented and web dependent to reflect increasing intensity of technology use. In the Bates and Poole continuum, 'blended learning' can cover classroom aids, laptops and hybrid learning, while 'distributed learning' can incorporate either hybrid or fully online learning.

It can be seen then that e-learning can describe a wide range of applications, and it is often by no means clear even in peer reviewed research publications which form of e-learning is being discussed. However, Bates and Poole argue that when instructors say they are using e-learning, this most often refers to the use of technology as classroom aids, although over time, there has been a gradual increase in fully online learning (see Market above).

COMPUTER-BASED LEARNING

Computer-based learning, sometimes abbreviated to CBL, refers to the use of computers as a key component of the educational environment. While this can refer to the use of computers in a classroom, the term more broadly refers to a structured environment in which computers are used for teaching purposes.

Cassandra B. Whyte researched about the ever increasing role that computers would play in higher education. This evolution, to include computer-supported collaborative learning, in addition to data management, has been realized. The type of computers has changed over the years from cumbersome, slow devices taking up much space in the classroom, home, and office to laptops and handheld devices that are more portable in form and size and this minimalization of technology devices will continue.

COMPUTER-BASED TRAINING

Computer-based trainings (CBTs) are self-paced learning activities accessible via a computer or handheld device. CBTs typically present content in a linear fashion, much like reading an online book or manual. For this reason they are often used to teach static processes, such as using software or completing mathematical equations. The term Computer-Based Training is often used interchangeably with Web-based training (WBT) with the primary difference being the delivery method. Where CBTs are typically delivered via CD-ROM, WBTs are delivered via the Internet using a web browser. Assessing learning in a CBT usually comes in form of multiple choice questions, or other assessments that can be easily scored by a computer such as drag-and-drop, radio button, simulation or other interactive means. Assessments are easily scored and recorded via online software, providing immediate end-user feedback and completion status. Users are often able to print completion records in the form of certificates.

CBTs provide learning stimulus beyond traditional learning methodology from textbook, manual, or classroom-based instruction. For example, CBTs offer user-friendly solutions for satisfying continuing education requirements. Instead of limiting students to attending courses or reading printed manuals, students are able to acquire knowledge and skills through methods that are much more conducive to individual learning preferences. For example, CBTs offer visual learning benefits through animation or video, not typically offered by any other means.

CBTs can be a good alternative to printed learning materials since rich media, including videos or animations, can easily be embedded to enhance the learning. Another advantage to CBTs is that they can be easily distributed to a wide audience at a relatively low cost once the initial development is completed.

However, CBTs pose some learning challenges as well. Typically the creation of effective CBTs requires enormous resources. The software for developing CBTs (such as Flash or Adobe Director) is often more complex than a subject matter expert or teacher is able to use. In addition, the lack of human interaction can limit both the type of content that can be presented as well as the type of assessment that can be performed. Many learning organizations are beginning to use smaller CBT/WBT activities as part of a broader online learning program which may include online discussion or other interactive elements.

Computer-supported collaborative learning (CSCL)

Computer-supported collaborative learning (CSCL) is one of the most promising innovations to improve teaching and learning with the help of modern information and communication technology. Most recent developments in CSCL have been called E-Learning 2.0, but the concept of collaborative or group learning whereby instructional methods are designed to encourage or require students to work together on learning tasks has existed much longer. It is widely agreed to distinguish collaborative learning from the traditional 'direct transfer' model in which the instructor is assumed to be the distributor of knowledge and skills, which is often given the neologism E-Learning 1.0, even though this direct transfer method most accurately reflects Computer-Based Learning systems (CBL).

Locus of Control remains an important consideration in successful engagement of E-learners. According to the work of Cassandra B. Whyte, the continuing attention to aspects of motivation and success in regard to E-learning should be kept in context and concert with other educational efforts. Information about motivational tendencies can help educators, psychologists, and technologists develop insights to help students perform better academically.

Technology-enhanced learning (TEL)

Technology enhanced learning (TEL) has the goal to provide socio-technical innovations (also improving efficiency and cost effectiveness) for e-learning practices, regarding individuals and organizations, independent of time, place and pace. The field of TEL therefore applies to the support of any learning activity through technology. TEL is often used synonymously with E-Learning even though there are significant differences. The main difference between the two expressions is that TEL focuses on the technological support of any pedagogical approach that utilizes technology. However this is rarely presented as including print technology or the developments around libraries, books and journals in the centuries before computers.

A learning activity can be described in terms of the

- resources: creation, distribution, access, compilation, consumption of digital content; tools and services
- actions: communication, collaboration, interaction with software tools
- context: time, duration, surrounding people and location
- roles: A learning activity is carried out by various actors in changing roles (e.g. student, teacher, facilitator, learning coach, human resource or education manager).
- objective: to support every human in achieving her or his learning goals, respecting individual as well as organizational learning preferences

Learning activities can follow different pedagogical approaches and didactic concepts. The main focus in TEL is on the interplay between these activities and respective technologies. This can range from enabling access to and authoring of a learning resource to elaborate software systems managing (e.g. learning management system, learning content management systems, learning repositories, adaptive learning hypermedia systems, etc.) and managing (human resource management systems; tools for self-directed learning, etc.) the learning process of learners with technical means.

Technology enhanced learning (TEL) has the goal of providing socio-technical innovations (also improving efficiency and cost effectiveness) for learning practices, regarding individuals and organizations, independent of time, place and pace. The field of TEL therefore describes the support of any learning activity through technology.

BENEFITS OF E-LEARNING

E-Learning can provide benefits for the organizations and individuals involved.

1. Improved performance: A 12-year meta-analysis of research by the U.S. Department of Education found that higher education students in online learning generally performed better than those in face-to-face courses.

2. Increased access: Instructors of the highest calibre can share their knowledge across borders, allowing students to attend courses across physical, political, and economic boundaries. Recognized experts have the opportunity of making information available internationally, to anyone interested at minimum costs. For example, the MIT OpenCourseWare program has made substantial portions of that university's curriculum and lectures available for free online.
3. Convenience and flexibility to learners: in many contexts, eLearning is self-paced and the learning sessions are available 24x7. Learners are not bound to a specific day/time to physically attend classes. They can also pause learning sessions at their convenience. The High technology is not necessary for all online courses. Basic internet access, audio, and video capabilities are common requirements. Depending on the technology used, students can begin their courses while at work and finish them at home on a different computer.
4. To develop the skills and competencies needed in the 21st century, in particular to ensure that learners have the digital literacy skills required in their discipline, profession or career Bates (2009) states that a major argument for e-learning is that it enables learners to develop essential skills for knowledge-based workers by embedding the use of information and communications technologies within the curriculum. He also argues that using e-learning in this way has major implications for course design and the assessment of learners.

Additional advantages of computer-based training over traditional classroom training include the ability to:

1. Pay less per credit hour
2. Reduce overall training time
3. Spread training out over extended periods of time (even months)
4. Bookmark progress (computer remembering where the student left off so they can resume the courses from there)
5. Remain in one location (e.g., home, office, airport, coffee shop, etc.) with no need to travel (also reduces transportation costs to physical classroom and benefits environment).
6. People no longer constrained to the course meeting times (in most cases).
7. Webcasts can be made public, and thus allow anyone to watch the course for free.
8. Allow people to be in multiple locations at their own leisure.
9. Receive quality training that bolsters job performance

Technology issues

Along with the terms learning technology, instructional technology, the term Educational Technology is generally used to refer to the use of technology in learning in a much broader sense than the computer-based training or Computer Aided Instruction of the 1980s. It is also broader than the terms Online Learning or Online Education which generally refer to purely web-based learning. In cases where mobile technologies are used, the term M-learning has become more common. E-learning, however, also has implications beyond just the technology and refers to the actual learning that takes place using these systems.

E-learning is naturally suited to distance learning and flexible learning, but can also be used in conjunction with face-to-face teaching, in which case the term Blended learning is commonly used. E-Learning pioneer Bernard Luskin argues that the "E" must be understood to have broad meaning if e-Learning is to be effective. Luskin says that the "e" should be interpreted to mean exciting, energetic, enthusiastic, emotional, extended, excellent, and educational in addition to "electronic" that is a traditional national interpretation. This broader interpretation allows for 21st century applications and brings learning and media psychology into the equation.

In higher education especially, the increasing tendency is to create a Virtual Learning Environment (VLE) (which is sometimes combined with a Management Information System (MIS) to create a Managed Learning Environment) in which all aspects of a course are handled through a consistent user interface standard throughout the institution. A growing number of physical universities, as well as newer online-only colleges, have begun to offer a select set of academic degree and certificate programs via the Internet at a wide range of levels and in a wide range of disciplines. While some programs require students to attend some campus classes or orientations, many are delivered completely online. In addition, several universities offer online student support services, such as online advising and registration, e-counseling, online textbook purchase, student governments and student newspapers.

E-Learning can also refer to educational web sites such as those offering learning scenarios, worksheets and interactive exercises for children. The term is also used extensively in the business sector where it generally refers to cost-effective online training.

The recent trend in the E-Learning sector is screencasting. There are many screencasting tools available but the latest buzz is all about the web based screencasting tools which allow the users to create screencasts directly from their browser and make the video available online so that the viewers can stream the video directly. The advantage of such tools is that it gives the presenter the ability to show his ideas and flow of thoughts rather than simply explain them, which may be more confusing when delivered via simple text instructions. With the combination of video and audio, the expert can mimic the one on one experience of the classroom and deliver clear, complete instructions. From the learner's point of view this provides the ability to pause and rewind and gives the learner the advantage of moving at their own pace, something a classroom cannot always offer.

Research on the use of video in lessons is preliminary, but early results show an increased retention and better results when video is used in a lesson. Creating a systematic video development method holds promise for creating video models that positively impact student learning.

COMMUNICATION TECHNOLOGIES USED IN E-LEARNING

Communication technologies are generally categorized as asynchronous or synchronous. Asynchronous activities use technologies such as blogs, wikis, and discussion boards. The idea here is that participants may engage in the exchange of ideas or information without the dependency of other participants involvement at the same time. Electronic mail (Email) is also asynchronous in that mail can be sent or received without having both the participants' involvement at the same time. Asynchronous learning also gives students the ability to work at their own pace. This is particularly beneficial for students who have health problems. They have the opportunity to complete their work in a low stress environment.

Synchronous activities involve the exchange of ideas and information with one or more participants during the same period of time. A face to face discussion is an example of synchronous communications. In an "E" learning environment, an example of synchronous communications would be a skype conversation or a chat room where everyone is online and working collaborativelly at the same time. Synchronous activities occur with all participants joining in at once, as with an online chat session or a virtual classroom or meeting.

Virtual classrooms and meetings can often use a mix of communication technologies. Participants in a virtual classroom use icons called emoticons to communicate feelings and responses to questions or statements. Students are able to 'write on the board' and even share their desktop, when given rights by the teacher. Other communication technologies available in a virtual classroom include text notes, microphone rights, and breakout sessions. Breakout sessions allow the participants to work collaboratively in a small group setting to accomplish a task as well as allow the teacher to have private conversations with his or her students.

The virtual classroom also provides the opportunity for students to receive direct instruction from a qualified teacher in an interactive environment. Students have direct and immediate access to their instructor for instant feedback and direction. The virtual classroom also provides a structured schedule of classes, which can be helpful for students who may find the freedom of asynchronous learning to be overwhelming. The virtual classroom also provides a social learning environment that closely replicates the traditional "brick and mortar" classroom. Most virtual classroom applications provide a recording feature. Each class is recorded and stored on a server, which allows for instant playback of any class over the course of the school year. This can be extremely useful for students to review material and concepts for an upcoming exam. This also provides students with the opportunity to watch any class that they may have missed, so that they never have to fall behind. It also gives parents the ability to monitor any classroom to insure that they are satisfied with the education their child is receiving.

In asynchronous online courses, students proceed at their own pace. If they need to listen to a lecture a second time, or think about a question for awhile, they may do so without fearing that they will hold back the rest of the class. Through online courses, students can earn their diplomas more quickly, or repeat failed courses without the embarrassment of being in a class with younger students. Students also have access to an incredible variety of enrichment courses in online learning, and can participate in college courses, internships, sports, or work and still graduate with their class.

In many models, the writing community and the communication channels relate with the E-learning and the M-learning communities. Both the communities provide a general overview of the basic learning models and the activities required for the participants to join the learning sessions across the virtual classroom or even across standard classrooms enabled by technology. Many activities, essential for the learners in these environments, require frequent chat sessions in the form of virtual classrooms and/or blog meetings.

LEARNING MANAGEMENT SYSTEM (LMS) AND LEARNING CONTENT MANAGEMENT SYSTEM (LCMS)

A learning management system (LMS) is software used for delivering, tracking and managing training/education. LMSs range from systems for managing training/educational records to software for distributing courses over the Internet and offering features for online collaboration.

A learning content management system (LCMS) is software for authontent (courses, reusable content objects). An LCMS may be solely dedicated to producing and publishing content that is hosted on an LMS, or it can host the content itself. The Aviation Industry Computer-Based Training Committee (AICC) specification provides support for content that is hosted separately from the LMS.

A LMS allows for teachers and administrators to track attendance, time on task, and student progress. LMS also allows for not only teachers and administrators to track these variables but parents and students as well. Parents can log on to the LMS to track grades. Students log on to the LMS to submit homework and to access the course syllabus and lessons.

Computer-aided assessment

Computer-aided Assessment (also but less commonly referred to as E-assessment), ranging from automated multiple-choice tests to more sophisticated systems is becoming increasingly common. With some systems, feedback can be geared towards a student's specific mistakes or the computer can navigate the student through a series of questions adapting to what the student appears to have learned or not learned.

The best examples follow a Formative Assessment structure and are called "Online Formative Assessment". This involves making an initial formative assessment by sifting out the incorrect answers. The author/teacher will then explain what the pupil should have done with each question. It will then give the pupil at least one practice at each slight variation of sifted out questions. This is the formative learning stage. The next stage is to make a Summative Assessment by a new set of questions only covering the topics previously taught. Some will take this even further and repeat the cycle such as BOFA which is aimed at the Eleven plus exam set in the UK.

The term learning design has sometimes come to refer to the type of activity enabled by software such as the open-source system LAMSwhich supports sequences of activities that can be both adaptive and collaborative. The IMS Learning Design specification is intended as a standard format for learning designs, and IMS LD Level A is supported in LAMS V2.elearning has been replacing the traditional settings due to its cost effectiveness.

Electronic performance support systems (EPSS)

Electronic performance support systems (EPSS) is a "computer-based system that improves worker productivity by providing on-the-job access to integrated information, advice, and learning experiences". 1991, Barry Raybould

Online Degrees

The term online degrees refers to college degrees (sometimes including high school diplomas and non-degree certificate programs) that can be earned primarily or entirely through the use of an Internet-connected computer, rather than attending college in a traditional campus setting. Improvements in technology and the increasing use of the Internet worldwide have led to a proliferation of online colleges that award associate's, bachelor's, master's and doctoral degrees.

Online Lecture

An online lecture is an educational lecture designed to be posted online. Lectures are recorded to video, audio or both, then uploaded and made viewable on a designated site. Students may go to a certain designated site to view the lecture online at a time which is convenient for them.

Traditionally, vocal education is possible only when the teacher and the pupil are together in the same room, where the teacher passes on the information in the same vicinity of the student. Online lectures are now possible with the advent of video communications. The development of the online lecture makes it possible so that the teacher and student no longer have to be in the same vicinity to teach and learn, respectively.

There are certain advantages to online lecturing. Students may access online lectures posted on their designated websites anywhere in the world, at any time they wish, as long as they have an internet connection. They can also be repeated for the sake of note taking. There are disadvantages to online lecturing, namely the lack of face to face interaction, and the fact that students cannot easily contact their instructors unless a communications link is created.

Content issues

Content is a core component of E-learning and includes issues such as pedagogy and learning object re-use.

Pedagogical elements

Pedagogical elements are an attempt to define structures or units of educational material. For example, this could be a lesson, an assignment, a multiple choice question, a quiz, a discussion group or a case study. These units should be format independent, so although it may be in any of the following methods, pedagogical structures would not include a textbook, a web page, a video conference or Podcast.

When beginning to create E-Learning content, the pedagogical approaches need to be evaluated. Simple pedagogical approaches make it easy to create content, but lack flexibility, richness and downstream functionality. On the other hand, complex pedagogical approaches can be difficult to set up and slow to develop, though they have the potential to provide more engaging learning experiences for students. Somewhere between these extremes is an ideal pedagogy that allows a particular educator to effectively create educational materials while simultaneously providing the most engaging educational experiences for students.

Pedagogical approaches or perspectives

It is possible to use various pedagogical approaches for eLearning which include:

- social-constructivist - this pedagogy is particularly well afforded by the use of discussion forums, blogs, wiki and on-line collaborative activities. It is a collaborative approach that opens educational content creation to a wider group including the students themselves. The One Laptop Per Child Foundation attempted to use a constructivist approach in its project
- Laurillard's Conversational Model is also particularly relevant to eLearning, and Gilly Salmon's Five-Stage Model is a pedagogical approach to the use of discussion boards.
- Cognitive perspective focuses on the cognitive processes involved in learning as well as how the brain works.
- Emotional perspective focuses on the emotional aspects of learning, like motivation, engagement, fun, etc.

- Behavioural perspective focuses on the skills and behavioural outcomes of the learning process. Role-playing and application to on-the-job settings.
- Contextual perspective focuses on the environmental and social aspects which can stimulate learning. Interaction with other people, collaborative discovery and the importance of peer support as well as pressure.
- Mode Neutral Convergence or promotion of 'transmodal' learning where online and classroom learners can coexist within one learning environment thus encouraging interconnectivity and the harnessing of collective intelligence.

Reusability, standards and learning objects

Much effort has been put into the technical reuse of electronically-based teaching materials and in particular creating or re-using Learning Objects. These are self contained units that are properly tagged with keywords, or other metadata, and often stored in an XML file format. Creating a course requires putting together a sequence of learning objects. There are both proprietary and open, non-commercial and commercial, peer-reviewed repositories of learning objects such as the Merlot repository.

A common standard format for e-learning content is SCORM whilst other specifications allow for the transporting of "learning objects" (Schools Framework) or categorizing metadata (LOM).

These standards themselves are early in the maturity process with the oldest being 8 years old. They are also relatively vertical specific: SIF is primarily pK-12, LOM is primarily Corp, Military and Higher Ed, and SCORM is primarily Military and Corp with some Higher Ed. PESC- the Post-Secondary Education Standards Council- is also making headway in developing standards and learning objects for the Higher Ed space, while SIF is beginning to seriously turn towards Instructional and Curriculum learning objects.

In the US pK12 space there are a host of content standards that are critical as well- the NCES data standards are a prime example. Each state government's content standards and achievement benchmarks are critical metadata for linking e-learning objects in that space.

An excellent example of e-learning that relates to knowledge management and reusability is Navy E-Learning, which is available to Active Duty, Retired, or Disable Military members. This on-line tool provides certificate courses to enrich the user in various subjects related to military training and civilian skill sets. The e-learning system not only provides learning objectives, but also evaluates the progress of the student and credit can be earned toward higher learning institutions. This reuse is an excellent example of knowledge retention and the cyclical process of knowledge transfer and use of data and records.

REASONS FOR ENGAGING IN ONLINE E-LEARNING

E-learning is not defined in most dictionaries that you pick up at the book store. An Internet search of the term, however, shows a general consensus that e-learning is the process of being educated through the use of electronic technology. In most cases, that means with the use of a computer, via the Internet. People engage in online e-learning for many reasons and most communities and colleges offer courses in this format today.

College Credit

- Most colleges, as of 2011, offer many online courses for students to choose from: everything from accounting to psychology, and even math. Online courses are a way for educators to reach more students without having to find a place to physically put them. Overcrowded classes make online e-learning beneficial for everyone. Some colleges even offer entire degree programs online, making education and a degree more accessible. Many people can not change their work schedule to accommodate school, but online courses are available 24/7. Online classes can also make it easier for students to increase their course load. While they may not be able to be physically present at five or six classes per session, they may be able to take four traditional classes and one or two online.

Career Advancement

- Many people take classes related to their careers in an attempt to remain current in standards and business practices. Business law, marketing, management and real estate are just a few of the professions where regulations change rapidly. By updating your skills and staying current with today's trends, you become more valuable in the workplace. Some companies will even pay for the classes if they are job related.

Career Change

- Online e-learning is a good way to gain new business skills. If you are interested in changing careers completely or just changing your path a little, online e-learning offers skills that enable you to expand your opportunities. Some career changes may require more study than others, but there is much more flexibility with the online educational format.

Personal Enrichment

- Online e-learning offers choices for learning that are almost endless. Some people may take online courses as a hobby to learn about things that they didn't get a chance to study in college, things like medieval history, religion, graphic design, or music history. Online e-learning is also a way for people to gain additional life skills. Writing courses, financial planning, healthy living, and computer skills are just a few of the things people often wish they could improve. The opportunities are endless, but with online e-learning, it is all accessible.

8

DISTANCE LEARNING

Distance learning is an increasingly popular method of gaining higher education with degrees available online ranging from certifications to doctoral degrees. Distance learning involves taking classes from a college or university from the comfort of your home. The college may be in the same town or could be on the other side of the world. Distance learning is great for adults who work during the day, or for parents that cannot attend traditional classes.

Distance education, or distance learning, is a field of education that focuses on the pedagogy, technology, and instructional system designs that aim to deliver education to students who are not physically "on site". According to the U.S. Department of Agriculture, it "is a process to create and provide access to learning when the source of information and the learners are separated by time and distance, or both." In other words, distance learning is the process of creating an educational experience of equal qualitative value for the learner to best suit their needs outside the classroom. Distance education courses that require a physical on-site presence for any reason including the taking of examinations is considered to be a hybrid or blended course of study. This emerging technology is becoming widely used in universities and institutions around the globe. With the recent trend of technological advance, distance learning is becoming more recognized for its potential in providing individualized attention and communication with students internationally. The most widely cited pedagogical theory of distance education is that of "transactional distance".

Distance learning opportunities are everywhere, which makes finding a program that is interesting to you quite easy. A quick search online will reveal a host of universities and colleges that offer degree programs through distance learning. Most colleges will require that you go through the typical admissions process involving submitting the application, the application fee, high school transcripts and college transcripts.

HISTORY

Distance education dates to at least as early as 1728, when "an advertisement in the Boston Gazette... 'Caleb Phillips, Teacher of the new method of Short Hand" was seeking students for lessons to be sent weekly. Modern distance education has been practiced at least since Isaac Pitman taught shorthand in Great Britain via correspondence in the 1840s. The development of the postal service in the 19th century led to the growth of commercial correspondence colleges with nationwide reach.

The University of London was the first university to offer distance-learning degrees, establishing its External Programme in 1858. The Society to Encourage Studies at Home was founded in 1873 in Boston, Massachusetts. In Australia, the University of Queensland established its Department of Correspondence Studies in 1911. Another pioneering institution was the University of South Africa, which has been offering Correspondence Education courses since 1946. In New Zealand, university-level distance education or extramural study began in 1960 at Massey University. The largest distance-education university in the United Kingdom is the Open University, founded 1969. Spain's Public UNED was founded in 1972. In Germany the FernUniversität in Hagen was founded 1974. There are now many similar institutions around the world, often with the name Open University (in English or in the local language). More than a dozen of them have grown to become 'mega-universities', a term coined to denote institutions with more than 100,000 students.

The first president of the University of Chicago, William Rainey Harper developed extended education and was considered one of the founders of "learning by correspondence programs." The University of Chicago instituted the first Extension Service in the United States through the use of mail, reaching out to a vast group of students internationally.

Charles Wedemeyer of the University of Wisconsin-Madison is considered one of the fathers of modern distance education in America. From 1964-1968 the Carnegie Foundation funded Wedemeyer's Articulated Instructional Media Project (AIM) which brought in a variety of communications technologies aimed at providing learning to an off-campus population. According to Moore's recounting, AIM impressed the British who imported these ideas and used them to create the first Open University, now called United Kingdom Open University (UKOU), to distinguish it from other open universities which have emerged. UKOU was established in the late 1960s and used television and radio as its primary delivery methodologies, thus placing it in the forefront of applying emerging technologies to learning. All "open universities" use distance-education technologies as delivery methodologies..

In addition, there are many private and public, non-profit and for-profit institutions offering courses and degree programs through distance education. The most successful example during this period was Coastline Community College, launched by Bernard Luskin having no campus and offering distance education telecourses through KOCE TV in Orange County, California. Levels of accreditation vary; some institutions offering distance education in the United States have received little outside oversight, and some may be fraudulent diploma mills. In many other jurisdictions, an institution may not use the term "University" without accreditation and authorisation, normally by the national government.

Online education is rapidly increasing among mainstream universities in the United States, where online doctoral programs have even developed at prestigious research institutions.

In the twentieth century, radio, television, and the Internet have all been used to further distance education. Computers and the Internet have made distance-learning distribution easier and faster. The private, for-profit University of Phoenix, which is primarily an online university, now has 200,000 students and expects to serve 500,000 by 2010, yet little is known about student success or lack of success in such a fast-growing institution. In 1996, Cable Pioneer Glenn Jones and Bernard Luskin launched Jones International University as the first accreddited fully online Wedemeyer's Articulated Instructional Media Project (AIM) which brought in a variety of communications technologies aimed at providing learning to an off-campus population. According to Moore's recounting, AIM impressed the British who imported these ideas and used them to create the first Open University, now called United Kingdom Open University (UKOU), to distinguish it from other open universities which have emerged. UKOU was established in the late 1960s and used television and radio as its primary delivery methodologies, thus placing it in the forefront of applying emerging technologies to learning. All "open universities" use distance-education technologies as delivery methodologies..

In 2006 the Sloan Consortium reported that more than 96 percent of the largest colleges and universities in the United States offered online courses and that almost 3.2 million U.S. students were taking at least one online course during the fall 2005 term.

Two of Canada's leading distance-education providers are Open Learning (TRU-OL) of Thompson Rivers University and Athabasca University (AU). TRU-OL educational goals are obtainable for anyone through accessible and varied courses that can be taken anytime and at an individually determined pace. With over 400 individual courses and more than 57 programs available for completion by distance and online learning, students can take a variety of programs such as: adult secondary school completion; certificates and diplomas, including advanced and post-baccalaureate; associate degrees; and bachelor's degrees. AU educational goals are the removal of barriers that restrict access to and success in university-level study and to increasing equality of educational opportunity for adult learners worldwide. AU offers over 700 courses in more than 90 undergraduate and graduate programs, including the Doctor of Education in Distance Education (D.Ed.) and the Doctor in Business Administration (DBA).

In Ontario, Canada the Ministry of Training, Colleges and Universities established the elearnnetwork.ca in 2007 to provide access to students in small and rural communities across Ontario who wanted to pursue college or university courses from their community by distance education.

In the province of Manitoba, the department of Education, Citizenship and Youth provides three options in distance education: Independent Study Option, Teacher Mediated Option and Web-based Course Option.

The Independent Study Option (ISO) provides the opportunity and flexibility for both school-age and adult learners to study a wide range of compulsory optional print based distance education courses from Grades 7 to 12. This form of distance education also provides students with support by email or phone. The Independent Study Option also offers several courses in French. In the event that a student leaves the province on a temporary or permanent basis, the ISO also provides the opportunity for continuing the study of Manitoba curriculum en route to receiving a Senior Years graduation diploma.

Teacher Mediated Option (TMO) supports the delivery of distance learning courses that are scheduled within the school day and use a variety of technologies to assist students including: instruction twice a school cycle for 40 minutes per class by audio teleconference, recording of classes as required for use up to five days after the class has occurred, and corresponding with an instructor between classes by email or phone. These courses are only available to students attending school or an adult learning centre.

METHODS

There are two main methods for taking distance education classes: online and by mail. Online classes involve logging on daily to a program, such as Blackboard or WebCT, to access assignments, class discussions and lecture notes. All assignments are usually submitted online.

Mail distance education classes involve communicating with your instructor through the postal service. This method usually comes with an additional fee for the printed materials, as well as a need to watch postage handling times to meet the proper deadlines for your classes.

Books

Your books for distance learning may come in two different ways. Some distance learning classes have the full textbook available online. However, most distance learning classes still use printed textbooks to go with their classes. Textbooks may be ordered online through sites such as Amazon.com, or they can be ordered and purchased through your school's bookstore and sent to your home.

Testing

Testing can also come in two forms. Some classes allow you to take the tests online, while others require you to find a proctor testing center. With online tests you may be able to use your book, but you may also be required to go by an honor system stating that you will not use a book during your test. This is why proctoring centers are becoming more popular with online learning classes as the teacher can assure that you will not be able to cheat. Also, some tests may be timed, while other may give you an unlimited amount of time to finish.

FACTS ABOUT DISTANCE LEARNING

Distance learning is becoming an accepted education-delivery method for schools, colleges, corporations, the government and the military. Once frowned upon by traditional bricks-and-mortar colleges, online courses are now offered by the majority of institutions of higher learning in the United States, and home schooling has taken on a whole new meaning

The term "distance learning" is used to describe any type of instruction that takes place outside of a classroom or training facility. It's most commonly applied to Internet-based education, but it can also include teleconferencing, audio and mail correspondence courses.

Students of all ages and circumstances now participate in distance learning, from pre-kindergarten to graduate school, along with workers in the corporate world, government, the military and medicine.

Distance learning (also known as "distance education") is a popular way to obtain a high school GED or a college education online. Students who are of pre-kindergarten age through grade 12 also use distance learning to get their schooling. Usually all you need is a computer with Internet access to further your education. It doesn't matter what your location is. You can sign up at any college across the United States that offers distance learning.

Instructions

- Realize that distance learning is usually done by using a computer and an Internet connection. You may also need to use printed materials that you receive by e-mail, fax or standard mail. You'll basically use the school's website to communicate back-and-forth with an instructor as you take each course.
- Get educated through distance learning by taking part in class discussions, hearing lectures and maybe even watching and listening to television and radio broadcasts.
- Complete your high school education by taking the required distance learning classes, passing the tests and earning a GED. You can then get your education online and study a specific area such as computer programming, data entry, creative writing or locksmithing. Taking one or more of these shortened programs can get you a certificate. You can sign-up and take additional distance learning classes to earn an Associate's degree and find employment in that field. If you wish, you can use/transfer your college credits and go on to earn a Bachelor's degree. You can even use a distance learning program to earn a Master's degree or a doctorate.
- Home school your children with the help of a distance learning school. Your students can study online to learn certain subjects, while you teach them the balance of their curriculum. Or, your children can take all their classes online.

THEORIES ON DISTANCE EDUCATION & LEARNING

Adults use distance-learning opportunities to obtain degrees more rapidly. Distance education also helps parents to acquire education and still maintain employment to care for their families. Corporations take advantage of distance learning to stretch budgetary dollars and to increase the knowledge base of employees. Faster Internet bandwidth and user-friendly training software spurs distance-learning usage within many demographic sectors. Adults ages 25 to 50 make up the main demographic group of distance-learning students, according to InstructionalDesign.gov. Moreover, adult-learning theory is a major basis for successfully designed e-learning courses and other distance-learning formats.

Malcolm Knowles

- Theoretical basis for distance-learning software, educational kits and eLearning tools are derived from some of the ideas of Malcolm Knowles. Knowles was an educational director for the Adult Education Association of the United States of America. The principle ideas that governed his intellectual contributions include the Adult Learning Theory, self-direction theory and his Andragogy Theory. Although some of his ideas were not unique, his concepts are influential over constructive framework for distance-learning models available today.

Knowles' Andragogy Model

- Implementation of distance-learning formats is directly linked to assumptions developed by the Andragogy Theory. The Andragogy Theory states that adults intrinsically have a self-directed expectation for learning, so any instructive model must accommodate this essential characteristic of education. Some assumptions within this theory state that adults are autonomous and self-directed, adults already know which education goals they want to achieve upon course enrollment and adults generally desire to learn because of intrinsic (internal) factors, rather than extrinsic (external) ones. Knowles utilized these assumptions to contrast the traditional model of Pedagogy, which is teacher-centered theory. For these reasons, distance education is firmly planted within today's society as a viable means of obtaining enrichment and degree certificates.

S.C.O.R.M.

- The Sharable Content Objective Resource Model uses current standards to make learning adaptive to multiple platforms for any member of the learning community, also suggested by Knowles. Moreover, it also encourages granularity in distance learning. Granularity breaks learning modules into smaller formats. For example, some developers present modules as a page, a paragraph or even a word study. Therefore, both traditional courses and smaller pieces of material are labeled under "content," instead of "courses" to create flexible-learning options for both developers and student. Furthermore, the model states that learning should be developed in "chunks" or as an object for repeatable development of student content. This theory refers developers back to the idea that the content they create must be adaptable and straightforward, so it can be used as a future reference or compiled with other learning material.

Informal Learning Revolutionized

- Knowles' theory on informal-adult education rests on the idea that education should remain flexible in its process. His principles also made reference to creating friendly and informal settings to allow students to utilize their experience and enthusiasm to grasp subject matters. Knowles' theory is closely linked to the Learning Management System (L.M.S.) used today. Learning Management Systems refer to the utilization of competency and knowledge-based content, discussion boards and mentoring through training modules within distance-learning course work. Through such software, corporations and institutions provide flexible-learning options that help learners meet workforce demands in a convenient manner.

Impacts of Distance Education on Teachers

Distance learning has varying positive and negative effects on teachers. Distance learning courses can give teachers more flexibility and let them perform their jobs from anywhere. Some teachers struggle to overcome technological barriers, but can find a variety of assistance if they have Internet access.

Adapting Teaching Strategies

Some educators struggle to adapt to distance instruction, because many strategies that are highly effective in person do not work online. For example, teachers cannot utilize body language and voice tone except through a webcam and podcasts, which take time and technical expertise to use effectively.

Greater Workload

Distance learning can force educators to work harder. Educators that teach more courses will have more papers to grade. Some educators are expected to give more students one-on-one interaction, which can consume more time. The Bureau of Labor Statistics reports that instructors must spend more time setting up online courses and answering emails than offline instructors spend with offline classroom activities.

Professional Development

Distance learning has enabled teachers to remain up-to-date with the latest educational research, allowing them to incorporate cutting-edge teaching strategies in the classroom. Some teachers work in rural areas and cannot travel to many conferences due to time and monetary constraints. Video cameras can record conferences and information can be sent to teachers, or posted on the Internet.

Professional Development

Teachers have complained that they do not receive enough instruction on effective teaching techniques in online courses. Most professional development courses focus on how to use the technology, but do not focus on instructional methods. Part of this comes from the fact that electronic distance learning is cutting-edge, and teachers need to be the innovators when finding out how to effectively teach content across long distances.

More Assistance

Teachers can receive more assistance when teaching distance learning courses. They can easily send information to other instructors or administrators, and ask for advice when overcoming a particular problem. When teachers run into a problem with a student in a physical classroom, the teacher often must make a quick decision without the help of other professionals. With distance learning classes, however, teachers can ask for help from other professionals before addressing a student.

Flexibility

Teachers participating in distance learning had more flexibility to engage in other activities, such as spending time with their families and attending community activities. Teachers can work more irregular hours when teaching, since they can respond to students at any time in the day.

Virtual Learning Environment

A virtual learning environment (VLE) is a software system designed to support teaching and learning in an educational setting, as distinct from a Managed Learning Environment, (MLE) where the focus is on management. A VLE will normally work over the Internet and provide a collection of tools such as those for assessment (particularly of types that can be marked automatically, such as multiple choice), communication, uploading of content, return of students' work, peer assessment, administration of student groups, collecting and organizing student grades, questionnaires, tracking tools, etc. New features in these systems include wikis, blogs, RSS and 3D virtual learning spaces.

TECHNOLOGIES USED IN DISTANCE EDUCATION

The types of available technologies used in distance education are divided into two groups: synchronous and asynchronous. Synchronous technology is a mode of online delivery where all participants are "present" at the same time requiring a timetable to be organized. Web Conferencing is an example of synchronous technology. Asynchronous technology is a mode of online delivery where participants access course materials on their own schedule. Students are not required to be together at the same time. Message board forums, e-mail and recorded video are examples of asynchronous technology.

Synchronous Technologies

- Web-based VoIP
- Telephone
- Videoconferencing
- Web conferencing
- Direct-broadcast satellite
- Internet radio
- Live streaming

Web-based VOIP

Web-based VoIP is based on the concept of click to talk, which is a form of Web-based communication in which a person clicks an object (i.e. button, image, or text) to request an immediate connection with another person in real-time either by phone call, Voice-over-Internet-Protocol (VoIP), or text. Click to talk requests are most commonly made through websites but can also be initiated by hyperlinks placed in email, blogs, flash animations, or video, and other Internet-based object or user interface.

Web-based VoIP uses the existing VoIP infrastructure but links the web object, which can be shown as Flash, Active X, or Silverlight by any kind of web page.

Call flow

Caller goes to a webpage and find the destination the caller want to communicate, a caller will be required or without a login process for identification, then click the object from the webpage which already connect to a phone or IP number, meanwhile, caller will also automatically allocate a caller number to make the communication link to the call receiver.

Current market

Web-based VoIP can be used for any kind of web communication services, such as yellow page service, web conference, e-Map, web toll free number or e-learning technology.

Telephone

The telephone is a telecommunications device that transmits and receives sound, most commonly the human voice. Telephones are a point-to-point communication system whose most basic function is to allow two people separated by large distances to talk to one another. It is one of the most common household appliances in the developed world, and has long been considered indispensable to business, industry and government. The word "telephone" has been adapted to many languages and is widely recognized around the world.

The device operates principally by converting sound waves into electrical signals, and electrical signals into sound waves. Such signals when conveyed through telephone networks - and often converted to electronic and/or optical signals - enable nearly every telephone user to communicate with nearly every other worldwide. Graphic symbols used to designate telephone service or phone-related information in print, signage, and other media include (U+2121), (U+260E), (U+260F), and (U+2706).

Video Conferencing

A videoconference or video conference (also known as a videoteleconference) is a set of interactive tele-communication technologies which allow two or more locations to interact via two-way video and audio transmissions simultaneously. It has also been called 'visual collaboration' and is a type of groupware.

Videoconferencing differs from videophone calls in that it's designed to serve a conference rather than individuals. It is an intermediate form of videotelephony, first deployed commercially by AT&T during the early 1970s using their Picturephone technology.

Technology

The core technology used in a videoteleconference (VTC) system is digital compression of audio and video streams in real time. The hardware or software that performs compression is called a codec (coder/decoder). Compression rates of up to 1:500 can be achieved. The resulting digital stream of 1s and 0s is subdivided into labelled packets, which are then transmitted through a digital network of some kind (usually ISDN or IP). The use of audio modems in the transmission line allow for the use of POTS, or the Plain Old Telephone System, in some low-speed applications, such as videotelephony, because they convert the digital pulses to/from analog waves in the audio spectrum range.

The other components required for a VTC system include:

- Video input : video camera or webcam
- Video output: computer monitor , television or projector
- Audio input: microphones, CD/DVD player, cassette player, or any other source of PreAmp audio outlet.
- Audio output: usually loudspeakers associated with the display device or telephone
- Data transfer: analog or digital telephone network, LAN or Internet

There are basically two kinds of VTC systems:

Dedicated systems have all required components packaged into a single piece of equipment, usually a console with a high quality remote controlled video camera. These cameras can be controlled at a distance to pan left and right, tilt up and down, and zoom. They became known as PTZ cameras. The console contains all electrical interfaces, the control computer, and the software or hardware-based codec. Omnidirectional microphones are connected to the console, as well as a TV monitor with loudspeakers and/or a video projector. There are several types of dedicated VTC devices:

1. Large group VTC are non-portable, large, more expensive devices used for large rooms and auditoriums.
2. Small group VTC are non-portable or portable, smaller, less expensive devices used for small meeting rooms.
3. Individual VTC are usually portable devices, meant for single users, have fixed cameras, microphones and loudspeakers integrated into the console.
2. Desktop systems are add-ons (hardware boards, usually) to normal PCs, transforming them into VTC devices. A range of different cameras and microphones can be used with the board, which contains the necessary codec and transmission interfaces. Most of the desktops systems work with the H.323 standard. Videoconferences carried out via dispersed PCs are also known as e-meetings.

Echo cancellation

A fundamental feature of professional VTC systems is acoustic echo cancellation (AEC). Echo can be defined as the reflected source wave interference with new wave created by source. AEC is an algorithm which is able to detect when sounds or utterances reenter the audio input of the VTC codec, which came from the audio output of the same system, after some time delay. If unchecked, this can lead to several problems including:

1. the remote party hearing their own voice coming back at them (usually significantly delayed)
2. strong reverberation, rendering the voice channel useless as it becomes hard to understand and
3. howling created by feedback. Echo cancellation is a processor-intensive task that usually works over a narrow range of sound delays.

Multipoint videoconferencing

Simultaneous videoconferencing among three or more remote points is possible by means of a Multipoint Control Unit (MCU). This is a bridge that interconnects calls from several sources (in a similar way to the audio conference call). All parties call the MCU unit, or the MCU unit can also call the parties which are going to participate, in sequence. There are MCU bridges for IP and ISDN-based videoconferencing. There are MCUs which are pure software, and others which are a combination of hardware and software. An MCU is characterised according to the number of simultaneous calls it can handle, its ability to conduct transposing of data rates and protocols, and features such as Continuous Presence, in which multiple parties can be seen onscreen at once. MCUs can be stand-alone hardware devices, or they can be embedded into dedicated VTC units.

Some systems are capable of multipoint conferencing with no MCU, stand-alone, embedded or otherwise. These use a standards-based H.323 technique known as "decentralized multipoint", where each station in a multipoint call exchanges video and audio directly with the other stations with no central "manager" or other bottleneck. The advantages of this technique are that the video and audio will generally be of higher quality because they don't have to be relayed through a central point. Also, users can make ad-hoc multipoint calls without any concern for the availability or control of an MCU. This added convenience and quality comes at the expense of some increased network bandwidth, because every station must transmit to every other station directly.

Web Conferencing

Web conferencing is used to conduct live meetings, training, or presentations via the Internet. In a web conference, each participant sits at his or her own computer and is connected to other participants via the internet. This can be either a downloaded application on each of the attendees' computers or a web-based application where the attendees access the meeting by clicking on a link distributed by e-mail (meeting invitation) to enter the conference.

A webinar is a neologism to describe a specific type of web conference. It is typically one-way, from the speaker to the audience with limited audience interaction, such as in a webcast. A webinar can be collaborative and include polling and question & answer sessions to allow full participation between the audience and the presenter. In some cases, the presenter may speak over a standard telephone line, while pointing out information being presented onscreen, and the audience can respond over their own telephones, speaker phones allowing the greatest comfort and convenience. There are web conferencing technologies on the market that have incorporated the use of VoIP audio technology, to allow for a completely web-based communication. Depending upon the provider, webinars may provide hidden or anonymous participant functionality, making participants unaware of other participants in the same meeting.

In the early years of the Internet, the terms "web conferencing" was often used to describe a group discussion in a message board and therefore not live. The term has evolved to refer specifically to live or "synchronous" meetings.

DIRECT-BROADCAST SATELLITE

Direct broadcast satellite (DBS) is a term used to refer to satellite television broadcasts intended for home reception.

A designation broader than DBS would be direct-to-home signals, or DTH. This was initially meant to distinguish the transmissions directly intended for home viewers from cable television distribution services that sometimes carried on the same satellite. The term DTH predates DBS satellites and is often used in reference to services carried by lower power satellites which required larger dishes (1.7m diameter or greater) for reception.

In Europe, prior to the launch of Astra 1A in 1988, the term DBS was commonly used to describe the nationally-commissioned satellites planned and launched to provide TV broadcasts to the home within several European countries (e.g., BSB in the UK, TV-Sat in Germany). These services were to use the D-Mac and D2-Mac format and BSS frequencies with circular polarization from orbital positions allocated to each country. Before these DBS satellites, home satellite television in Europe was limited to a few channels, really intended for cable distribution, and requiring dishes typically of 1.2m SES Astra launched the Astra 1A satellite to provide services to homes across Europe receivable on dishes of just 60 cm-80 cm and, although these mostly used PAL video format and FSS frequencies with linear polarization, the DBS name slowly came to applied to all Astra satellites and services too.

INTERNET RADIO

Internet radio (also known as web radio, net radio, streaming radio and e-radio) is an audio service transmitted via the Internet. Music streaming on the Internet is usually referred to as webcasting since it is not transmitted broadly through wireless means. Internet radio involves streaming media presenting listeners with a continuous stream of audio that cannot be paused or replayed, much like traditional broadcast media; in this respect, it is distinct from on-demand file serving. Internet radio is also distinct from podcasting, which involves downloading rather than streaming. Many Internet radio services are associated with a corresponding traditional (terrestrial) radio station or radio network. Internet-only radio stations are independent of such associations.

Internet radio services are usually accessible from anywhere in the world-for example, one could listen to an Australian station from Europe or America. Some major networks like Clear Channel in the US and Chrysalis in the UK restrict listening to in country because of music licensing and advertising concerns. Internet radio remains popular among expatriates and listeners with interests that are often not adequately served by local radio stations (such as eurodance, progressive rock, ambient music, folk music, classical music, and stand-up comedy). Internet radio services offer news, sports, talk, and various genres of music-every format that is available on traditional radio stations.

STREAMING MEDIA

Streaming media are multimedia that are constantly received by, and normally presented to, an end-user while being delivered by a streaming provider (the term "presented" is used in this article in a general sense that includes audio or video playback). The name refers to the delivery method of the medium rather than to the medium itself. The distinction is usually applied to media that are distributed over telecommunications networks, as most other delivery systems are either inherently streaming (e.g., radio, television) or inherently non-streaming (e.g., books, video cassettes, audio CDs). The verb 'to stream' is also derived from this term, meaning to deliver media in this manner. Internet television is a commonly streamed media.

ASYNCHRONOUS TECHNOLOGIES

Compact Cassette

The Compact Cassette, often referred to as audio cassette, cassette tape, cassette, or simply tape, is a magnetic tape sound recording format. Although originally designed for dictation, improvements in fidelity led the Compact Cassette to supplant reel-to-reel tape recording in most non-professional applications. Its uses ranged from portable audio to home recording to data storage for early microcomputers. Between the early 1970s and late 1990s, the cassette was one of the two most common formats for prerecorded music, first alongside the LP and later the Compact Disc. Cassette is a French word meaning "little box."

Compact Cassettes consist of two miniature spools, between which a magnetically coated plastic tape is passed and wound. These spools and their attendant parts are held inside a protective plastic shell. Two stereo pairs of tracks (four total) or two monaural audio tracks are available on the tape; one stereo pair or one monophonic track is played or recorded when the tape is moving in one direction and the second pair when moving in the other direction. This reversal is achieved either by manually flipping the cassette or by having the machine itself change the direction of tape movement ("auto-reverse").

E-MAIL

Electronic mail, most commonly abbreviated email or e-mail, is a method of exchanging digital messages. E-mail systems are based on a store-and-forward model in which e-mail server computer systems accept, forward, deliver and store messages on behalf of users, who only need to connect to the e-mail infrastructure, typically an e-mail server, with a network-enabled device for the duration of message submission or retrieval. Originally, e-mail was always transmitted directly from one user's device to another's; nowadays this is rarely the case.

An electronic mail message consists of two components, the message header, and the message body, which is the email's content. The message header contains control information, including, minimally, an originator's email address and one or more recipient addresses. Usually additional information is added, such as a subject header field.

Originally a text-only communications medium, email was extended to carry multi-media content attachments, which were standardized in with RFC 2045 through RFC 2049, collectively called, Multipurpose Internet Mail Extensions (MIME).

The foundation for today's global Internet e-mail service was created in the early ARPANET and standards for encoding of messages were proposed as early as

1973 (RFC 561). An e-mail sent in the early 1970s looked very similar to one sent on the Internet today. Conversion from the ARPANET to the Internet in the early 1980s produced the core of the current service.

Network-based email was initially exchanged on the ARPANET in extensions to the File Transfer Protocol (FTP), but is today carried by the Simple Mail Transfer Protocol (SMTP), first published as Internet standard 10 (RFC 821) in 1982. In the process of transporting e-mail messages between systems, SMTP communicates delivery parameters using a message envelope separately from the message (header and body) itself.

Internet Forum

An Internet forum, or message board, is an online discussion site. It originated as the modern equivalent of a traditional bulletin board, and a technological evolution of the dialup bulletin board system. From a technological standpoint, forums or boards are web applications managing user-generated content.

People participating in an Internet forum may cultivate social bonds and interest groups for a topic made from the discussions.

Voicemail

Voicemail (or voice mail, voice-mail, vmail or VMS, sometimes called messagebank) is a centralized system of managing telephone messages for a large group of people. The term is also used more broadly, to denote any system of conveying voice message, including the answering machine.

Videotape

Videotape is a means of recording images and sound onto magnetic tape as opposed to movie film or random access digital media. Videotapes are also used for storing scientific or medical data, such as the data produced by an electrocardiogram. In most cases, a helical scan video head rotates against the moving tape to record the data in two dimensions, because video signals have a very high bandwidth, and static heads would require extremely high tape speeds. Videotape is used in both video tape recorders (VTRs) or, more commonly, video cassette recorders (VCRs) and video cameras. Tape is a linear method of storing information and, since nearly all video recordings made nowadays are digital, it is expected to gradually lose importance as non-linear/random-access methods of storing digital video data become more common.

Distance Classroom

Distance Classroom is a facility standard for distance learning that focuses on the pedagogy, technology, and instructional systems design that aim to deliver education to students who are not physically "on site". Rather than attending courses in person, teachers and students may communicate at times of their own choosing by exchanging printed or electronic media, or through technology that allows them to communicate in real time and through other online ways. Distance education courses that require a physical on-site presence for any reason including the taking of examinations is considered to be a hybrid or blended course of study.

TESTING AND EVALUATION IN DISTANCE EDUCATION

Distance education has long had trouble with testing. The delivery of testing materials is fairly straightforward, which makes sure it is available to the student and he or she can read it at their leisure. The problem arises when the student is required to complete assignments and testing. Online courses have had difficulty controlling cheating in quizzes, tests, or examinations because of the lack of teacher control. In a classroom situation a teacher can monitor students and visually uphold a level of integrity consistent with an institution's reputation. However, with distance education the student can be removed from supervision completely. Some schools address integrity issues concerning testing by requiring students to take examinations in a controlled setting.

Assignments have adapted by becoming larger, longer, and more thorough so as to test for knowledge by forcing the student to research the subject and prove they have done the work. Quizzes are a popular form of testing knowledge and many courses go by the honor system regarding cheating. Even if the student is checking questions in the textbook or online, there may be an enforced time limit or the quiz may be worth so little in the overall mark that it becomes inconsequential. Exams and bigger tests may be harder to regulate.

Used in combination with invigilators, a pre-arranged supervisor trusted with overseeing big tests and examinations may be used to increase security. Many Midterms and Final examinations are held at a common location so that professors can supervise directly. When the Internet became a popular medium for distance education many websites were founded offering secure exam software and packages to help professors manage their students more effectively.

CLEP

In recent years, the CollegeBoard has been promoting its College Level Examination Program (CLEP) tests. These tests are fully accredited and can be used for many of the general education and even core requirements of many degree templates. The tests are administered in approved testing centers and are closely proctored to prevent cheating. CLEP tests are computer-based, online tests that consist of roughly 80-120 multiple choice questions. Because the test is computer-based, the candidate's score can be tallied as soon as the test is completed. CLEP's passing grade is a 50 (roughly equivalent to a C-grade) and is scaled all the way to 80 (roughly the equivalent of an A-grade) for a perfect score. CLEP operates on a pass or fail basis, in that the actual grade does not determine credit awarded, but is strictly based on whether the candidate passes or not.

DSST

In addition to CLEP tests, the DANTES Standardized Subject Tests (DSST) is also frequently used to cover areas that CLEP does not offer tests in. These are very similar in format and administration to CLEP, being computer-based, online, and proctored, with immediate test results available. DSST also offers a number of its exams in paper based format, though they must be sent in to DSST's offices for grading, resulting in a delay for application of credit. Traditionally, DSST has used a grading system nearly identical to that of CLEP, but has recently been overhauling its tests and applying a new grading system, with a 300-500 point grade, with 400 as the passing grade. Credit is awarded based on pass or fail.

In the form of Virtual School

A virtual school or cyberschool describes an institution that teaches courses entirely or primarily through online methods. Though there are tens of thousands of commercial and non-accredited courses available online, the term "virtual school" is generally reserved for accredited schools that teach a full-time (or nearly full-time) course of instruction designed to lead to a degree. Virtual public and private schools serving every grade level including graduate programs may elect to pursue accreditation through various regional and national organizations. Accredited schools must meet rigorous standards as defined by the issuing organization and are designed to insure that students are receiving the highest quality instruction and education. Examples of organizations that issue school accreditation include: Middle States Association of Schools and Colleges, Northwest Association of Accredited Schools.

All student services are conducted through Internet technology. The virtual school differ/contrasts from the traditional school through the physical media that links administrators, teachers and students and is an alliance of public distance learning schools. Many states in the United States have their own virtual school, and many of them have students numbering in the thousands. By providing a student's social security number the person is then entered into a database where they can choose which classes they want to take.

There are many different virtual school instructional and enrollment models. Instructional models range from fully independent self paced courses to semester based, teacher facilitated courses. Class sizes range widely with anywhere from 25 students to as many as 200 students in each class section. Students keep in contact with teachers and collaborate with other students through web communication tools provided in the course delivery platforms like Blackboard or Desire2Learn or Moodle. In some cases students communicate by phone with instructors. To help with communication many virtual schools have implemented their own system programs to help build courses and maintain student profiles. There are also many books and training manuals to aid in the development of such schools and courses.

The Form of Virtual University

The term "virtual university" is used to describe any organization that provides higher education programs through electronic devices such as the computer or a TV Screen. Some of the Universities are real institutes, the bricks and mortar type that provide online learning as part of their extended university courses while others provide courses only on-line.

Some of these organizations exist only as loosely tied combines of universities, institutes or departments that together provide a number of courses over the Internet, television or other media, that are separate and distinct from programs offered by the single institution outside of the combine. Others are actual organizations with a legal framework, yet named virtual because they appear only on the internet, without a physical location aside from administration units. Still other virtual universities can be organized through specific or multiple physical locations, with some having actual campuses to receive program delivery through technological media that is broadcast from another location, where real professors give televised lectures.

The goal of Virtual Universities is to provide access to that part of the population who would not be able to attend a physical campus, for reasons such as: (1)distance-where students live too far from a physical campus to attend regular classes; (2) need for flexibility-some students need the flexibility to study at home whenever it is convenient for them to do so.

Program delivery in a virtual university is administered through information communication technology such as web pages, e-mail and other networked sources. When the term "virtual" was first coined in the computational sense, it applied to things that were simulated by the computer like virtual memory. Over time, the adjective has been applied to things that really exist and are created or carried on by means of computers.

Students taking so called "virtual" courses are doing "real" work to get their degrees and educators preparing and teaching those courses spend plenty of "real" time in doing so. That is, students meet rigorous academic learning outcomes and evaluations through programs constructed by credible academics according to standard university-level criteria. Many Virtual Universities are accredited in the same way as traditional universities and operate according to the same academic standards. These universities can grant degrees that will be recognized around the world. Online programs can be marketed to any person who has on-line access to provide learning experiences and training in an open access format.

STATUS OF DISTANCE LEARNING IN INDIA

Amrita Learning

Amrita Learning is a computer-based 'adaptive learning' program in English and Mathematics. It provides interactive, audio-visual supplementary education for children of three-and-a-half years to 7th grade, for home and classroom use. Developed in collaboration with Amrita University, the content of this research-based software is in line with the NCERT/CBSE syllabi.

Adaptive Assessment

Under the 'Adaptive Assessment' concept, as a student learns, s/he is continually assessed by the programme and the software adapts to their level. "The programme is also being used at some schools...to administer the CBSE mandated Continuous and Comprehensive Evaluation (CCE). Teachers can replace a large portion of paper-based CCE with computer based assessment. After the teacher teaches a set of topics in the classroom, students are immediately taken to the computer and evaluated... Students who have mastered one topic move on to the next level and those who have not mastered a topic are provided with more practice."

Sikkim Manipal University of Distance Education

Sikkim Manipal University Directorate of Distance Education was established in 2001 by the Sikkim Manipal University of Health, Medical and Technological Sciences as part of its efforts to bring education to the masses to fulfil the growing demand for professionals. SMU is university in Sikkim which is joint venture in between Government of Sikkim & Manipal Education to offer regular & Distance education course.

Accreditations/Recognition

The University is recognized by DEC, UGC, & Ministry of HRD to offer program in 9 discipline. The Association of Indian Universities (AIU) recognises SMUDE conferred degrees as on par with the degrees conferred by its members. Sikkim Manipal University Directorate of Distance Education provides courses in the follwoing disciplines:

- Information Technology
- Management
- Commerce
- Journalism & Mass Com
- Apparel & Fashion Design
- Telecom technology
- Allied Health Science
- Bio Informatics & Biotechnology
- Hospitality & Tourism

DISTANCE EDUCATION COUNCIL

Distance Education Council (DEC) is an organisation based in New Delhi, India responsible for the promotion and coordination of the open university and distance education system and for determination of its standards in India. The Council was constituted under the Indira Gandhi National Open University Act (1985). Its consistent with the duty of the University that takes all such steps as it may deem fit for the promotion of the Open University and distance education systems in the educational pattern of the country and for the coordination and determination of standards of teaching, evaluation & research in such systems; and in pursuance of the objects of the University to encourage greater flexibility, diversity, accessibility, mobility and innovation in education at the University level by making full use of the latest scientific knowledge and new educational technology, and to further cooperation between the existing Universities. It is considered necessary and expedient to establish a Distance Education Council as an authority of the University under Section 16 of the Act.

Initiatives of DEC

DEC coordinated in development of learner-centric open and distance learning (ODL) system and ensures high quality of education, meet challenges of access and equity to reach the un-reached, the Distance Education Council (DEC) has following initiatives:

- DES started state governments/conventional universities to establish open universities/ distance education institutes and create a network of such institutions
- Provides financial support and grants and academic guidelines to institutions of open and distance education
- Evolve norms, procedures and guidelines in respect of admission, evaluation, and certification
- Assess and accredit institutions of open and distance learning to ensure quality
- It uses of technology in education and provide opportunities for sharing technological resources and competencies through inter-university partnerships/ consortia

G

- It facilitate development and sharing of self-instructional (multiple media) materials amongst different open universities/distance education institutions
- DEC helps sharing of student support services created by various State Open Universities (SOUs) and correspondence course Institutes (CCIs)
- Promotes convergence of conventional, ODL and other systems to facilitate mobility of learners through credit transfer/sharing
- Promotes research and innovation in ODL systems
- Facilitate training for indigenous capacity building in ODL systems
- Created databases for SOUs, CCIs, distance educators and functionaries associated with ODL systems

Eklavya Technology Channel

Eklavya Technology Channel is a distant learning joint initiative between the

IIT and IGNOU. It was inaugurated by Prof. Murli Manohar Joshi, Honourable Minister, HRD, S&T and Ocean Development on 26 January 2003.

The objective of this initiative is to bring to the audience the actual IIT classrooms virtually at their door steps. It is a channel dedicated to technical education and shall run programs generated at different IITs. The channel is designed to carry video courses in different disciplines generated at various IITs on weekdays and special interest programs on Sundays. Currently, eight complete courses are being run in parallel, contributed by IIT Delhi, IIT Kharagpur and IIT Madras and are repeated in the same sequence without a break. It always is tough to contact authorities concerned to downlink this channel...

Indira Gandhi National University

The Indira Gandhi National Open University, (known as IGNOU) is a national university with its headquarters in New Delhi, Delhi, India. Named after former Prime Minister of India, Indira Gandhi, the university was established in 1985 with a budget of INR 2000 crore, when the Parliament of India passed the Indira Gandhi National Open University Act, 1985 (IGNOU Act 1985).

IGNOU, one of the largest universities in the world; was founded to impart education by means of distance and open education, provide higher education opportunities particularly to the disadvantaged segments of society, to encourage, coordinate and set standards for distance and open education in India and strengthen the human resources of India through education.

Apart from teaching and research, extension and training form the mainstay of its academic activities. It also acts as a national resource centre, and serves to promote and maintain standards of distance education in India. IGNOU hosts the Secretariats of the SAARC Consortium on Open and Distance Learning (SACODiL) and the Global Mega Universities Network (GMUNET) initially supported by UNESCO.

National Institute on Open Schooling

The National Institute of Open Schooling, commonly known as NIOS , NOS or National Open School, is the Board of Education for school level in India. It was established by the Ministry of Human Resource Development of the Government of India in 1989. The NIOS is a national board for Secondary and Senior Secondary examinations similar to the CBSE and the CISCE.

It has a current enrollment of about 1.5 million students at Secondary and Senior Secondary levels which makes it the largest open schooling system in the world.

School of Open Learning

The School of Open Learning (a part of the Campus of Open Learning) formerly known as The School of Correspondence Courses and Continuing Education, established under the University of Delhi in 1962, is a pioneer Institution in the field of Distance Education in India.

The country witnessed the beginning of an alternate mode of education when the School started with a modest admission of 900 students in 1962. The School enrolled more than two lakhs students in the Academic Session 2006-2007. On many occasions our students have been toppers in various disciplines. The admission process for various courses in the School is governed by the norms established by the University of Delhi. The examination is also conducted by the University of Delhi. The University of Delhi confers the degree to the students of the School as it does in the case of its other constituent colleges. There is no differentiation in the course curriculum followed by the School of Open Learning and other constituent colleges and Departments of the University of Delhi. In an effort to cater to the needs of a growing number of students the School established the South Study Centre at Moti Bagh from the academic session 1990-91. In an effort to reach out to a larger number of students the school is in the process of opening up Study Centre in the Eastern and the Western part of the National Capital Region of Delhi.

The School offers Undergraduate/Postgraduate Degree courses in the subjects of Arts/Humanities and Commerce. The medium of instruction is primarily through well- prepared printed course material which is distributed by mail to all the enrolled students. This is also supplemented through Personal Contact Program conducted for the benefit of students at various study centers run by the School. An experienced faculty is always available at the main campus for academic interaction with students.

The School offers learning through the distance education mode which is a viable alternative for students who need a flexible medium of instruction to attain higher education and vocational skills.

In addition, the School maintains a well-stocked library to facilitate wide exposure to contemporary developments in streams of courses offered. The School also has a South Study Centre at South Moti Bagh, New Delhi.

A well appointed faculty is always available at the main campus for academic interaction with students.

9

AUDIO-VISUAL MEDIA

Audiovisual (AV) means possessing both a sound and a visual component, such as slide-tape presentations,films, television programs, church services and live theater productions.

Audiovisual service providers frequently offer web streaming, video conferencing and live broadcast services.

Computer-based audiovisual equipment is often used in education, with many schools and universities installing projection equipment and using interactive whiteboard technology.

Another audiovisual expression is the visual presentation of sound (visual music).

Importance

Residential audiovisual

Generally, residential audiovisual encompasses in-ceiling speakers, flat panel TVs, projectors and projector screens. This could include lighting, blinds, cinema rooms.

Commercial audiovisual

The professional audiovisual industry is a multibillion-dollar industry, comprising the manufacturers, dealers, systems integrators, consultants, programmers, presentations professionals and technology managers of audiovisual products and services.

Commercial audiovisual can sometimes be a very lengthy process to get it right. Boardroom audio visual can be installed for a number of reasons, but usually it is because the executives of the organization/business wants to have meetings with colleagues/customers/suppliers around the world. When creating an array of boardrooms for customers it has been seen that you have to be able to balance the pattern from the audio and microphone so there is no interruption in the sound quality for the individual/s listening in.

The proliferation of audiovisual communications technologies, including sound, video, lighting, display and projection systems, is evident in every sector of society: in business, education, government, the military, healthcare, retail environments, worship, sports and entertainment, hospitality, restaurants, and museums. The application of audiovisual systems is found in collaborative conferencing (which includes video-conferencing, audio-conferencing, web-conferencing and data-conferencing); presentation rooms, auditoriums, and lecture halls; command and control centers; digital signage, and more. Concerts and corporate events are among the most obvious venues where audiovisual equipment is used in a staged environment. Providers of this type of service are known as rental and staging companies, although they may also be served by an in-house technology team (e.g., in a hotel or conference center).

According to a 2006 market forecast study by InfoComm International, a leading trade association representing the audiovisual industry, 2006 was the fourth consecutive year that significant growth was projected for the industry. Revenue for surveyed North American companies was expected to grow by 40% in 2006, and by 10.7% for European audiovisual companies. The single biggest factor for this increase is the increased demand for networked audiovisual products due to the integration of audiovisual and IT technology. The two leading markets for AV equipment in North America and Europe continue to be business/IT and education, especially as conference room technologies become more advanced.

Audiovisual education

Audiovisual education is instruction where particular attention is paid to the audio and visual presentation of the material, with the goal of improving comprehension and retention.

Various Forms

The main advantage of audio-visual communication is the ability for one to convey what they are communicating in an effective way. There are two main types of audio-visual communication, live communication at an event and communication through published content. The use of audio-visual aids can help one communicate in both instances:

- Sound: the most important part of communication is for the listeners at a live event to hear what is being said, if they can't hear what the speaker is saying clearly it makes the communication rather useless.
- Visual Aids: the use of presentations on a screen can aid with communication greatly and can provide another platform for one to share their thoughts and ideas with an audience. It is much more interesting for the audience if they can view and comprehend what is being said through means other than speech. Visual aids, such as graphs, diagrams and photographs, also help display information concisely and help the audience retain the information after the event.
- Video Content: videos are a really great way to communicate something to an audience, they are able to clearly inform the viewer in a concise and fun way, much like visual aids. Being able to deploy videos of recorded events as well as videos in general definitely helps with user engagement or distributing content

to a much wider viewership in the case of advertising.

- Recording and Broadcasting: AV systems can usually support the recording and live broadcasting of events. This can be very useful for engaging with a wider audience by providing the content to people who are not able to be at an event in person.
- Lighting: through lighting one can make an event much more fit for purpose, whether it be stage lighting for productions or lighting in a filmed video. Lighting can help the viewers focus on what you want them to and makes an event much more interesting as opposed to having no lighting variation.
- Signage: the use of signage around an event can be a great way to communicate to the attendees, providing the latest updates (through a live Twitter feed for example), photos and information (such as social media links or the schedule for the day) to them live. From experience Planet eSign is a really great solution for this.
- And there are many more examples of audio-visual communication, such as posters, video-conferencing and telecommunication that you can research the benefits of in your own time.

However, the underlying disadvantage of audio-visual is by far the costs and expertise associated with developing an infrastructure necessary to provide these aids. It goes without saying that if you want a high quality AV system you will have to pay a fairly large amount of money. The pricing for this can get as high as six-figures depending on the size of the system you are trying to implement. Maintenance and management are also other costly factors, in many cases the solutions implemented do not run themselves and require someone to be present on-site in order to run the system - especially if it is a hall. The cost of maintaining a system can be very high for audio-visual communication systems, especially if using projectors, which tend to break or require maintenance (e.g. replacing bulbs) very often. Also remember that you need space to install an audio-visual system and in some cases the system may require special requirements such as cable routing, installation of ceiling lighting, mounting of wall speakers or a dedicated audio-visual desk to name a few.

One of the other disadvantages with audio-visual communication is the high standards associated with it. If an AV system is not working properly because it is a cheap solution that has cut corners, it is nearly as useless as having no system in the first place. You only have to look as far as the classroom to see this in reality; if a projector in the classroom is experiencing issues or the sound from the computer is not working, the teacher will most likely just not use the whole system altogether. When implementing an AV solution it is important to ensure that it works and it works well, the last thing people want is to have a system that requires an expert to use and manage on a day-to-day basis. Even with audio-visual communication through published content, people expect the content be of very high quality, for example video content is expected to be in 1080p and have clear sound without any background noises. People do not want to see a live broadcast that is having buffering issues or a video recording where the filming is unstable and the person filming takes time to move the camera.

Audia/Radio:

Broadcast and audio recordings-Strengths and Limitations

Broadcasting is the distribution of audio or video content to a dispersed audience via any electronic mass communications medium, but typically one using the electromagnetic spectrum (radio waves), in a one-to-many model. Broadcasting began with AM radio, which came into popular use around 1920 with the spread of vacuum tuberadio transmitters and receivers. Before this, all forms of electronic communication (early radio, telephone, and telegraph) were one-to-one, with the message intended for a single recipient. The term broadcasting evolved from its use as the agricultural method of sowing seeds in a field by casting them broadly about. It was later adopted for describing the widespread distribution of information by printed materials or by telegraph. Examples applying it to "one-to-many" radio transmissions of an individual station to multiple listeners appeared as early as 1898.

Over the air broadcasting is usually associated with radio and television, though in recent years, both radio and television transmissions have begun to be distributed by cable (cable television). The receiving parties may include the general public or a relatively small subset; the point is that anyone with the appropriate receiving technology and equipment (e.g., a radio or television set) can receive the signal. The field of broadcasting includes both government-managed services such as public radio, community radio and public television, and private commercial radio and commercial television. The U.S. Code of Federal Regulations, title 47, part 97 defines "broadcasting" as "transmissions intended for reception by the general public, either direct or relayed". Private or two-way telecommunications transmissions do not qualify under this definition. For example, amateur ("ham") and citizens band (CB) radio operators are not allowed to broadcast. As defined, "transmitting" and "broadcasting" are not the same.

Transmission of radio and television programs from a radio or television station to home receivers by radio waves is referred to as "over the air" (OTA) or terrestrial broadcasting and in most countries requires a broadcasting license. Transmissions using a wire or cable, like cable television (which also retransmits OTA stations with their consent), are also considered broadcasts but do not necessarily require a license (though in some countries, a license is required). In the 2000s, transmissions of television and radio programs via streaming digital technology have increasingly been referred to as broadcasting as well.

History of broadcasting

It is generally recognised that the first radio transmission was made from a temporary station set up by Guglielmo Marconi in 1895. This followed on from pioneering work in the field by a number of people including Alessandro Volta, André-Marie Ampère, Georg Ohm and James Clerk Maxwell.

The radio broadcasting of music and talk intended to reach a dispersed audience started experimentally around 1905-1906, and commercially around 1920 to 1923. VHF (very high frequency) stations started 30 to 35 years later. In the early days, radio stations broadcast on the long wave, medium wave and short wave bands, and later on VHF (very high frequency) and UHF (ultra high frequency). However, in the United Kingdom, Hungary, France and some other places, from as early as 1890 there was already a system whereby news, music, live theatre, music hall, fiction readings, religious broadcasts, etc., were available in private homes [and other places] via the conventional telephone line, with subscribers being supplied with a number of special, personalised headsets. In Britain this system was known as Electrophone, and was available as early as 1895 or 1899 [sources vary] and up until 1926. In Hungary, it was called Telefon Hírmondó [1893-1920s], and in France, Théâtrophone [1890-1932]). The Wikipedia Telefon Hírmondó page includes a 1907 program guide which looks remarkably similar to the types of schedules used by many broadcasting stations some 20 or 30 years later.

By the 1950s, virtually every country had a broadcasting system, typically one owned and operated by the government. Alternative modes included commercial radio, as in the United States; or a dual system with both state sponsored and commercial stations, introduced in Australia as early as 1924, with Canada following in 1932. Today, most countries have evolved into a dual system, including the UK. By 1955, practically every family in North America and Western Europe, as well as Japan, had a radio. A dramatic change came in the 1960s with the introduction of small inexpensive portable transistor radio, the greatly expanded ownership and usage. Access became practically universal across the world.

Early broadcasting

Argentina

Argentina was a world pioneer in broadcasting, being the third country in the world to make its first regular broadcasts in 1920, having been the first Spanish-speaking country in Latin America to offer daily radio broadcasts. The main stations were in Buenos Aires and Córdoba. Among the historical facts related to Argentine radio, it can be mentioned that the first radio broadcast was made with the live broadcast of Richard Wagner's opera Parsifal from the Teatro Coliseo in Buenos Aires, on August 27, 1920, in charge of the Radio Argentina Society of Enrique Susini, César Guerrico, Miguel Mugica, Luis Romero and Ignacio Gómez, who installed a transmitting device on the roof of the building, for which they are remembered as "The crazy people on the roof".

In 1921, the transmission of classical music became a daily occurrence. The following year, the assumption of President Marcelo Torcuato de Alvear was broadcast live. In September 1923 the famous "fight of the century" was issued between Luis Ángel Firpo and Jack Dempsey from the Polo Grounds in New York, and in October of the following year the match between the Argentine and Uruguayan national teams was broadcast. Also at that time the first advertisements, called "reclames", were put on the air. At the end of the decade the radio drama was born. In those years several radio stations arose, Argentina (originally Radio Argentina), Culture, Excelsior, Mitre (originally South American), Splendid (originally Grand Splendid), Belgrano (originally National), Prieto (originally Broadcasting Critic), Del Pueblo - (originally Quilmes Broadcasting), America-, Antartida (originally Fénix), Municipal, Rivadavia (originally Muebles Díaz), Porteña and Stentor (originally Sarmiento).

The introduction of the loudspeakers substantially modified the listening conditions. The receiving apparatus was gaining an important place in the home, gathering around the family. Meanwhile, the multiplication of the stations generated the first conflicts over the airwaves, which led to the first regulations on emission frequencies at the end of the 20s.

Australia

The History of broadcasting in Australia has been shaped for over a century by the problem of communication across long distances, coupled with a strong base in a wealthy society with a deep taste for aural communications. Australia developed its own system, through its own engineers, manufacturers, retailers, newspapers, entertainment services, and news agencies. The government set up the first radio system, and business interests marginalized the hobbyists and amateurs. The Labor Party was especially interested in radio because it allowed them to bypass the newspapers, which were mostly controlled by the opposition. Both parties agreed on the need for a national system, and in 1932 set up the Australian Broadcasting Commission, as a government agency that was largely separate from political interference. The first commercial broadcasters, originally known as "B" class stations, were on the air as early as 1925. The number of stations (commercial and national) remained relatively dormant throughout World War II and in the post-war era.

Formative years

Australian radio hams can be traced to the early 1900s. The 1905 Wireless Telegraphy Act whilst acknowledging the existence of wireless telegraphy, brought all broadcasting matters in Australia under the control of the Federal Government. In 1906, the first official Morse code transmission in Australia was by the Marconi Company between Queenscliff, Victoria and Devonport, Tasmania.

Experiments with broadcasting music

The first broadcast of music was made during a demonstration on 13 August 1919 by Ernest Fisk (later Sir Ernest) of AWA – Amalgamated Wireless (Australasia).

A number of amateurs commenced broadcasting music in 1920 and 1921. Many other amateurs soon followed. 2CM was run by Charles MacLuran who started the station in 1921 with regular Sunday evening broadcasts from the Wentworth Hotel, Sydney. 2CM is often regarded as Australia's first, regular, non-official station.

Sealed set system

It was not until November 1923 when the government finally gave its approval for a number of officially recognised medium wave stations. All stations operated under a unique Sealed Set system under which each set was sealed to the frequency of one station. Part of the price of the set went to the government via the Postmaster-General's Department (PMG), with money also going to the broadcaster. Apart from extremely limited advertising, this was the broadcasters' only source of income. From the outset problems with the system came to the fore. Many young people built their own sets, which could receive all the stations. The sealed set system was devised by broadcasting pioneer Ernest Fisk of AWA – Amalgamated Wireless (Australasia).

Categories in Australia from 1924

As quickly as July 1924, the Sealed Set system was declared to be unsuccessful and it was replaced by a system of A Class and B Class stations. There were one or two A Class stations in each major market and these were paid for by a listener's licence fee imposed on all listeners-in. The five former sealed set stations became A Class stations, and they were soon joined by stations in other State capitals.

From 1929, all A Class stations received all their programs from the one source, the Australian Broadcasting Company which was made up of the following shareholders: Greater Union Theatres (a movie theatre chain), Fuller's Theatres (a live theatre chain) and J. Albert & Sons (music publishers and retailers). A number of B Class stations were also licensed. These did not receive any government monies and were expected to derive their income from advertising, sponsorship, or other sources. Within a few years B Class stations were being referred to as "commercial stations".

Amateur broadcasters continued to operate in the long wave and short wave bands.

A national service, the Australian Broadcasting Commission, was formed in July 1932, when the Australian Broadcasting Company's contract expired. The Corporation took over the assets of all A Class stations. It still exists as the Australian Broadcasting Corporation. The Australian Broadcasting Co changed its name to the Commonwealth Broadcasting Company and later the Australian Radio Network. It soon purchased Sydney commercial station 2UW and now has an Australia-wide network of commercial stations.

Types of programs

As with most countries, most Australian stations originally broadcast music interspersed with such things as talks, coverage of sporting events, church broadcasts, weather, news and time signals of various types. Virtually all stations also had programs of interest to women, and children's sessions. From the outset, A Class stations' peak-hour evening programs often consisted of live broadcasts from various theatres, i.e. dramas, operas, musicals, variety shows, vaudeville, etc. The first dramas especially written for radio were transmitted in the mid-1920s. By the 1930s, the ABC was transmitting a number of British programs sourced from the BBC, and commercial stations were receiving a number of US programs, particularly dramas. However, in the 1940s, war-time restrictions made it difficult to access overseas programs and, therefore, the amount of Australian dramatic material increased. As well as using original ideas and scripts, there were a number of local versions of overseas programs. Initially, much of the music broadcast in Australia was from live studio concerts. However, the amount of gramophone (and piano roll) music soon increased dramatically, particularly on commercial stations.

In the late 1930s, the number of big production variety shows multiplied significantly, particularly on the two major commercial networks, Macquarie and Major. After World War II the independent Colgate-Palmolive radio production unit was formed. It poached most major radio stars from the various stations. Until the 1950s, the popular image of the whole family seated around a set in the living room was the most accepted way of listening to radio. Therefore, most stations had to be all things to all people, and specialised programming was not really thought about at this stage (it did not come in until the late 1950s). Because of this, programming on most stations was pretty much the same.

Early experiments with television

As early as 1929, two Melbourne commercial radio stations, 3UZ and 3DB were conducting experimental mechanical television broadcasts – these were conducted in the early hours of the morning, after the stations had officially closed down. In 1934 Dr Val McDowall at amateur station 4CM Brisbane conducted experiments in electronic television.

Mobile stations

Two of Australia's most unusual medium wave stations were mobile stations 2XT and 3YB. They both operated in eras prior to the universal establishment of rural radio stations. 2XT was designed and operated by AWA within the State of New South Wales, from a NSW Railways train, between November 1925 and December 1927. 2XT, which stood for experimental train, visited over 100 rural centres. Engineers would set up a transmitting aerial and the station would then begin broadcasting. This led to the further sales of AWA products. 3YB provided a similar service in rural Victoria between October 1931 and November 1935. Initially, the station operated from a Ford car and a Ford truck, but from 17 October 1932 they operated from a converted 1899 former Royal Train carriage. Whilst the engineers were setting up the station's 50-watt transmitter in the town being visited, salesmen would sign up advertisers for the fortnight that 3YB would broadcast from that region. The station was on the air from 6.00 and 10.00 pm daily, and its 1,000-record library was divided into set four-hour programs, one for each of 14 days. In other words, the music broadcast from each town was identical. The station was operated by Vic Dinenny, but named after announcer Jack Young from Ballarat. On 18 January 1936, Dinenny set up 3YBWarnambool, followed on 18 May 1937 by 3ULWarragul.

The merchant vesselMV Kanimbla is believed to be the world's only ship built with an inbuilt broadcasting station. The Kanimlba was constructed in Northern Ireland in 1936 and was primarily designed for McIlwraith McEachern Limited to ply passengers between Cairns, Queensland and Fremantle, Western Australia. The broadcasting station was constructed and operated by AWA and was initially given the ham radio callsign VK9MI but was later 9MI. (At this time, the "9" in the callsign was aberrationary [see "Call Signs, above].) The station made an experimental broadcast before leaving Northern Ireland, and a number of such broadcasts at sea, on the way to Australia. 9MI's first official broadcast in April 1939 was made from the Great Australian Bight. The station broadcast on short wave, usually a couple of times per week, but many of its programs were relayed to commercial medium wave stations that were also owned by AWA. The 9MI manager and announcer (and probably the only member of staff) was Eileen Foley. 9MI ceased broadcasting at the commencement of World War II in September 1939. The Kanimbla was commissioned as a Royal Navy (later Royal Australian Navy) vessel with the name HMS/HMAS Kanimbla. It had an extremely prominent and successful war-time career.

Canada

The history of broadcasting in Canada begins as early as 1919 with the first experimental broadcast programs in Montreal. Canadians were swept up in the radio craze and built crystal sets to listen to American stations while The Marconi Wireless Telegraph Company of Canada offered its first commercially produced radio-broadcast receiver (Model "C") in 1921, followed by its "Marconiphone" Model I in 1923. Main themes in the history include the development of the engineering technology; the construction of stations across the country and the building of networks; the widespread purchase and use of radio and television sets by the general public; debates regarding state versus private ownership of stations; financing of the broadcasts media through the government, license fees, and advertising; the changing content of the programming; the impact of the programming on Canadian identity; the media's influence on shaping audience responses to music, sports and politics; the role of the Québec government; Francophone versus Anglophone cultural tastes; the role of other ethnic groups and First Nations; fears of American cultural imperialism via the airwaves; and the impact of the Internet and smartphones on traditional broadcasting media.

Radio signals carried long distances, and a number of American stations could easily be received in parts of Canada. The first Canadian station was CFCF, originally an experimental station from the Marconi Company in Montreal. Civilian use of Wireless Telegraphy had been forbidden in Canada for the duration of World War I. The Marconi Wireless Telegraph Company of Canada was the only one to retain the right to continue radio experiments for military use. This proved instrumental in giving the company a lead in developing an experimental radio broadcasting station immediately after the war. The first radio broadcast in Canada was accomplished by The Marconi Wireless Telegraph Company of Canada in Montreal on December 1, 1919 under the call sign XWA (for "Experimental Wireless Apparatus") from its Williams Street factory. The station began regular programming on May 20, 1920 and its call letters were changed to CFCF on November 4, 1920. In Toronto, the first radio station was operated by the Toronto Star newspaper. Station CKCE began in April 1922. and were so well received that the Star pushed forward with its own studios and transmitting facilities, returning to the air as CFCA in late June 1922. In Montreal, another newspaper, La Presse, put its own station, CKAC on the air in late September 1922. Because there were governmental limitations on radio frequencies back then, CKAC and CFCF alternated—one would broadcast one night, and the other would broadcast the night after that. For a time, CKAC was broadcasting some programs in French, and some in English: in 1924, for example, the station rebroadcast fifteen Boston Bruins hockey games from station WBZ in Boston. Meanwhile, in other Canadian provinces, 1922 was also the year for their first stations, including CJCE in Vancouver, and CQCA (which soon became CHCQ) in Calgary.

As radio grew in popularity during the mid-1920s, a problem arose: the U.S. stations dominated the airwaves and with a limited number of frequencies available for broadcasters to use, it was the American stations that seemed to get most of them. This was despite an agreement with the US Department of Commerce (which supervised broadcasting in the years prior to the Federal Radio Commission) that a certain number of frequencies were reserved exclusively for Canadian signals. But if a US station wanted one of those frequencies, the Department of Commerce seemed unwilling to stop it, much to the frustration of Canadian owners who wanted to put stations on the air. The Canadian government and the US government began negotiations in late 1926, in hopes of finding a satisfactory solution. Meanwhile, in 1928, Canada got its first network, operated by the Canadian National Railways. CNR had already made itself known in radio since 1923, thanks in large part to the leadership of CNR's president, Sir Henry Thornton. The company began equipping its trains with radio receivers, and allowed passengers to hear radio stations from Canada and the US. In 1924, CN began building its own stations, and by 1928, it was able to create a network. In 1932, the Canadian Radio Broadcasting Commission was formed, and in 1936, the Canadian Broadcasting Corporation, the country's national radio service, made its debut.

Cuba

There was interest in radio almost from broadcasting's earliest days. Due to the proximity of Cuba to the U.S. state of Florida, some Cubans would try to listen to the American stations whose signals reached the island. But there was no radio station in Cuba until 1922. The arrival of the first radio station, PWX, was greeted with enthusiasm. PWX, owned by the Cuban Telephone Company, was located in Havana. It was a joint venture with the International Telephone and Telegraph Company of New York. PWX debuted on the air on October 10, 1922. PWX broadcast programs in both English and Spanish, and its signal was easily received at night in a number of American cities. Another early station in Cuba was owned by Frank Jones, an American amateur radio operator and Chief Engineer of the Tuinucu Sugar Company. The station used amateur call letters, and went on the air as 6KW. In late 1928, PWX began using the call letters CMC. Its slogan was "If you hear 'La Paloma,' you are in tune with CMC." As with many other countries, interest in radio expanded, and by 1932, Cuba had more than thirty stations, spread out in cities all over the island.

France

Radio Paris began operations in 1922, followed by Radio Toulouse and Radio Lyon. Before 1940, 14 commercial and 12 public sector radio stations were in operation. The government exerted tight control over radio broadcasting. Political debate was not encouraged. In the 1932 election campaign, for example, the opposition was allowed one broadcast while the incumbent made numerous campaign broadcasts. Radio was a potentially powerful new medium, but France was quite laggard in consumer ownership of radio sets, With 5 million radio receivers in 1937, compared to over 8 million and both Britain and Germany, and 26 million in the United States. The government imposed very strict controls on news dissemination. After 1938, stations were allowed only three brief daily bulletins, of seven minutes each, to cover all the day's news. The Prime Minister's office closely supervised the news items that were to be broadcast. As war approached, Frenchmen learned little or nothing about it from the radio. The government thought that policy wise, because it wanted no interference in its policies. The unexpected result, however, was the Frenchman were puzzled and uncertain great crises erupted in 1938-39, and their morale and support for government policies was much weaker than in Britain.

Germany

The first radio station in Germany went on the air in Berlin in late 1923, using the call letters "LP." Before 1933, German radio broadcasting was Conducted by 10 regional broadcasting monopolies, each of which had a government representative on its board. The Post Office Provided overall supervision. A listening fee of 2 Reichsmark per receiver paid most costs, and radio station frequencies were limited, which even restricted the number of amateur radio operators. Immediately following Hitler's assumption of power in 1933, Joseph Goebbels became head of the Ministry for Propaganda and Public Enlightenment and took full control of broadcasting. Non-Nazis were removed from broadcasting and editorial positions. Jews were fired from all positions.

Germany was easily served by a number of European mediumwave stations, including the BBC, but the Nazis made it illegal for Germans to listen to foreign broadcasts. During the war, German stations broadcast not only war propaganda and entertainment for German forces dispersed through Europe, as well as air raid alerts. There was heavy use of short wave for "Germany Calling" programmes directed at Britain and Allied forces around the world. Goebbels Also set up numerous Nazi stations that pretended to be from the Allied world. Germany experimented with television broadcasting, using a 180-line raster system beginning before 1935. German propaganda claimed the system was superior to the British mechanical scanning system.

Japan

The first radio station in Japan was JOAK, which opened in Tokyo in March 1925. It was founded by Masajiro Kotamura, an inventor and engineer. It was unique in that at least one of its announcers was a woman, Akiko Midorikawa. JOAK was followed soon after by JOBK in Osaka and JOCK in Nagoya. The National Broadcasting Service, today known as NHK (Nippon Hoso Kyokai), began in August 1926. All stations were supported by licensing fees: in 1926, for example, people wishing to receive a permit to own a radio set paid a fee of one yen a month to the government. Programming on Japanese stations of the 1920s included music, news, language instruction (lessons were offered in English, French and German) and educations talks. These early stations broadcast on average about eight hours of programs a day.

Mexico

Amateur radio was very popular in Mexico; while most of the hams were male, notably Constantino de Tarnava, acknowledged in some sources as Mexico's first amateur radio operator, one of the early ham radio operators was female—Maria Dolores Estrada. But commercial radio was difficult to achieve, due to a federal regulation forbidding any broadcasts that were not for the benefit of the Mexican government. Still, in November 1923, CYL in Mexico City went on the air, featuring music (both folk songs and popular dance concerts), religious services, and news. CYL used as its slogans "El Universal" and "La Casa del Radio", and it won over the government, by giving political candidates the opportunity to use the station to campaign. Its signal was so powerful that it was even received in Canada sometimes. Pressure from listeners and potential station owners also contributed to the government relenting and allowing more stations to go on the air. In 1931, the "C" call letters were all changed to "X" call letters (XE being reserved for broadcasting), and by 1932, Mexico had nearly forty radio stations, ten of which were in Mexico City.

Netherlands

On the 6th of November 1919, the Dutch radio pioneer Hans Henricus Schotanus à Steringa Idzerda started regular radio transmissions from The Hague. As these were regular transmissions and the program was announced beforehand in the newspaper NRC, this is seen as the start of commercial broadcasting.

Philippines

Interest in amateur radio was noted in the Philippines in the early 1920s. There were radio stations operating in the Philippines, including one owned by American businessman named Henry Hermann, as early as 1922, according to some sources; not much documentation about that period of time exists. In the autumn of 1927, KZRM in Manila, owned by the Radio Corporation of the Philippines, went on the air. The Radio Corporation of the Philippines was a subsidiary of American company RCA (Radio Corporation of America). By 1932, the island had three radio stations: KRZC in Cebu, as well as KZIB (owned by a department store) and KZFM, the government-owned station in Manila. Of the stations listed by Pierre Key, KZFM was the strongest, with 50,000 watts. Two radio networks were ultimately created: one, the Manila Broadcasting Company, began as a single station, KZRH in Manila, in July 1939, and after World War II, in 1946, the station's owners began to develop their network by buying other radio properties. As for the Philippine Broadcasting Company, it too began with one station (KZFM), and received its new name in mid-1946, after the Philippines became an independent country. At the end of 1946, the new network had six stations. Both KZRH and KZFM also affiliated with American networks; the stations wanted to have access to certain popular American programs, and the American networks wanted to sell products in the Philippines.

Sri Lanka

Sri Lanka has the oldest radio station in Asia (world's second oldest). The station was known as Radio Ceylon. It developed into one of the finest broadcasting institutions in the world. It is now known as the Sri Lanka Broadcasting Corporation. Sri Lanka created broadcasting history in Asia when broadcasting was started in Ceylon by the Telegraph Department in 1923 on an experimental footing, just three years after the inauguration of broadcasting in Europe. Gramophone music was broadcast from a tiny room in the Central Telegraph Office with the aid of a small transmitter built by the Telegraph Department engineers from the radio equipment of a captured German submarine. This broadcasting experiment was successful; barely three years later, on December 16, 1925, a regular broadcasting service came to be instituted. Edward Harper who came to Ceylon as Chief Engineer of the Telegraph Office in 1921, was the first person to actively promote broadcasting in Ceylon. Sri Lanka occupies an important place in the history of broadcasting with broadcasting services inaugurated just three years after the launch of the BBC in the United Kingdom. Edward Harper launched the first experimental broadcast as well as founding the Ceylon Wireless Club, together with British and Ceylonese radio enthusiasts on the island. Edward Harper has been dubbed ' the Father of Broadcasting in Ceylon,' because of his pioneering efforts, his skill and his determination to succeed. Edward Harper and his fellow Ceylonese radio enthusiasts, made it happen.

Kingdo

The first experimental music broadcasts, from Marconi's factory in Chelmsford, began in 1920. Two years later, in October 1922, a consortium of radio manufacturers formed the British Broadcasting Company (BBC); they allowed some sponsored programs, although they were not what we would today consider a fully commercial station. Meanwhile, the first radio stations in England were experimental station 2MT, located near Chelmsford, and station 2LO in London: both were operated by the Marconi Company. By late 1923, there were six stations broadcasting regularly in the United Kingdom: London's 2LO, Manchester's2ZY, and stations in Birmingham (5IT), Cardiff, Newcastle, and Glasgow. As for the consortium of radio manufacturers, it dissolved in 1926, when its license expired; it then became the British Broadcasting Corporation, a non-commercial organization. Its governors are appointed by the British government, but they do not answer to it. Lord Reith took a formative role in developing the BBC, especially in radio. Working as its first manager and Director-General, he promoted the philosophy of public service broadcasting, firmly grounded in the moral benefits of education and of uplifting entertainment, eschewing commercial influence and maintaining a maximum of independence from political control.

Commercial stations such as Radio Normandie and Radio Luxembourg broadcast into the UK from other European countries. This provided a very popular alternative to the rather austere BBC. These stations were closed during the War, and only Radio Luxembourg returned afterward. BBC television broadcasts in Britain began on November 2, 1936, and continued until wartime conditions closed the service in 1939.

United States

Reginald Fessenden did ground-breaking experiments with voice and music by 1906.Charles "Doc" Herrold of San Jose, California sent out broadcasts as early as April 1909 from his Herrold School electronics institute in downtown San Jose, using the identification San Jose Calling, and then a variety of different call signs as the Department of Commerce began to regulate radio. He was on the air daily for nearly a decade when the World War interrupted operations.

Pioneer radio station 2XG, also known as the "Highbridge station", was an experimental station located in New York City and licensed to the DeForest Radio Telephone and Telegraph Company. It was the first station to use a vacuum tube transmitter to make radio broadcasts on a regular schedule. From 1912 to 1917 Charles Herrold made regular broadcasts, but used an arc transmitter. He switched to a vacuum tube transmitter when he restarted broadcasting activities in 1921. Herrold coined the terms broadcasting and narrowcasting,. Herrold claimed the invention of broadcasting to a wide audience, through the use of antennas designed to radiate signals in all directions. David Sarnoff has been considered by many as "the prescient prophet of broadcasting who predicted the medium's rise in 1915", referring to his radio music box concept.

A few organizations were allowed to keep working on radio during the war. Westinghouse was the most well-known of these. Frank Conrad, a Westinghouse engineer, had been making transmissions from 8XK since 1916 that included music programming. A team at the University of Wisconsin–Madison headed by Professor Earle M. Terry was also on the air. They operated 9XM, originally licensed by Professor Edward Bennett in 1914, and experimented with voice broadcasts starting in 1917.

1920s

By 1919, after the war, radio pioneers across the country resumed transmissions. The early stations gained new call signs. A few early stations, notably 8MK (later known as WWJ in Detroit) were started by newspapers, but in those early years, radio and newspapers regarded each other as competitors. One early station, 8XK in Pittsburgh, became KDKA in 1920; its ownership has asserted that it was the first radio station in the USA, but that claim is controversial There were other stations on the air around the same time as KDKA, including a station at Union College in Schenectady, New York that became known as WRUC; 8MK in Detroit; 1XE in Medford Hillside MA, and several others. KDKA received a commercial license and began broadcasting on November 2, 1920.

Madison Avenue early on recognized the importance of radio as a new advertising medium. Advertising provided the major funding for most stations. The United States never had a licensing fee for set users. The National Broadcasting Company began regular broadcasting in 1926, with telephone links between New York and other Eastern cities. NBC became the dominant radio network, splitting into Red and Blue networks. The Columbia Broadcasting System began in 1927 under the guidance of William S. Paley.

Radio in education began as early as April 1922, when Medford Hillside's WGI Radio broadcast the first of an ongoing series of educational lectures from Tufts College professors. These lectures were described by the press as a sort of "wireless college." Soon, other colleges across the U.S. began adding radio broadcasting courses to their curricula; some, like the University of Iowa, even provided what today would be known as distance-learning credits.Curry College, first in Boston and then in Milton, Massachusetts, introduced one of the nation's first broadcasting majors in 1932 when the college teamed up with WLOE in Boston to have students broadcast programs. This success led to numerous radio courses in the curriculum which has taught thousands of radio broadcasters from the 1930s to today.

In 1934, several independent stations formed the Mutual Broadcasting System to exchange syndicated programming, including The Lone Ranger and Amos 'n' Andy. Prior to 1927, U.S. radio was supervised by the Department of Commerce. Then, the Radio Act of 1927 created the Federal Radio Commission (FRC); in 1934, this agency became known as the Federal Communications Commission (FCC). A Federal Communications Commission decision in 1939 required NBC to divest itself of its Blue Network. That decision was sustained by the Supreme Court in a 1943 decision, National Broadcasting Co. v. United States, which established the framework that the "scarcity" of radio-frequency meant that broadcasting was subject to greater regulation than other media. This Blue Network network became the American Broadcasting Company (ABC). Around 1946, ABC, NBC, and CBS began regular television broadcasts. Another TV network, the DuMont Television Network, was founded earlier, but was disbanded in 1956; later in 1986 the surviving DuMont independent stations formed the nucleus of the new Fox Broadcasting Company.

1950s and 1960s

Australia

Norman Banks was one of Melbourne's (and Australia's) most prominent broadcasters at 3KZ (1930-1952) and 3AW (1952-1978). He is remembered for founding Carols by Candlelight, as a pioneer football commentator, and for hosting both musical and interview programs. In later years he was one of Melbourne's first and most prominent talk back hosts. At the commencement of his career, Banks was known for his double entendres and risque remarks; as a talk back host he was outspoken in his conservative views, especially regarding the White Australia policy and Apartheid. In 1978 his 47-year career in radio was hailed as the longest in world history. Not including the early television experiments (see above), mainstream television transmission commenced in Sydney and Melbourne in the latter part of 1956, that is, in time for the 1956 MelbourneOlympic Games in November/December 1956. It was then phased in to other capital cities, and then into rural markets. Many forms entertainment, particularly drama and variety, were considered more suited to television than radio, and many such programs were gradually deleted from radio schedules.

The transistor radio first appeared on the market in 1954. In particular, it made portable radios even more transportable. All sets quicklly became smaller, cheaper and more convenient. The aim of radio manufacturers became a radio in every room, in the car, and in the pocket. The upshot of these two changes was that stations started to specialise and concentrate on specific markets. The first areas to see specialised stations were the news and current affairs market, and stations specialising in pop music and geared toward the younger listener who was now able to afford his/her own radio. Talk back ("talk radio") became a major radio genre by the end of the 1960s, but it was not legalised in Australia until October 1967. The fears of intrusion were addressed by a beep that occurred every few seconds, so that the caller knew that his/her call was being broadcast. There was also a seven-second delay so that obscene or libelous material could be monitored. By the end of the 1960s, specialisation by radio stations had increased dramatically and there were stations focusing on various kinds of music, talk back, news, sport, etc.

Germany

When the Federal Republic of Germany was organized in 1949, its Enabling Act established strong state government powers. Broadcasting was organized on a state, rather than a national, basis. Nine regional radio networks were established. A technical coordinating organization, the Arbeitsgemeinschaft der offentlich-rechtlichen Rundfunkanstalten der Bundesrepublik Deutschland (ARD), came into being in 1950 to lessen technical conflicts. The Allied forces in Europe developed their own radio networks, including the U.S. American Forces Network (AFN). Inside Berlin, Radio in the American Sector (RIAS) became a key source of news in the German Democratic Republic. Germany began developing a network of VHF FM broadcast stations in 1955 because of the excessive crowding of the mediumwave and shortwave broadcast bands.1933

Sri Lanka

Radio Ceylon ruled the airwaves in the 1950s and 1960s in the Indian sub-continent. The station developed into the most popular radio network in South Asia. Millions of listeners in India for example tuned into Radio Ceylon. Announcers like Livy Wijemanne, Vernon Corea,Pearl Ondaatje, Tim Horshington, Greg Roskowski, Jimmy Bharucha, Mil Sansoni, Eardley Peiris, Shirley Perera, Bob Harvie, Christopher Greet, Prosper Fernando, Ameen Sayani (of Binaca Geetmala fame),Karunaratne Abeysekera, S.P.Mylvaganam (the first Tamil Announcer on the Commercial Service) were hugely popular across South Asia. The Hindi Service also helped build Radio Ceylon's reputation as the market leader in the Indian sub-continent. Gopal Sharma, Sunil DuttAmeen Sayani, Hamid Sayani, were among the Indian announcers of the station. The Commercial Service of Radio Ceylon was hugely successful under the leadership of Clifford Dodd, the Australian administrator and broadcasting expert who was sent to Ceylon under the Colombo Plan. Dodd hand picked some of the most talented radio presenters in South Asia. They went on to enjoy star status in the Indian sub-continent. This was Radio Ceylon's golden era.

United Kingdom

Radio Luxembourg remained popular during the 1950s but saw its audience decline as commercial television and pirate radio, combined with a switch to a less clear frequency, began to erode its influence. BBC television resumed on June 7, 1946, and commercial television began on September 22, 1955. Both used the pre-war 405-line standard. BBC2 came on the air on April 20, 1964, using the 625-line standard, and began PAL colour transmissions on July 1, 1967, the first in Europe. The two older networks transmitted in 625-line colour from 1969. During the 1960s there was still no UK-based commercial radio. A number of 'pirate' radio ships, located in international waters just outside the jurisdiction of English law, came on the air between 1964 and 1967. The most famous of these was Radio Caroline, which was the only station to continue broadcasting after the offshore pirates were effectively outlawed on August 14, 1967 by the Marine Broadcasting Offences Act. It was finally forced off air due to a dispute over tendering payments, but returned in 1972 and continued on and off until 1990. (The station subsequently broadcast legally, initially under 28-day Restricted Service Licences and subsequently via satellite - since closed - internet streams and, since 2017, a local AM transmitter.)

United States

Television began to replace radio as the chief source of revenue for broadcasting networks. Although many radio programs continued through this decade, including Gunsmoke and The Guiding Light, by 1960 networks had ceased producing entertainment programs. As radio stopped producing formal fifteen-minute to hourly programs, a new format developed. "Top 40" was based on a continuous rotation of short pop songs presented by a "disc jockey." Famous disc jockeys in the era included Alan Freed, Dick Clark, Don Imus and Wolfman Jack. Top 40 playlists were theoretically based on record sales; however, record companies began to bribedisc jockeys to play selected artists, in a controversy that was called "payola". In the 1950s, American television networks introduced broadcasts in color. The Federal Communications Commission approved the world's first monochrome-compatible color television standard in December 1953. The first network colorcast followed on January 1, 1954, with NBC transmitting the annual Tournament of Roses Parade in Pasadena, California to over 20 stations across the country. An educational television network, National Educational Television (NET), predecessor to PBS, was founded. Shortwave broadcasting played an important part of fighting the cold war with Voice of America and the BBC World Service, Radio Free Europe and Radio Liberty transmitting through the "Iron Curtain", and Radio Moscow and others broadcasting back, as well as "jamming" (transmitting to cause intentional interference) the Western stations in the Soviet bloc.

1970s, 1980s, and 1990s

Australia

After much procrastination on the part of various federal governments, FM broadcasting was eventually introduced in 1975. (There had been official experiments with FM broadcasting as far back as 1948.) Only a handful of radio stations were given new licences during the 1940s, 50s & 60s but, since 1975, many hundreds of new broadcasting licences have been issued on both the FM and AM bands. In the latter case, this was made possible by having 9 kHz between stations, rather 10 kHz breaks, as per the Geneva Frequency Plan. The installation of directional aerials also encouraged more AM stations. The type of station given FM licences reflects the policies and philosophies of the various Australian governments. Initially, only the ABC and community radio stations were granted FM licences. However, after a change of government, commercial stations were permitted on the band, as from 1980. At first, one or two brand new stations were permitted in each major market. However, in 1990, one or two existing AM stations in each major market were given FM licences; the stations being chosen by an auction system. Apart from an initial settling-in period for those few stations transferred from AM to FM, there has been no simulcasting between AM and FM stations. In major cities, a number of brand new FM licences were issued in the 1990s and 2000s. All rural regions which traditionally had only one commercial station now have at least one AM and one FM commercial station. In many cases, the owner of the original station now has at least two outlets. The number of regional transmitters for the ABC's five networks also increased dramatically during this era.

Europe

Commercial radio (re-)legalisation in most European countries occurred in this era, starting with United Kingdom in 1973 (see Independent Local Radio) and ending with Austria in 1995.

In 1987, stations in the European Broadcasting Union began offering Radio Data System (RDS), which provides written text information about programs that were being broadcast, as well as traffic alerts, accurate time, and other teletext services.

Sri Lanka

The Government of Sri Lanka opened up the market in the late 1970s and 1980s allowing private companies to set up radio and television stations. Sri Lanka's public services broadcasters are the Sri Lanka Broadcasting Corporation (SLBC), Independent Television Net Work (ITN) and the affiliated radio station called Lak-handa. They had stiff competition on their hands with the private sector. Broadcasting in Sri Lanka went through a transformation resulting in private broadcasting institutions being set up on the island among them Telshan

Network (Pvt) Ltd (TNL), Maharaja Television – TV, Sirasa TV and Shakthi TV, and EAP Network (Pvt) Ltd – known as Swarnawahini – these private channels all have radio stations as well. The 1990s saw a new generation of radio stations being established in Sri Lanka among them the 'Hiru' radio station. In the 1980s public service broadcasters like the Sri Lanka Broadcasting Corporation set up their own FM arm. Sri Lanka celebrated 80 years of broadcasting in December 2005. In January 2007 the Sri Lanka Broadcasting Corporation celebrated 40 years as a public corporation.

United Kingdom

A new pirate station, Swiss-owned Radio Nordsee International, broadcast to Britain and the Netherlands from 1970 until outlawed by Dutch legislation in 1974 (which meant it could no longer be supplied from the European mainland). The English service was heavily jammed by both Labour and Conservative Governments in 1970 amid suggestions that the ship was actually being used for espionage. Radio Caroline returned in 1972 and continued until its ship sank in 1980 (the crew were rescued). A Belgian station, Radio Atlantis, operated an English service for a few months before the Dutch act came into force in 1974. Land-based commercial radio finally came on air in 1973 with London's LBC and Capital Radio. Channel 4 television started in November 1982. Britain's UHF system was originally designed to carry only four networks. Pirate radio enjoyed another brief resurgence with a literal re-launch of Radio Caroline in 1983, and the arrival of American-owned Laser 558 in 1985. Both stations were harassed by the British authorities; Laser closed in 1987 and Caroline in 1989, since then it has pursued legal methods of broadcasting, such as temporary FM licences and satellite. Two rival satellite television systems came on the air at the end of the 1980s: Sky Television and British Satellite Broadcasting. Huge losses forced a rapid merger, although in many respects it was a takeover of BSB (Britain's official, Government-sanctioned satellite company) by Sky. Radio Luxembourg launched a 24-hour English channel on satellite, but closed its AM service in 1989 and its satellite service in 1991.

The Broadcasting Act 1990 in UK law marked the establishment of two licensing authorities – the Radio Authority and the Independent Television Commission – to facilitate the licensing of non-BBC broadcast services, especially short-term broadcasts. Channel 5 went on the air on March 30, 1997, using "spare" frequencies between the existing channels.

United States

The rise of FM changed the listening habits of younger Americans. Many stations such as WNEW-FM in New York City began to play whole sides of record albums, as opposed to the "Top 40" model of two decades earlier. In the 1980s, the Federal Communications Commission, under Reagan Administration and Congressional pressure, changed the rules limiting the number of radio and television stations a business entity could own in one metropolitan area. This deregulation led to several groups, such as Infinity Broadcasting and Clear Channel to buy many stations in major cities. The cost of these stations' purchases led to a conservative approach to broadcasting, including limited playlists and avoiding controversial subjects to not offend listeners, and increased commercials to increase revenue. AM radio declined throughout the 1970s and 1980s due to various reasons including: Lower cost of FM receivers, narrow AM audio bandwidth, and poor sound in the AM section of automobile receivers (to combat the crowding of stations in the AM band and a "loudness war" conducted by AM broadcasters), and increased radio noise in homes caused by fluorescent lighting and introduction of electronic devices in homes. AM radio's decline flattened out in the mid-1990s due to the introduction of niche formats and over commercialization of many FM stations.

The 2000s

The "Kerbango Internet Radio" was the first stand-alone product that let users listen to Internet radio without a computer.

The 2000s saw the introduction of digital radio and direct broadcasting by satellite (DBS) in the USA. Digital radio services, except in the United States, were allocated a new frequency band in the range of 1,400 MHz. Regular shortwave broadcasts using Digital Radio Mondiale (DRM), a digital broadcasting scheme for short and medium wave broadcasts have begun. This system makes the normally scratchy international broadcasts clear and nearly FM quality, and much lower transmitter power. This is much better to listen to and has more languages.

Australia

In Australia, from August 2009, digital radio was phased in by geographical region. Today, the ABC, SBS, commercial and community radio stations operate on the AM and FM bands. Most stations are available on the internet and most also have digital outlets. By 2007, there were 261 commercial stations in Australia. The ABC currently has five AM/FM networks and is in the process of establishing a series of supplementary music stations that are only available on digital radios and digital television sets. SBS provides non-English language programs over its two networks, as do a number of community radio stations.

The earliest broadcasting consisted of sending telegraph signals over the airwaves, using Morse code, a system developed in the 1830s by Samuel F.B. Morse, physicistJoseph Henry and Alfred Vail. They developed an electrical telegraph system which sent pulses of electric current along wires which controlled an electromagnet that was located at the receiving end of the telegraph system. A code was needed to transmit natural language using only these pulses, and the silence between them. Morse therefore developed the forerunner to modern International Morse code. This was particularly important for ship-to-ship and ship-to-shore communication, but it became increasingly important for business and general news reporting, and as an arena for personal communication by radio amateurs (Douglas, op. cit.). Audio broadcasting began experimentally in the first decade of the 20th century. By the early 1920s radio broadcasting became a household medium, at first on the AM band and later on FM. Television broadcasting started experimentally in the 1920s and became widespread after World War II, using VHF and UHF spectrum. Satellite broadcasting was initiated in the 1960s and moved into general industry usage in the 1970s, with DBS (Direct Broadcast Satellites) emerging in the 1980s.

Originally all broadcasting was composed of analog signals using analog transmission techniques but in the 2000s, broadcasters have switched to digital signals using digital transmission. In general usage, broadcasting most frequently refers to the transmission of information and entertainment programming from various sources to the general public.

- Analog audio vs. HD Radio
- Analog television vs. Digital television
- Wireless

The world's technological capacity to receive information through one-way broadcast networks more than quadrupled during the two decades from 1986 to 2007, from 432 exabytes of (optimally compressed) information, to 1.9 zettabytes. This is the information equivalent of 55 newspapers per person per day in 1986, and 175 newspapers per person per day by 2007.

Script Writing

Screenplay

A screenplay, or script, is a written work by screenwriters for a film, television program or video game. These screenplays can be original works or adaptations from existing pieces of writing. In them, the movement, actions, expression and dialogues of the characters are also narrated. A screenplay written for television is also known as a teleplay.

Originality is the aspect of created or invented works as being new or novel, and thus distinguishable from reproductions, clones, forgeries, or derivative works. An original work is one not received from others nor one copied from or based upon the work of others.. It is a work created with a unique style and substance. The term "originality" is often applied as a compliment to the creativity of artists, writers, and thinkers. The modern idea of originality is tied to Romanticism, by a notion that is often called romantic originality.

The concept of originality is culturally contingent. At the time of Shakespeare, it was more common to appreciate the similarity with an admired classical work, and Shakespeare himself avoided "unnecessary invention". It wasn't until the start of the 18th century that the concept of originality became an ideal in Western culture.

Originality in law

In law, originality has become an important legal concept with respect to intellectual property, where creativity and invention have manifest as copyrightable works. In the patent law of the United States and most other countries, only original inventions are subject to protection. In addition to being original, inventions submitted for a patent must also be useful and nonobvious.

In United States copyright law and the law of many other states, copyrights protect only original works of authorship, a property which has been historically and legally linked to a concept of "creativity". A work must pass a threshold of originality in order to be copyrightable.

In United Kingdomintellectual property law, a derived work can demonstrate originality, and must do so if it is to respect copyright.

Originality under the United States Copyright Law

In the Copyright Law of the United States, more specifically under 17 U.S.C 102, the work that is sought to be protected must satisfy the threshold for originality. Though most of the countries require certain degree of originality in the work sought to be protected, such requirement does not stem from either the Berne Convention or the TRIPS Agreement. Therefore, there is no uniformity in the standard for originality. In the United States, originality necessitates bare minimum degree of creativity and independent creation. The Supreme Court of the United States in the case of Feist Publications v. Rural Telephone Service Co. held that the work must be independently created and must possess minimum degree of creativity. This interpretation requires an extremely low level of creativity and in the words of the court, "must possess some creative spark no matter how crude, humble or obvious it might be." The court also took the opportunity to reject the previously judicially-established and followed the sweat of the brow doctrine. According to the said doctrine, labour and hard-work alone could suffice to establish originality. After the dosctrine was rejected by the Supreme Court in 1991, in the Bridgeman

Art Library v. Corel Corpcase, the court held that the copies of public domain photographs could not be copyrighted since they lacked originality and while such reproductions may have involved skill and labour, no protection could be granted to them, on account of lack of originality.

While the current legal requirements of originality viz. minimum level of creativity and independent labour can be easily assessed and applied in case of literary works, the courts are required to undertake a deeper legal and factual inquiry in photographic works. The United States District Court for Southern District of New York in Mannion v. Coors Brewing Company considered originality in terms of timing, subject and rendition, and held that the nature and extent of the copyright would be independent in the three aspects. The requirement for originality was incorporated in the statute only in the Copyright Act, 1976 and over the course of time, the courts have evolved various metrics to apply the test. Unlike, Patents, novelty is not required for a work to be considered as original. The United States Court of Appeals for the Second Circuit in Sheldon (1936) had clarified that sometimes it is relevant for other purposes. Therefore, if the work created by you is identical to a pre-existing work but you are unaware of the latter's existence, you may still enjoy copyright protection for your work.

Apart from novelty, the work is not required to be made with an intent to be original. What is considered is only that it is actually an independent creation in effect. In 1951, the court in Alfred Bell Co. v. Catalda Arts held that the question as to whether there was intent to be original was not to be considered. The Supreme Court of the United States has also clarified that it is not necessary for the work to be artistic to qualify as original. Furthermore, in the landmark ruling, the court observed that it would be a dangerous undertaking for persons trained only to the law to constitute themselves final judges of the worth of pictorial illustrations, outside of the narrowest and most obvious limits. At the one extreme, some works of genius would be sure to miss appreciation. Their very novelty would make them repulsive until the public had learned the new language in which their author spoke. It may be more than doubted, for instance, whether the etchings of Goya or the paintings of Monet would have been sure of protection when seen for the first time. At the other end, copyright would be denied to pictures which appealed to a public less educated than the judge. This observation was an embodiment of the principle of artistic or aesthetic neutrality which seeks to eliminate the inherent subjectivity involved in the judges deciding whether the work is artistic, and hence, the question as to whether it warrants protection. The principle finds four broad justifications- (i) lack of expertise in the judges (ii) fear of elitism (iii) fear of paternalism (also called parentalism) (iv) lack of consensus on what constitutes art. However, scholars note that the principle of aesthetic neutrality is often violated as the adjudicators end up favouring creators of what they believe is deserving of copyright grant. In the United States, the work is not required to be non-commercial in nature for copyright protection and unlike the US trademark law, the work need to be necessarily lawful.

Therefore, works created for commercial purposes, such as advertisements can also be granted a copyright.

Originality Under Indian Copyright Law

Section 13(1)(a) of the Indian Copyright Act, 1957 mentions 'originality' as a requirement for copyright protection to literary, dramatic, musical and artistic works. Courts have interpreted this requirement of 'originality' in different ways. This has given rise to various doctrines/tests that can be helpful in determining whether a work meets the threshold of originality. The most prominent case with respect to 'originality' under the Indian Copyright Law is the Eastern Book Company v DCB Modak. This judgment gave rise to two doctrines i.e. modicum of creativity and the skill and judgment test. This remains the accepted and current position of law in India as of now. However, prior to this, the Indian Courts used to follow the Sweat of the Brow approach.

Sweat of the Brow theory

This theory bases the grant of copyright protection on the effort and labour that an author puts into her work as opposed to the creativity involved. Locke's theory of labour as property has often been extended to give jurisprudential basis to this theory of copyright law. In the case of V. Govindan v E.M. Gopalakrishna Kone, it was held that compilations of information would meet the threshold of 'originality' under the Indian Copyright Act since it involves some level of 'skill, labour and brain'. A similar line of reasoning was adopted in the case of Burlington Home Shipping Pvt Ltd v Rajnish Chibber where a database was held to be original enough to be protected by copyright under Indian law. However, like in other jurisdictions, this theory was discarded by the Indian Courts also and the focus was shifted to the creativity involved in any work.

EBC Modak Case (Modicum of Creativity & Skill and Judgment Test)

The EBC Modak case is the Indian counterpart of the Feist Publications case in terms of the test it laid down. It concerned the copyrightability of Supreme Court judgments that were copy-edited and published by Eastern Book Company. These judgments were published along with 'headnotes' that were written by the Company itself. While explicitly discarding the Sweat of the Brow theory, the Court held that simply copy editing would not meet the threshold of originality under copyright law since it would only demonstrate an "amount of skill, labour and capital put in the inputs of the copy-edited judgments and the original or innovative thoughts for the creativity would be completely excluded.". Thus, it introduced the requirement of 'creativity' under originality. With respect to the level of creativity involved, the court adopted the 'minimal degree of creativity' approach. Following this standard, the headnotes that did not copy from the judgment verbatim were held to be copyrightable.

Finally, the Court also gave way to the 'Skill and Judgment Test' which is more or less a compromise between the sweat of the brow theory and the modicum of creativity test. While relying on the CCH Canadian Case, the Court essentially held that a work would meet the originality standard as long as there is labour or effort involved but not only labour. It must involve some level of skill and judgment as well. However, this approach mirrors the Sweat of the Brow theory more closely and is therefore a difficult theory to defend. Further, the Court held the division of a judgment into paragraphs and numbering them was enough to meet this standard of 'Skill and Judgment'. Whether this is the correct interpretation of the test as given in the CCH Canadian Case remains debatable.

Originality in science

Scientific literature considered as primary must contain original research, and even review articles contain original analysis or interpretation.

Originality of ideas and creative works

An original idea is one not thought up by another person beforehand. Sometimes, two or more people can come up with the same idea independently.

The evaluation of originality depends not only on the creative work itself, but also on the temporal context, the zeitgeist. In a study of the musical originality of 15,618 classical music themes, the importance of objective characteristics and the zeitgeist for popularity was examined. Both the musical originality of a theme relative to its contemporary works (the zeitgeist), as well as its "absolute" originality influenced in similar magnitude the popularity of a theme. Similarly, objective features and temporal context both influenced the evaluation of linguistic originality.

Original recording

An original painting, photographic negative, analog audio, or video recording, will contain qualities that can be difficult, or under current technology may be impossible to copy in its full integrity. That can also apply for any other artifact.

That is why it is often necessary to preserve the original, in order to preserve its original integrity. The copy is made to preserve the original recording by saving the original from degenerating as it is being played, rather than to replace the original.

Teleplay

A teleplay is a screenplay or script used in the production of a scripted television program or series. In general usage, the term is most commonly seen in reference to a standalone production, such as a television film, a television play or an episode of an anthology series; in internal industry usage, however, all television scripts (including episodes of ongoing drama or comedy series) are teleplays, although a "teleplay" credit may be subsumed into a "written by" credit depending on the circumstances of its creation.

The term first surfaced during the 1950s with wide usage to distinguish teleplays from stage plays written for theater and screenplays written for films. All three have different formats, conventions, and constraints.

Usage

According to current Writers Guild of America guidelines, a television script consists of two distinct parts: "story" and "teleplay". The story comprises "basic narrative, idea, theme or outline indicating character development and action", while the teleplay consists of "individual scenes and full dialogue or monologue (including narration in connection therewith), and camera set-ups, if required". Simply put, this distinguishes the contribution of ideas toward the story from the actual writing of the dialogue and stage directions present on the page in the finished product.

Accordingly, story and teleplay will appear as distinct credits on a television script if different people played those roles in the script's creation; if the same person or people performed both roles equally (unless they also worked on the concept with one or more people not directly involved in writing the script or developing the story concept), then the story and teleplay credits will not be used and instead a merged "written by" credit will be given. However, a written by credit may be given to only three people maximum; if more than three people were involved, then the credits must distinguish those who were "story" contributors from those who were "teleplay" contributors.

History

On the hour-long TV anthology drama shows of the Golden Age of Television, such as The United States Steel Hour, The Goodyear Television Playhouse, The Philco Television Playhouse, The Alcoa Hour, Armstrong Circle Theatre, and Studio One, productions often were telecast live from studios with limited scenery and other constraints similar to theatrical presentations. These constraints made a teleplay quite different from a screenplay.

However, television dramatists, such as Paddy Chayefsky, JP Miller and Tad Mosel, turned such limitations to their advantage by writing television plays with intimate situations and family conflicts characterized by naturalistic, slice of life dialogue. When seen live, such productions had a real-time quality not found in films (shot out of sequence), yet they employed tight close-ups, low-key acting and other elements not found in stage productions. For many viewers, this was equivalent to seeing live theater in their living rooms, an effect enhanced when television plays expanded from 60-minute time slots to a 90-minute series with the introduction of Playhouse 90 in the late 1950s.

Format and style

The format is structured so that one page equates to roughly one minute of screen time, though this is only used as a ballpark estimate and often bears little resemblance to the running time of the final movie. The standard font is 12 point, 10 pitch Courier Typeface.

The major components are action (sometimes called "screen direction") and dialogue. The action is written in the present tense and is limited to what can be heard or seen by the audience, for example descriptions of settings, character movements, or sound effects. The dialogue is the words the characters speak, and is written in a center column.

Unique to the screenplay (as opposed to a stage play) is the use of slug lines. A slug line, also called a master scene heading, occurs at the start of every scene and typically contains three pieces of information: whether the scene is set inside (interior/INT.) or outside (exterior/EXT.), the specific location, and the time of day. Each slug line begins a new scene. In a "shooting script" the slug lines are numbered consecutively for ease of reference.

Physical format

American screenplays are printed single-sided on three-hole-punched paper using the standard American letter size (8.5 x 11 inch). They are then held together with two brass brads in the top and bottom hole. The middle hole is left empty as it would otherwise make it harder to quickly read the script.

In the United Kingdom, double-hole-punched A4 paper is normally used, which is slightly taller and narrower than US letter size. Some UK writers format the scripts for use in the US letter size, especially when their scripts are to be read by American producers, since the pages would otherwise be cropped when printed on US paper. Because each country's standard paper size is difficult to obtain in the other country, British writers often send an electronic copy to American producers, or crop the A4 size to US letter.

A British script may be bound by a single brad at the top left hand side of the page, making flicking through the paper easier during script meetings. Screenplays are usually bound with a light card stock cover and back page, often showing the logo of the production company or agency submitting the script, covers are there to protect the script during handling which can reduce the strength of the paper. This is especially important if the script is likely to pass through the hands of several people or through the post.

Increasingly, reading copies of screenplays (that is, those distributed by producers and agencies in the hope of attracting finance or talent) are distributed printed on both sides of the paper (often professionally bound) to reduce paper waste. Occasionally they are reduced to half-size to make a small book which is convenient to read or put in a pocket; this is generally for use by the director or production crew during shooting.

Although most writing contracts continue to stipulate physical delivery of three or more copies of a finished script, it is common for scripts to be delivered electronically via email.

Screenplay formats

Screenplays and teleplays use a set of standardizations, beginning with proper formatting. These rules are in part to serve the practical purpose of making scripts uniformly readable "blueprints" of movies, and also to serve as a way of distinguishing a professional from an amateur.

Feature film

Motion picture screenplays intended for submission to mainstream studios, whether in the US or elsewhere in the world, are expected to conform to a standard typographical style known widely as the studio format which stipulates how elements of the screenplay such as scene headings, action, transitions, dialog, character names, shots and parenthetical matter should be presented on the page, as well as font size and line spacing.

One reason for this is that, when rendered in studio format, most screenplays will transfer onto the screen at the rate of approximately one page per minute. This rule of thumb is widely contested — a page of dialogue usually occupies less screen time than a page of action, for example, and it depends enormously on the literary style of the writer — and yet it continues to hold sway in modern Hollywood.

There is no single standard for studio format. Some studios have definitions of the required format written into the rubric of their writer's contract. The Nicholl Fellowship, a screenwriting competition run under the auspices of the Academy of Motion Picture Arts and Sciences, has a guide to screenplay format. A more detailed reference is The Complete Guide to Standard Script Formats.

Spec screenplay

A "spec script" or speculative screenplay is a script written to be sold on the open market with no upfront payment, or promise of payment. The content is usually invented solely by the screenwriter, though spec screenplays can also be based on established works, or real people and events.

Television

For American TV shows, the format rules for hour-long dramas and single-camera sitcoms are essentially the same as for motion pictures. The main difference is that TV scripts have act breaks. Multi-camera sitcoms use a different, specialized format that derives from stage plays and radio. In this format, dialogue is double-spaced, action lines are capitalized, and scene headings, character entrances and exits, and sound effects are capitalized and underlined.

Drama series and sitcoms are no longer the only formats that require the skills of a writer. With reality-based programming crossing genres to create various hybrid programs, many of the so-called "reality" programs are in a large part scripted in format. That is, the overall skeleton of the show and its episodes are written to dictate the content and direction of the program. The Writers Guild of America has identified this as a legitimate writer's medium, so much so that they have lobbied to impose jurisdiction over writers and producers who "format" reality-based productions. Creating reality show formats involves storytelling structure similar to screenwriting, but much more condensed and boiled down to specific plot points or actions related to the overall concept and story.

Documentaries

The script format for documentaries and audio-visual presentations which consist largely of voice-over matched to still or moving pictures is different again and uses a two-column format which can be particularly difficult to achieve in standard word processors, at least when it comes to editing or rewriting. Many script-editing software programs include templates for documentary formats.

Screenwriting software

Various screenwriting software packages are available to help screenwriters adhere to the strict formatting conventions. Detailed computer programs are designed specifically to format screenplays, teleplays, and stage plays. Such packages include BPC-Screenplay, Celtx, Fade In, Final Draft, FiveSprockets, Montage, Movie Magic Screenwriter, Movie Outline 3.0, Scrivener, Movie Draft SE and Zhura. Software is also available as web applications, accessible from any computer, and on mobile devices, such as Fade In Mobile and Scripts Pro.

The first screenwriting software was SmartKey, a macro program that sent strings of commands to existing word processing programs, such as WordStar, WordPerfect and Microsoft Word. SmartKey was popular with screenwriters from 1982 to 1987, after which word processing programs had their own macro features.

Script coverage

Script coverage is a filmmaking term for the analysis and grading of screenplays, often within the script-development department of a production company. While coverage may remain entirely verbal, it usually takes the form of a written report, guided by a rubric that varies from company to company. The original idea behind coverage was that a producer's assistant could read a script and then give their producer a breakdown of the project and suggest whether they should consider producing the screenplay or not.

Pre-production

Pre-production is the process of planning some of the elements involved in a film, play, or other performance. There are three parts in a production: pre-production,

production, and post-production. Pre-production ends when the planning ends and the content starts being produced.

In film

In filmmaking and video production, pre-production formally begins once a project has been greenlit. At this stage, finalizing preparations for production go into effect. Financing will generally be confirmed and many of the key elements such as principal cast members, director and cinematographer are set. By the end of pre-production, the screenplay is usually finalized and satisfactory to all the financiers and other stakeholders.

During pre-production, the script is broken down into individual scenes storyboards and all the locations, props, cast members, costumes, special effects and visual effects are identified. An extremely detailed schedule is produced and arrangements are made for the necessary elements to be available to the film-makers at the appropriate times. Sets are constructed, the crew is hired, financial arrangements are put in place and a start date for the beginning of principal photography is set. At some point in pre-production there will be a read-through of the script which is usually attended by all cast members with speaking parts, the director, all heads of departments, financiers, producers, and publicists.

In music

In the music industry, pre-production is a process whereby a recording artist spends time creating and refining their musical ideas. The artist thus produces a song's demo recording, or rough draft, in order to pre-establish the song's creative premise. This reduces the time and money spent in expensive studios. The goal is to enter into the major recording phase of production with the basic and most promising ideas having been already established.

Notable producers who preferred this process have included Bruce Fairbairn and Bob Rock. They have both produced successful albums such as Bon Jovi's Slippery When Wet, Mötley Crüe's Dr. Feelgood, Metallica's The Black Album and Aerosmith's Permanent Vacation.

Pre-production

In pre-production, every step of actually creating the film is carefully designed and planned. The production company is created and a production office established. The film is pre-visualized by the director, and may be storyboarded with the help of illustrators and concept artists. A production budget is drawn up to plan expenditures for the film. For major productions, insurance is procured to protect against accidents.

The nature of the film, and the budget, determine the size and type of crew used during filmmaking. Many Hollywood blockbusters employ a cast and crew of hundreds, while a low-budget, independent film may be made by a skeleton crew of eight or nine (or fewer). These are typical crew positions:

- Storyboard artist: creates visual images to help the director and production designer communicate their ideas to the production team.
- Director: is primarily responsible for the storytelling, creative decisions and acting of the film.
  - o Assistant director (AD): manages the shooting schedule and logistics of the production, among other tasks. There are several types of AD, each with different responsibilities.
- Film producer: hires the film's crew.
  - o Unit production manager: manages the production budget and production schedule. They also report, on behalf of the production office, to the studio executives or financiers of the film.
  - o Location manager: finds and manages film locations. Nearly all pictures feature segments that are shot in the controllable environment of a studio sound stage, while outdoor sequences call for filming on location.
- Production designer: the one who creates the visual conception of the film, working with the art director, who manages the art department, which makes production sets.
  - o Costume designer: creates the clothing for the characters in the film working closely with the actors, as well as other departments.
  - o Makeup and hair designer: works closely with the costume designer in order to create a certain look for a character.
- Casting director: finds actors to fill the parts in the script. This normally requires that actors audition.
  - o Choreographer: creates and coordinates the movement and dance – typically for musicals. Some films also credit a fight choreographer.
- Director of photography (DP): the head of the photography of the entire film, supervises all cinematographers and Camera Operators.
- Production sound mixer: the head of the sound department during the production stage of filmmaking. They record and mix the audio on set – dialogue, presence and sound effects in mono and ambience in stereo. They work with the boom operator, Director, DA, DP, and First AD.
  - o Sound designer: creates the aural conception of the film, working with the supervising sound editor. On Bollywood-style Indian productions the sound designer plays the role of a director of audiography.
  - o Composer: creates new music for the film. (usually not until post-production)

Production

In production, the film is created and shot. More crew will be recruited at this stage, such as the property master, script supervisor, assistant directors, stills photographer, picture editor, and sound editors. These are just the most common roles in filmmaking; the production office will be free to create any unique blend of roles to suit the various responsibilities possible during the production of a film.

A typical day's shooting begins with the crew arriving on the set/location by their call time. Actors usually have their own separate call times. Since set construction, dressing and lighting can take many hours or even days, they are often set up in advance.

The grip, electric and production design crews are typically a step ahead of the camera and sound departments: for efficiency's sake, while a scene is being filmed, they are already preparing the next one.

While the crew prepare their equipment, the actors do their costumes and attend the hair and make-up departments. The actors rehearse the script and blocking with the director, and the camera and sound crews rehearse with them and make final tweaks. Finally, the action is shot in as many takes as the director wishes. Most American productions follow a specific procedure:

The assistant director (AD) calls "picture is up!" to inform everyone that a take is about to be recorded, and then "quiet, everyone!" Once everyone is ready to shoot, the AD calls "roll sound" (if the take involves sound), and the production sound mixer will start their equipment, record a verbal slate of the take's information, and announce "sound speed", or just "speed", when they are ready. The AD follows with "roll camera", answered by "speed!" by the camera operator once the camera is recording. The clapper, who is already in front of the camera with the clapperboard, calls "marker!" and slaps it shut. If the take involves extras or background action, the AD will cue them ("action background!"), and last is the director, telling the actors "action!". The AD may echo "action" louder on large sets.

A take is over when the director calls "cut!", and camera and sound stop recording. The script supervisor will note any continuity issues and the sound and camera teams log technical notes for the take on their respective report sheets. If the director decides additional takes are required, the whole process repeats. Once satisfied, the crew moves on to the next camera angle or "setup," until the whole scene is "covered." When shooting is finished for the scene, the assistant director declares a "wrap" or "moving on," and the crew will "strike," or dismantle, the set for that scene.

At the end of the day, the director approves the next day's shooting schedule and a daily progress report is sent to the production office. This includes the report sheets from continuity, sound, and camera teams. Call sheets are distributed to the cast and crew to tell them when and where to turn up the next shooting day. Later on, the director, producer, other department heads, and, sometimes, the cast, may gather to watch that day or yesterday's footage, called dailies, and review their work.

With workdays often lasting 14 or 18 hours in remote locations, film production tends to create a team spirit. When the entire film is in the can, or in the completion of the production phase, it is customary for the production office to arrange a wrap party, to thank all the cast and crew for their efforts.

For the production phase on live-action films, synchronizing work schedules of key cast and crew members is very important, since for many scenes, several cast members and most of the crew must be physically present at the same place at the same time (and bankable stars may need to rush from one project to another).

Animated films have different workflow at the production phase, in that voice talent can record their takes in the recording studio at different times and may not see one another until the film's premiere, while most physical live-action tasks are either unnecessary or are simulated by various types of animators.

Post-production process and practices

Here the video/film is assembled by the film editor. The shot film material is edited. The production sound (dialogue) is also edited; music tracks and songs are composed and recorded, if a film is sought to have a score; sound effects are designed and recorded. Any computer-graphic visual effects are digitally added by an artist. Finally, all sound elements are mixed into "stems", which are then married to picture, and the film is fully completed ("locked").

Distribution

This is the final stage, where the film is released to cinemas or, occasionally, directly to consumer media (VHS, VCD, DVD, Blu-ray) or direct download from a digital media provider. The film is duplicated as required (either onto film or hard disk drives) and distributed to cinemas for exhibition (screening). Press kits, posters, and other advertising materials are published, and the film is advertised and promoted. A B-roll clip may be released to the press based on raw footage shot for a "making of" documentary, which may include making-of clips as well as on-set interviews.

Film distributors usually release a film with a launch party, a red-carpet premiere, press releases, interviews with the press, press preview screenings, and film festival screenings. Most films are also promoted with their own special website separate from those of the production company or distributor. For major films, key personnel are often contractually required to participate in promotional tours in which they appear at premieres and festivals, and sit for interviews with many TV, print, and online journalists. The largest productions may require more than one promotional tour, in order to rejuvenate audience demand at each release window.

Since the advent of home video in the early 1980s, most major films have followed a pattern of having several distinct release windows. A film may first be released to a few select cinemas, or if it tests well enough, may go directly into wide release. Next, it is released, normally at different times several weeks (or months) apart, into different market segments like rental, retail, pay-per-view, in-flight entertainment, cable, satellite, or free-to-air broadcast television. The distribution rights for the film are also usually sold for worldwide distribution. The distributor and the production company share profits and manage losses.

Independent filmmaking

Filmmaking also takes place outside of the mainstream and is commonly called independent filmmaking. Since the introduction of DV technology, the means of production have become more democratized and economically viable. Filmmakers can conceivably shoot and edit a film, create and edit the sound and music, and mix the final cut on a home computer. However, while the means of production may be democratized, financing, traditional distribution, and marketing remain difficult to accomplish outside the traditional system. In the past, most independent filmmakers have relied on film festivals (such as Sundance, Venice, Cannes and Toronto film festivals) to get their films noticed and sold for distribution and production. However, the Internet has allowed for relatively inexpensive distribution of independent films on websites such as YouTube. As a result, several companies have emerged to assist filmmakers in getting independent movies seen and sold via mainstream internet marketplaces, often adjacent to popular Hollywood titles. With internet movie distribution, independent filmmakers who choose to forgo a traditional distribution deal now have the ability to reach global audiences.

Use of RCCP in teaching

Overview

The Resolving Conflict Creatively Program (RCCP) is a comprehensive, school-based, violence-prevention program designed for use with children in kindergarten through eighth grade. The 51-lesson program curriculum and accompanying activities are tailored to be developmentally appropriate for a given age group. Through promoting positive conflict resolution and understanding of different cultures, the program strives to create a more caring and peaceful school environment. RCCP now serves over 400 schools in 16 urban, suburban, and rural districts across the country.

The program is based on the theory that aggressive and violent behaviors are learned and therefore can be affected through education. The primary goal of RCCP is to increase children's levels of knowledge regarding ways in which to approach conflict situations, to develop children's conflict resolution skills, and to promote children's positive interpersonal and intergroup relations. In addition, RCCP attempts to combat prejudice and stereotypes, and the various types of conflict and violence that may arise as a result of these issues, by teaching children how to recognize and oppose prejudice and by increasing their respect for and understanding of diversity. Finally, RCCP aims to transform the overall school culture into one that exemplifies nonviolent conflict resolution and a respect for and openness to diversity.

RCCP involves classroom instruction of children by trained teachers. In addition, the program includes the recruitment, training, and supervision of children to act as peer mediators. These mediators help facilitate the resolution of conflicts among children both in the classroom and elsewhere in school.

Evaluation Methods

The first study of RCCP was conducted by the National Center for Children in Poverty (Aber et al., 1998, and Aber, Brown, and Henrich, 1999). The evaluation employed a quasi-experimental research design, with a sample of 5,053 children in grades two through six and nearly 400 teachers in 15 public elementary schools across four major school districts in New York City. At the start of the study (fall 1994), the participating classrooms were divided into four groups in varying stages of intervention: non-intervention (control), the beginning stage of intervention, integration of some program components, and integration of all program components. The schools participating in the evaluation were drawn from among the 87 schools across New York City already involved with RCCP (with the exception of the year-one "no-intervention" group). Schools were selected equally from the four school districts and were chosen so that student race/ethnicity, poverty status, and school size were comparable. Participating children were evenly distributed across the grades. Overall, 48 percent of the sample was female; 43 percent was black, 36 percent was Latino, 16 percent was white, and 6 percent was of another race/ethnicity; and 82 percent received free lunch. Data were collected in fall 1994 and spring 1995. Outcomes, such as aggressive fantasies, attributional biases about aggression, interpersonal negotiation strategies, psychological symptomatology (e.g., fighting, teasing), and depression, were assessed at the end of the first year of the study (spring 1995).

For analytic purposes, classrooms were observed to assess teacher level of RCCP implementation and then grouped accordingly. Three distinct profiles of implementation were identified. The High Lessons profile was characterized by teachers who received a moderate amount of training and taught many RCCP lessons (an average of 23 lessons), and had a classroom composition with relatively few peer mediators (children nominated for additional training in mediation skills; see Implementation Detail at the end of this program description). The Low Lessons profile was characterized by teachers who received the most training and coaching and taught few RCCP lessons (an average of two lessons) and had a classroom composition with the highest percentage of peer mediators. Finally, the No Lessons profile was characterized by teachers who received no RCCP training and taught no RCCP lessons. They may, however, have had some peer mediators included in their classroom. Teachers were not assigned to their implementation profile — in other words, they self-selected the amount of lessons they taught and the amount of training they received.

Aber, Brown, and Jones (2003) reported a second study of the effects of RCCP in a sample of 11,160 first through sixth graders from the same 15 New York City public elementary schools. The study took place in the 1994-1995 and 1995-1996 academic years. As in the first study, the elementary schools were initially divided into four groups on the basis of stage of intervention: nonintervention, the beginning stage of intervention, integration of some program components, and integration of all program components. Among those in the sample, 48 percent were female, 41 percent were Hispanic, 40 percent were black, 14 percent were white, and 5 percent were of another race/ethnicity. Approximately 86 percent of the students were receiving free school lunches. Data were collected at four points in time in the fall and spring over the two academic years. Of the 11,160 children, approximately 9 percent participated at only one data-collection time point, 42 percent participated at two time points, 4 percent participated at three times points, and 45 percent participated at all four time points. Children who participated at fewer time points scored significantly lower in reading and math achievement in the spring of 1994 (Year 1) and had higher rates of absence during Years 1 and 2 than did children who participated more frequently. Multilevel growth curve modeling (a statistical technique that looks at children's developmental trajectories, or rates of change, over time) was used to analyze program outcomes similar to those explored in Aber et al. (1998).

A dissertation by Brown (2003) addressed a quasi-experimental study of RCCP in a sample of predominantly low-income, minority children in the second and third grades. The students were from 15 New York City public elementary schools in four school districts, and the study took place over three years in the mid-1990s, with data collected at three or four points in time, depending on the outcome studied. The schools were initially divided into four groups in varying stages of intervention of RCCP: non-intervention, beginning stage, integration of some program components, and integration of all program components. Groups of schools were chosen whose student race/ethnic background, poverty status, and school sizes were comparable both across the districts and across stages of RCCP implementation. Among the total sample, 49 percent were female, 40 percent were Hispanic, 39 percent were black, 16 percent were white, and 4 percent were of another race/ethnicity. A total of 2,543 children had California Achievement Test math scores at pretest in spring 1994, with 22.5 percent (n = 572) missing in spring 1995 and/or spring 1996. Compared with children who completed follow-up math tests, children with missing math scores had significantly lower math scores in spring 1994, were more likely to be Hispanic, and were more likely to receive free lunch. In addition to math achievement, other outcome measures included teachers' perceptions of children's aggressive behavior. Latent growth curve modeling was used to analyze program outcomes.

Key Evaluation Findings

Aber et al. (1998) and Aber, Brown, and Henrick (1999) found the following:

- Children in all three analytic profiles (High Lessons, Low Lessons, and No Lessons) experienced an increase over time in their hostile attributions (e.g., when presented with a hypothetical ambiguous vignette, the child was more likely to attribute hostile, rather than benign, intent to the actors in the scene). In addition, children in all three profiles experienced an increase over time in their aggressive interpersonal negotiation strategies (i.e., by selecting from responses to hypothetical situations categorized on a four-point scale ranging from aggressive to nonagressive) and a decrease in their positive, proactive interpersonal negotiation strategies.
    - The rate of negative changes was significantly slowed for those children in the High Lessons profile as compared with children in the other two groups.
    - The High-Lessons profile children did not experience a significant decrease

in their ability to positively and proactively problem-solve and negotiate, whereas for both the Low Lessons and No Lessons (control) group, the decrease was significant.

- o The largest negative increases were found in the Low-Lessons profile children. Their rate of increase in negative behaviors exceeded that of the No Lessons population.

- Children in all three analytic profiles experienced an increase over time in their aggressive fantasies (e.g., responses to questions such as, Do you sometimes have daydreams about hitting or hurting someone you don't like?) and conduct problems.
  - o Among children in the High Lessons profile, the increase in aggressive fantasies was not statistically significant, although children experienced a significant increase in conduct problems.

o The size of the increase in both aggressive fantasies and conduct problems was significant for both the Low Lessons and the No Lessons profiles. The average level of increase of aggressive fantasies and conduct problems at the end of the year in children in the Low Lessons profile was significantly larger than the average level of increase in both the High Lessons and Low Lessons groups.

- Program impact was different for boys than it was for girls. While boys in the High Lessons profile did not have a significant decrease over time in their positive negotiation strategies and behaviors as compared with the girls in the High Lessons profile, boys in the other two profiles had a significantly larger decrease than did girls in those groups.
- Program impact was found to be slightly less effective with older children and children in high-risk classrooms and neighborhoods. This finding was consistent across the analytic profiles.

Aber, Brown, and Jones (2003) reported the following:

- Higher levels of classroom instruction in RCCP were associated with lower levels of hostile attribution bias, aggressive strategies, depression, and conduct problems, and with higher levels of competent interpersonal strategies.
- In contrast, higher levels of teacher training and coaching were significantly associated with an increase in hostile attribution bias, aggressive strategies, depression, and conduct problems, as well as with a decline in competent interpersonal strategies.
- Children receiving higher levels of classroom instruction relative to teacher training and coaching ("high lessons") had a slower rate of increase in aggressive fantasies than did children receiving higher levels of teacher training and coaching relative to classroom instruction ("high training and coaching").
- Children in the High Lessons group were reported by teachers as being generally consistent in their levels of aggressive behavior over time compared with the "high training and coaching" children, whose aggressive behavior was reported as steadily increasing over time.

- Similarly, the High Lessons children's teacher-reported prosocial behavior steadily increased over time, whereas such behavior in "high training and coaching" children declined slightly during the same period.
- Intervention effects were for the most part consistent across different demographic groups, such as race/ethnicity, gender, and economic resources (as defined by school lunch eligibility).

The study by Brown (2003) found the following:

- A higher level of exposure to RCCP lessons (analyzed on a continuum) predicted significant growth in math achievement, as well as significant decreases in teacher perceptions of negative behavior. In addition, a significant, negative relationship was found between teacher perceptions of negative behavior and growth in math achievement.
- The program was effective for both boys and girls, and for both students receiving free/reduced-price lunch and those receiving full-priced lunch.
- Differences between groups based on race/ethnicity included the following:
    - The direct effect of RCCP lessons on math achievement was significant for black and Hispanic children but not for white children.
    - The relationship between RCCP lessons and teachers' perceptions was not significant for black children, nor was the relationship between teachers' perceptions and math achievement. These findings suggest that the indirect effects of lessons on math achievement through reductions in teachers' perceptions of negative behavior are evident only for white and Hispanic children.

Implementation Detail

Program Design

- RCCP is introduced into a school gradually over the course of several years. Initially, a few motivated teachers are recruited to participate, and a relatively low number of RCCP lessons is offered. This marks the "beginning" phase of implementation. From that phase, a school moves to the "consolidation" phase, in which additional teachers are added and the administrator training and peer mediation components are introduced. Next comes the "saturation" phase, in which even more classrooms are added to the program. Finally, a school reaches the "full model" of intervention, in which the program has been implemented schoolwide and a targeted intervention for high-risk youth has been added.
- The peer mediation component of the program is designed to give children opportunities to practice skills they have learned. Children in grades four through six are nominated by their classmates or appointed by teachers. Nominated children receive a three-day training session and are then identified as peer mediators who may intervene in conflicts during non-classroom time. Mediators wear special T-shirts and work in pairs. They do not intervene in physical fights.

- RCCP offers instruction to school administrators to educate them about the program and to provide implementation support.

Curriculum

RCCP has a set curriculum. The number of lessons included in the curriculum, however, varies with the individual teacher and level of implementation. The number of lessons given over the course of the years can range from zero to 55, with an average of 13 lessons. The number of lessons included is determined by the level of implementation in the school. As the school moves through the four levels of implementation (beginning, consolidation, saturation, and full model), additional lessons are added to participating classrooms. The RCCP curriculum is designed around several core skill areas: building communication, learning to effectively recognize and express feelings, dealing with anger, resolving conflicts, fostering cooperation, respecting and appreciating diversity, and countering prejudice. The lessons are organized into units based on these skills. Each unit is designed to take from one-half to one full hour. Lessons are presented in a "workshop" format, that is, the teacher's role in the lesson is not to lecture and impart specific knowledge, but rather to facilitate student-directed discussions and learning. Skills are taught through role-playing, interviewing, brainstorming, and small-group discussions. Different versions of the curriculum have been developed for children in the lower and upper elementary school grades and for students in junior high and high school.

Staffing

The program is implemented by classroom teachers. In addition to an 18- to 24-hour introductory course in which teachers learn about and practice the skills they will be teaching in the RCCP, curriculum teachers receive follow-up support and development from RCCP program staff.

Issues to Consider

This program received a "promising" rating. The research was conducted using a well-implemented, semi-randomized controlled experiment and involved a large sample size. Despite some positive findings, there are some methodological limitations to the evaluations, and there were conflicting outcomes. The first study suggests that while there were positive findings, those outcomes were limited to one intervention group—the High-Lessons students. Further, the findings indicated that the program may not be as effective with higher-risk populations that are likely to be more prone to violent and aggressive behaviors. In addition, the individual program components were not analyzed to assess their relative contributions to outcomes (positive or negative) or level of implementation (High or Low). As such, it may be difficult to determine what aspects of the program are producing the positive or negative outcomes.

While children's assignment to classrooms was random, teacher participation was not. Only teachers who agreed to participate in RCCP training, or who had completed RCCP training, participated in the evaluation. The program's materials describe the teachers who are recruited to participate in the program as "highly motivated." It is possible that the characteristics of teachers who are willing and interested in participating in the RCCP program differ from the characteristics of other teachers, and that it is these differences among teachers, rather than the program curriculum, that are producing the observed outcomes.

An issue of considerable concern from the first study (Aber et al., 1998) is in regard to the findings that indicate that individuals who received low numbers of lessons had poorer outcomes relative to those in the other two groups. It is worth noting that if low levels of lessons are detrimental or in fact produce worse outcomes than no exposure to the program whatsoever, then the issues of fidelity of implementation and teacher motivation become very important to the success of the program.

A finding of interest from Aber, Brown, and Jones (2003) is that higher levels of classroom instruction and lower levels of teacher training and coaching were related to significant reductions in the risk of a child having poorer outcomes. The authors suggest that this somewhat counterintuitive finding may be due to the positive relationship between classroom instruction and teacher training. In other words, if RCCP program staff perceived that a teacher needed additional help, in part because they believed the teachers were not delivering the intended amount of RCCP classroom instruction, they focused more intently on training those teachers. Therefore, those teachers who received lower rates of training and coaching may be those who were successfully implementing the classroom instruction to begin with, which in turn led to the children's observed positive outcomes.

Finally, it is important to note that positive program effects may not be consistent across all populations. The findings from Aber et al. (1998) and Aber, Brown, and Henrich (1999) indicate that the program is less effective on older children. At the same time, the baseline measures indicate that the behaviors and attitudes that the program targets increase with age. The program has been evaluated to date with children of elementary school age only. Additionally, the results from Brown (2003) suggest that the RCCP lessons' direct effects on math achievement extend only to Hispanic and black children and not to white children, while the effects of RCCP on reductions in teachers' perceptions of negative behavior are evident only for Hispanic and white children.

Role of AIR/Gyanvani

History of AIR/Gyanvani

In March 2000, when FM frequency licenses were auctioned, the Ministry of

Human Resource Development (MHRD) had been given a frequency for educational broadcasting in each of the 40 cities. The ministry handed the task to IGNOU as it already had some experience telecasting education on Gyan Darshan. IGNOU signed a MOU with Prasar Bharati with an understanding that Prasar Bharati shall provide its infrastructure and also set up and operate the FM stations for educational broadcasts. The signatory of MOU were Shri K. S. Prasada Rao Registrar, IGNOU and Hari Om Srivastava, Chief Engineer from All India radio. The MOU was signed in Presence of Shri H. P. Dixit, Vice Chancellor of IGNOU and Shri Anil Baijal, CEO, Prasar Bharati. IGNOU started broadcasting in Allahabad, Bangalore, Bhopal, Coimbatore, Lucknow and Vishakhapatnam. This was to expand to 40 other cities in two years. Gyan Vani's Educational FM Radio Network has spread to 37 cities and towns across the country. A proposal to start Gyan Vani Stations at another 15 places is under consideration of the Ministries of HRD and Information & Broadcasting.

Description

Gyan Vani is an educational FM radio station in several cities of India. Gyan Vani stations operate as a media cooperative with the day-to-day programmes being contributed by various educational institutions, NGOs, government and semi-government organizations, UN agencies, ministries such as Agriculture, Environment, Health, Women and Child Welfare, Science & Technology, etc. besides national level institutions such as NCERT, NIOS and state open universities. Each Gyan Vani station has a range of about 60 km and covers an entire city including the adjoining rural areas.

The medium of broadcast is English, Hindi or language of the region. Gyan Vani FM radio uses stereophonic FM transmitters, and professionals operate the radio stations. Each nodal centre is provided with media from Indira Gandhi National Open University's (IGNOU) Electronic Media Production Centre. The centre serves purposes of production, dissemination and transmission of educational material. The facilities available at the media production centre are shared with various educational and training institutions, state open universities, central and state government ministries or departments, non governmental organizations, corporate bodies and other sectors. Once the Government of India through a cabinet decision decided to allot one frequency for Education with IGNOU as the nodal agency, Dr R Sreedher, then the director of EMPC designed the network by organising a series of brain storming sessions. His idea was to use the audio video studios available with the educational institutions for producing the programmes and use the AIR or the Doordarshan, public broadcasters' towers and technical facilities for transmission. He wanted to hire these facilities instead of creating his own infrastructure and appointing technical persons. A memorandum of understanding was signed between IGNOU and Prasar Bharati to share the towers. But as of 2013 there are 37 stations functioning. But the original concept of localised broadcasts have been given a go by and most of them are relaying the Delhi programmes. The second phase of radio privatisation even though reserved one frequency for education, neither the MHRD, the nodal ministry nor IGNOU, has taken any interest in pursuing the network. Change of governments and the party in power at the centre, resulted in step-motherly treatment of the network. Dr Sreedher left IGNOU in 2003 and thereafter the EMPC centre is not having any other dynamic director. The regular director, VK Arora was able to complete the task of installing 37 transmitters but was responsible for deviating from original programmes to a relay concept. After Arora left, a new regular full-time director has not been appointed and also the autonomous status of EMPC has been withdrawn making the centre really helpless in expanding the network

Audio Conferencing and Interactive radio conference.

Audio Conferencing Defined

Audio conferencing is the practice of connecting multiple called parties on a single audio conference call, with multiple lines connected through a conferencing bridge.

We've put together this guide to help you successfully connect, host and participate in audio conference calls.

Connecting to an Audio Conference Call

Audio conferencing participants can either be dialed directly by the meeting host or dial in manually to the conferencing bridge to join the call. Modern audio conferencing solutions allow for alternate connections methods such as cloud-based web connections using VoIP or connecting through smartphone or tablet applications.

Hosting an Audio Conference Call

Audio conference hosts are typically given a dial-in number and passcode to distribute to meeting attendees who use to join the conference call. Hosts can also control features like volume, muting, locking/unlocking the call, removing guests and more using so-called "star commands," or key combinations involving the "*" button on the phone and a series of numbers that correspond to the feature being used.

Modern audio conferencing solutions often include a visual software component that can control many of these features using the host's desktop or laptop to manipulate settings, control guest volume, etc. You can now find audio integrated into video conferencing and web conferencing tools for a single, all-in-one conferencing solution.

Participating in an Audio Conference

Audio conferencing participants typically also have access to star commands, although a more limited set than the audio conference host. These commands allow them to mute their lines or control their volumes. Participants have a variety of ways they can join an audio conference, including traditional dial-in, through mobile apps or through VoIP connections on a desktop or laptop.

Choosing an Audio Solution

Audio quality is a critical component to the day-to-day enterprise. However, oftentimes businesses put their audio solution on the backburner because of the complexity of other communication and collaboration software. Audio conferencing has grown increasingly more complex, and there are several key things to consider when choosing a solution:

A conference call is a telephone call in which someone talks to several people at the same time. The conference calls may be designed to allow the called party to participate during the call, or the call may be set up so that the called party merely listens into the call and cannot speak. It is sometimes called ATC (audio tele-conference).

Conference calls can be designed so that the calling party calls the other participants and adds them to the call; however, participants are usually able to call into the conference call themselves by dialing a telephone number that connects to a "conference bridge" (a specialized type of equipment that links telephone lines).

Companies commonly use a specialized service provider who maintains the conference bridge, or who provides the phone numbers and PIN codes that participants dial to access the meeting or conference call. These service providers can often dial-out to participants, connecting them to call and introducing them to the parties who are on-the-line. The operators can also take additional information such as question and answer details and also enable and disable advanced conferencing features such as muting lines, muting participants and enabling a recording feature. An operator can often be summoned to conference call hosted by a service provider using a combination of keys on a users' (sometimes only the moderator) telephone keypad. The most common recall function is *0. (asterisk and the zero/operator key)

The more limited three-way calling is available (usually at an extra charge) on home or office phone lines. For a three-way call, the first called party is dialed. Then the hook flash button (or recall button) is pressed and the other called party's phone number is dialed. While it is ringing, flash/recall is pressed again to connect the three people together. This option allows callers to add a second outgoing call to an already connected call.

Usage

Business

Businesses use conference calls daily to meet with remote parties, both internally and outside of their company. Common applications are client meetings or sales presentations, project meetings and updates, regular team meetings, training classes and communication to employees who work in different locations. Conference calling is viewed as a primary means of cutting travel costs and allowing workers to be more productive by not having to go out-of-office for meetings.

Conference calls are used by nearly all United Statespublic corporations to report their quarterly results. These calls usually allow for questions from stock analysts and are called earnings calls. A standard conference call begins with a disclaimer stating that anything said in the duration of the call may be a forward-looking statement, and that results may vary significantly. The CEO, CFO, or investor relations officer then will read the company's quarterly report. Lastly, the call is opened for questions from analysts.

Conference calls are increasingly used in conjunction with web conferences, where presentations or documents are shared via the internet. This allows people on the call to view content such as corporate reports, sales figures and company data presented by one of the participants. The main benefit is that the presenter of the document can give clear explanations about details within the document, while others simultaneously view the presentation. Care should be taken not to mix video and audio source on the same network since the video feed can cause interruptions on sound quality.

It is important to pay attention to conference call etiquette when participating; for example, one should refrain from shouting and multitasking in certain cases. Care should also be taken to schedule a call at a convenient time.

Business conference calls are usually hosted or operator-assisted, with a variety of features.

Conference calls are also beginning to cross over into the world of podcasting and social networking, which in turn fosters new kinds of interaction patterns. Live streaming or broadcasting of conference calls allows a larger audience access to the call without dialing into a bridge. In addition, organizers of conference calls can publish a dial-in number alongside the audio stream, creating potential for audience members to dial in and interact.

The UK government has changed flexible working rights since 2014, so that employees who have been working full-time for a company or organisation can lawfully request flexible working. In recent years, there have been a number of different types of flexible working options as a result of conference calling technology enabling employees to work remotely.

Flat-rate conferencing

Flat-rate conferencing services are being offered which give unlimited access to a conference bridge at a fixed monthly cost. Because telecommunication carriers offer free long-distance bundled with local service, this alternative is gaining widespread popularity for budget conscious businesses and non-profits.

In the UK, there are conference services offered on a pay-as-you-go basis where the cost of the phone calls (using 0843/0844, or 0871/0872 non-geographic revenue sharing numbers) from each of the participants covers the cost of the conference service. With this service type there is no monthly charge and usually no contracts to sign.

Prepaid conference calls

Prepaid conference call services allow businesses and individuals to purchase conferencing services online, and conduct conference calls on a pay-as-you-go basis. Typically, a conference call PIN and its associated calling instructions are displayed immediately online after being purchased and/or sent via email. Generally, prepaid conference call services are used with a landline telephone, mobile phone, or computer, and there is no need to buy additional expensive telecommunications hardware or add/switch long distance service. Some services allow one to start or join a conference call from virtually any country worldwide—with appropriate telephone access.

Large telecommunications providers such as AT&T, Embarq (formerly Sprint), Verizon and other large to medium conferencing service providers maintain a dominant position in the conferencing niche; servicing many of the world's biggest brands. However, the Internet and improved global VoIP networks have helped to significantly reduce the barrier of entry into this niche.

Free conference calling

Free conferencing is different from traditional conference calling in that it has no organizer fees and allows for multiple people to meet for the price of their long distance connections. Companies that provide free conference call services are usually compensated through a revenue sharing arrangement with the local phone company, sharing the terminating access charge for all incoming calls to a phone carrier.

Some background on the terminating access charge: On every long distance call in the United States including toll conference calls, the consumer is paying for origination (dial tone), transport, and termination (connecting the call). Each of these phone companies share a piece of the cost of the call. If it is the same phone company performing all three tasks (most likely the two largest phone companies – AT&T and Verizon), they keep all of the charge. This is known as intercarrier compensation (ICC) and is intended to keep the telecommunications system functioning by having every phone company receive compensation for using their network.

In the case of free conference calling, the conferencing company strikes an agreement with the local phone company that hosts the conferencing bridge to receive a share of the terminating access charge received for connecting the call. At large carriers such as AT&T and Verizon, they keep these access charges for their own conferencing services in addition to charging the customer for the conference service. With free conference calling, as mentioned above, there are no organizer fees so these services do not double-dip: the consumer pays for a regular call with the same three components – origination, transport, and termination – of any call. In other words, the call costs the same as any other call under the customer's calling plan, but the conferencing is included for free to the host and participants of the conference call.

This added competition in the conferencing market has brought average rates down from over 20 cents per minute to under 10 cents per minute. In addition, it is more efficient and less expensive to speak to many people on one call (a conference call) than on multiple person-to-person calls.

In November 2011, the Federal Communications Commission (FCC) published a 732-page Order on InterCarrier Compensation (ICC), including rules governing revenue sharing. Citing Section 251(b)(5) of the Telecommunications Act of 1996, the FCC mandated that terminating access rates for all calls (not just conference calls) be leveled in 2012 and 2013, then reduced in three increments over the subsequent three years until they reach $0 in 2017. These mostly sub-1 cent charges are replaced with an access recovery charge (ARC) that is added onto every customers' bill by their phone carriers. In other words, every phone company will get to keep the terminating access charges they had to pay out to connect each call while charging consumers more whether they make calls or not. This order has been challenged at the Federal Appeals Court by several parties.

As for revenue sharing, the order adds a measure for high volume call traffic which triggers an immediate terminating access charge reduction to the lowest rate of any carrier in that state.

In the United Kingdom, the 0870 prefix was originally used by UK-based free conference calling providers in order to receive a rebate from every call from a telephone company that owns the number. However, in April 2009 Ofcom, the independent regulator and competition authority for the UK communications industries, announced that the rebate that is payable to the telecom's supplier when an 0870 number is used would be removed. Systems were soon moved to 0844 and 0871 prefixes in order to retain the revenue sharing arrangement.

Recently in the UK, a very small number of conference call providers have begun to use 03 numbers, which are included in bundled minutes under Ofcom regulations. This has provided the option to hold conference calls without any costs whatsoever, as call are included in the minutes bundles provided by most UK network operators. There is a general trend for companies in the UK to more to 03 numbers for inbound services because these numbers are more palatable to the caller.

A distinct difference between sound quality of paid and free conference calls has been noted by customers who have claimed to hear background noises when using the free conferencing services, which rarely happens on paid conference calling services.

Premium conferencing

Here participants dial in on a premium-rate number such as a toll free number in the US. The conference is typically hosted by the party that perceives value in the call in order to justify the cost: this could be a business owner, a non-profit board member, an educator, lawyer, or expert in any given field. That person then usually pays for the cost of the call. Premium conferencing can also be used for charitable fundraisers.

Premium Conferencing Feature Sets

- Reservationless or operator assisted conferencing
- Host PINs
- Name announce
- Roll-call (unique and superior)
- Moderator/participant codes
- Live web-based call management with mute/unmute, drop one/all, and dial out
- Recording with .wav file access through an online account
- High-quality on-demand transcriptions (with 4-hour turnaround on request)
- Customizable, "branded" greetings(unique)

10

COMMUNICATION PROCESS

Communication requires a sender, a message, and an intended recipient, although the receiver need not be present or aware of the sender's intent to communicate at the time of communication; thus communication can occur across vast distances in time and space. Communication requires that the communicating parties share an area of communicative commonality. The communication process is complete once the receiver has understood the sender.

HUMAN COMMUNICATION

Human spoken and picture languages can be described as a system of symbols (sometimes known as lexemes) and the grammars (rules) by which the symbols are manipulated. The word "language" also refers to common properties of languages. Language learning normally occurs most intensively during human childhood. Most of the thousands of human languages use patterns of sound or gesture for symbols which enable communication with others around them. Languages seem to share certain properties, although many of these include exceptions. There is no defined line between a language and a dialect. Constructed languages such as Esperanto, programming languages, and various mathematical formalisms are not necessarily restricted to the properties shared by human languages.

Human **Communication process by 6 steps** *Communication is a dynamic, transactional (two way) process that can be broken into six phases.*

1. The sender has an idea: You conceive an idea and want to share it.
2. The sender encodes the idea: When you put the idea into a message that your receiver will understand, you are encoding it. You decide on the message's form (word, facial expression, and gesture), length, organization, tone, and style –all of which depend on your idea, your audiences, and your personal style of mode.
3. The sender transmits the message: To physically transmit your message to your receiver, you select a communication channel (verbal or nonverbal, spoken or written) and a medium (telephone, letter, memo, report, face to face conservation, etc). This choice depends on your message, your audience's location, your need for speed, and the formality required.
4. The receiver gets the message: For communication to occur, your receiver must first get the message. If you send a letter, you receiver has to read it

before understanding it. If you're giving a speech, your listeners have to be able to hear you, and they have to be paying attention.

5. The receiver decodes the message: You receiver must decode (absorb and understand) your message. The decode message must then be stores in the receiver's mind. If all goes well, the receiver interprets your message correctly, assigning the same meaning to your words as you intended and responding in the desired way.
6. The receiver sends feedback: After decoding your message, the receiver responds in some way and signals that response to you. This feedback enables you to evaluate the effectiveness of your message. If your audience doesn't understand what you mean, you can tell by the response and refine your message.

A variety of verbal and non-verbal means of communicating exists such as body language; eye contact, sign language, paralanguage, haptic communication, chronemics, and media such as pictures, graphics, sound, and writing.

Convention on the Rights of Persons with Disabilities also defines the communication to include the display of text, Braille, tactile communication, large print, accessible multimedia, as well as written and plain language, human reader, and accessible information and communication technology.

Nonverbal Communication

Nonverbal communication describes the process of conveying meaning in the form of non-word messages through e.g. gesture, body language or posture; facial expression and eye contact, object communication such as clothing, hairstyles, architecture, symbols and infographics, as well as through an aggregate of the above. Non-verbal communication is also called silent language and plays a key role in human day to day life from employment relations to romantic engagements.

Speech also contains nonverbal elements known as paralanguage. These include voice quality, emotion and speaking style as well as prosodic features such as rhythm, intonation and stress. Likewise, written texts include nonverbal elements such as handwriting style, spatial arrangement of words and the use of emoticons to convey emotional expressions in pictorial form.

Visual Communication

Visual communication is the conveyance of ideas and information through creation of visual representations. Primarily associated with two dimensional images, it includes: signs, typography, drawing, graphic design, illustration, colours, and electronic resources, video and TV. Recent research in the field has focused on web design and graphically oriented usability. Graphic designers use methods of visual communication in their professional practice.

Oral Communication

Oral communication, while primarily referring to spoken verbal communication, typically relies on both words, visual aids and non-verbal elements to support the conveyance of the meaning. Oral communication includes discussion, speeches, presentations, interpersonal communication and many other varieties. In face to face communication the body language and voice tonality plays a significant role and may have a greater impact on the listener than the intended content of the spoken words.

A great presenter must capture the attention of the audience and connect with them. For example, out of two persons telling the same joke one may greatly amuse the audience due to his body language and tone of voice while the second person, using exactly the same words, bores and irritates the audience. Visual aid can help to facilitate effective communication and is almost always used in presentations for an audience.

A widely cited and widely misinterpreted figure used to emphasize the importance of delivery states that "communication comprise 55% body language, 38% tone of voice, 7% content of words", the so-called "7%-38%-55% rule". This is not however what the cited research shows – rather, when conveying *emotion,* if body language, tone of voice, and words *disagree,* then body language and tone of voice will be believed more than words. For example, a person saying "I'm delighted to meet you" while mumbling, hunched over, and looking away will be interpreted as insincere.

Over time the forms of and ideas about communication have evolved through progression of technology. Advances include communications psychology and media psychology; an emerging field of study. Researchers divides the progression of written communication into three revolutionary stages called "Information Communication Revolutions" (Source needed).

During the 1st stage written communication first emerged through the use of pictographs. The pictograms were made in stone, hence written communication was not yet mobile.

During the 2nd stage writing began to appear on paper, papyrus, clay, wax, etc. Common alphabets were introduced and allowed for the uniformity of language across large distances. A leap in technology occurred when the Gutenberg printing-press was invented in the 15th century.

The 3rd stage is characterised by the transfer of information through controlled waves and electronic signals.

Communication is thus a process by which meaning is assigned and conveyed in an attempt to create shared understanding. This process, which requires a vast repertoire of skills in interpersonal processing, listening, observing, speaking, questioning, analyzing, gestures and evaluating enables collaboration and cooperation.

TRANSACTIONAL MODEL OF COMMUNICATION

The first major model for communication came in 1949 by Claude Shannon and Warren Weaver for Bell Laboratories The original model was designed to mirror the functioning of radio and telephone technologies. Their initial model consisted of three primary parts: sender, channel, and receiver. The sender was the part of a telephone a person spoke into, the channel was the telephone itself, and the receiver was the part of the phone where one could hear the other person. Shannon and Weaver also recognized that often there is static that interferes with one listening to a telephone conversation, which they deemed noise.

In a simple model, often referred to as the transmission model or standard view of communication, information or content (e.g. a message in natural language) is sent in some form (as spoken language) from an emisor/ sender/ encoder to a destination/ receiver/ decoder. This common conception of communication simply views communication as a means of sending and receiving information. The strengths of this model are simplicity, generality, and quantifiability. Social scientists Claude Shannon and Warren Weaver structured this model based on the following elements:

1. An information source, which produces a message.
2. A transmitter, which encodes the message into signals
3. A channel, to which signals are adapted for transmission
4. A receiver, which 'decodes' (reconstructs) the message from the signal.
5. A destination, where the message arrives.

Shannon and Weaver argued that there were three levels of problems for communication within this theory.

The technical problem: how accurately can the message be transmitted?

The semantic problem: how precisely is the meaning 'conveyed'?

The effectiveness problem: how effectively does the received meaning affect behavior?

Daniel Chandler critiques the transmission model by stating:

It assumes communicators are isolated individuals.

No allowance for differing purposes.

No allowance for differing interpretations.

No allowance for unequal power relations.

No allowance for situational contexts.

In 1960, David Berlo expanded on Shannon and Weaver's (1949) linear model of communication and created the SMCR Model of Communication. The Sender-Message-Channel-Receiver Model of communication separated the model into clear parts and has been expanded upon by other scholars.

Communication is usually described along a few major dimensions: Message (what type of things are communicated), source / emisor / sender / encoder (by whom), form (in which form), channel (through which medium), destination / receiver / target / decoder (to whom), and Receiver. Wilbur Schram (1954) also indicated that we should also examine the impact that a message has (both desired and undesired) on the target of the message. Between parties, communication includes acts that confer knowledge and experiences, give advice and commands, and ask questions. These acts may take many forms, in one of the various manners of communication. The form depends on the abilities of the group communicating. Together, communication content and form make messages that are sent towards a destination. The target can be oneself, another person or being, another entity (such as a corporation or group of beings).

Communication can be seen as processes of information transmission governed by three levels of semiotic rules:

1. Syntactic (formal properties of signs and symbols),
2. Pragmatic (concerned with the relations between signs/expressions and their users) and
3. Semantic (study of relationships between signs and symbols and what they represent).

Therefore, communication is social interaction where at least two interacting agents share a common set of signs and a common set of semiotic rules. This commonly held rules in some sense ignores autocommunication, including intrapersonal communication via diaries or self-talk, both secondary phenomena that followed the primary acquisition of communicative competences within social interactions.

In light of these weaknesses, Barnlund (2008) proposed a transactional model of communication. The basic premise of the transactional model of communication is that individuals are simultaneously engaging in the sending and receiving of messages.

In a slightly more complex form a sender and a receiver are linked reciprocally. This second attitude of communication, referred to as the constitutive model or constructionist view, focuses on how an individual communicates as the determining factor of the way the message will be interpreted. Communication is viewed as a conduit; a passage in which information travels from one individual to another and this information becomes separate from the communication itself. A particular instance of communication is called a speech act. The sender's personal filters and the receiver's personal filters may vary depending upon different regional traditions, cultures, or gender; which may alter the intended meaning of message contents. In the presence of "communication noise" on the transmission channel (air, in this case), reception and decoding of content may be faulty, and thus the speech act may not achieve the desired effect. One problem with this encode-transmit-receive-decode model is that the processes of encoding and decoding imply that the sender and receiver each possess something that functions as a codebook, and that these two code books are, at the very least, similar if not identical. Although something like code books is implied by the model, they are nowhere represented in the model, which creates many conceptual difficulties.

Theories of coregulation describe communication as a creative and dynamic continuous process, rather than a discrete exchange of information. Canadian media scholar Harold Innis had the theory that people use different types of media to communicate and which one they choose to use will offer different possibilities for the shape and durability of society (Wark, McKenzie 1997). His famous example of this is using ancient Egypt and looking at the ways they built themselves out of media with very different properties stone and papyrus. Papyrus is what he called '**Space Binding**'. it made possible the transmission of written orders across space, empires and enables the waging of distant military campaigns and colonial administration. The other is stone and 'Time Binding', through the construction of temples and the pyramids can sustain their authority generation to generation, through this media they can change and shape communication in their society (Wark, McKenzie 1997).

Bernard Luskin, UCLA, 1970, advanced computer assisted instruction and began to connect media and psychology into what is now the field of media psychology. In 1998, the American Association of Psychology, Media Psychology Division 46 Task Force report on psychology and new technologies combined media and communication as pictures, graphics and sound increasingly dominate modern communication.

Communication Noise

In any communication model, noise is interference with the decoding of messages sent over a channel by an encoder. There are many examples of noise:

Environmental Noise: Noise that physically disrupts communication, such as standing next to loud speakers at a party, or the noise from a construction site next to a classroom making it difficult to hear the professor.

Physiological-Impairment Noise: Physical maladies that prevent effective communication, such as actual deafness or blindness preventing messages from being received as they were intended.

Semantic Noise: Different interpretations of the meanings of certain words. For example, the word "weed" can be interpreted as an undesirable plant in your yard, or as a euphemism for marijuana.

Syntactical Noise: Mistakes in grammar can disrupt communication, such as abrupt changes in verb tense during a sentence.

Organizational Noise: Poorly structured communication can prevent the receiver from accurate interpretation. For example, unclear and badly stated directions can make the receiver even more lost.

Cultural Noise: Stereotypical assumptions can cause misunderstandings, such as unintentionally offending a non-Christian person by wishing them a "Merry Christmas".

Psychological Noise: Certain attitudes can also make communication difficult. For instance, great anger or sadness may cause someone to lose focus on the present moment. Disorders such as Autism may also severely hamper effective communication.

Communication Theory

Human communication is understood in various ways by those who identify with the field. This diversity is the result of communication being a relatively young field of study, composed of a very broad constituency of disciplines. It includes work taken from scholars of Rhetoric, Journalism, Sociology, Psychology, Anthropology, and Semiotics, among others.

Cognate areas include biocommunication, which investigates communicative processes within and among non-humans such as bacteria, animals, fungi and plants, and information theory, which provides a mathematical model for measuring communication within and among systems.

Generally, human communication is concerned with the making of meaning and the exchange of understanding. One model of communication considers it from the perspective of transmitting information from one person to another. In fact, many scholars of communication take this as a working definition, and use Lasswell's maxim, "who says what to whom in which channel with what effect," as a means of circumscribing the field of communication theory. Among those who subscribe to the transmission model are those who identify themselves with the communication sciences, and finds its roots in the studies of propaganda and mass media of the early 20th century.

Other commentators claim that a ritual process of communication exists, one not artificially divorcible from a particular historical and social context. This tradition is largely associated with early scholars of symbolic interactionism as well as phenomenologists.

Constructionist Models

There is an additional working definition of communication to consider that authors like Richard A. Lanham (2003) and as far back as Erving Goffman (1959) have highlighted. This is a progression from Lasswell's attempt to define human communication through to this century and revolutionized into the constructionist model. Constructionists believe that the process of communication is in itself the only messages that exist. The packaging can not be separated from the social and historical context from which it arose, therefore the substance to look at in communication theory is style for Richard Lanham and the performance of self for Erving Goffman.

Lanham chose to view communication as the rival to the over encompassing use of CBS model (which pursued to further the transmission model). CBS model argues that clarity, brevity, and sincerity are the only purpose to prose discourse, therefore communication. Lanham wrote, "If words matter too, if the whole range of human motive is seen as animating prose discourse, then rhetoric analysis leads us to the essential questions about prose style" (Lanham 10). This is saying that rhetoric and style are fundamentally important; they are not errors to what we actually intend to transmit. The process which we construct and deconstruct meaning deserves analysis.

Erving Goffman sees the performance of self as the most important frame to understand communication. Goffman wrote, "What does seem to be required of the individual is that he learn enough pieces of expression to be able to 'fill in' and manage, more or less, any part that he is likely to be given" (Goffman 73) Goffman is highlighting the significance of expression. The truth in both cases is the articulation of the message and the package as one. The construction of the message from social and historical context is the seed as is the pre-existing message is for the transmission model. Therefore any look into communication theory should include the possibilities drafted by such great scholars as Richard A. Lanham and Erving Goffman that style and performance is the whole process.

Communication stands so deeply rooted in human behaviors and the structures of society that scholars have difficulty thinking of it while excluding social or behavioral events. Because communication theory remains a relatively young field of inquiry and integrates itself with other disciplines such as philosophy, psychology, and sociology, one probably cannot yet expect a consensus conceptualization of communication across disciplines.

Communication Model Terms as provided by Rothwell (11-15):

- *Noise*; interference with effective transmission and reception of a message.
    - For example;
        - physical noise or external noise which are environmental distractions such as poorly heated rooms, startling sounds, appearances of things, music playing some where else, and someone talking really loudly near you.
        - psychological noise are biological influences that distract you from communicating competently such as sweaty palms, pounding heart, butterfly in the stomach, induced by speech anxiety, or feeling sick, exhausted at work, the ringing noise in your ear, being really hungry, and if you have a runny noise or a cough.
        - physiological noise are the preconception bias and assumptions such as thinking someone who speaks like a valley girl is dumb, or someone from a foreign country can't speak English well so you speak loudly and slowly to them.
        - semantic noise are word choices that are confusing and distracting such as using the word tri-syllabic instead of three syllables.
- *Sender*; the initiator and encoder of a message
- *Receiver*; the one that receives the message (the listener) and the decoder of a message
- *Decode*; translates the senders spoken idea/message into something the receiver understands by using their knowledge of language from personal experience.
- *Encode*; puts the idea into spoken language while putting their own meaning into the word/message.
- *Channel*; the medium through which the message travels such as through oral communication (radio, television, phone, in person) or written communication (letters, email, text messages)

- *Feedback*; the receivers verbal and nonverbal responses to a message such as a nod for understanding (nonverbal), a raised eyebrow for being confused (nonverbal), or asking a question to clarify the message (verbal).
- *Message*; the verbal and nonverbal components of language that is sent to the receiver by the sender which conveys an idea.

Linear Model – is a one way model to communicate with others. It consists of the sender encoding a message and channeling it to the receiver in the presences of noise. Draw backs – the linear assumes that there is a clear cut beginning and end to communication. It also displays no feedback from the receiver.

Interactive Model – is two linear model stacked on top of each other. So the sender channels a message to the receiver and the receiver then becomes the sender and channels a message to the original sender. So this model has added feedback, indicates that communication is not a one way but a two way process. It also has "field of experience" which includes our cultural background, ethnicity geographic location, extend of travel, and general personal experiences accumulated over the course of your lifetime. Draw backs – there is feedback but it is not simultaneous.

For example – instant messaging. The sender sends an IM to the receiver, then the original sender has to wait for the IM from the original receiver to react. Or a question/answer session where you just ask a question then you get an answer.

Transactional Model – assumes that people are connected through communication; they engage in transaction. Firstly, it recognizes that each of us is a sender-receiver, not merely a sender or a receiver. Secondly, it recognizes that communication affects all parties involved. So communication is fluid/simultaneous. This is how most conversation are like. The transactional model also contains ellipses that symbolize the communication environment (how you interpret the data that you are given). Where the ellipse meet is the most effect communication area because both communicators share the same meaning of the message.

For example – talking/listening to friends. While your friend is talking you are constantly giving them feedback on what you think through your facial expression verbal feedback without necessarily stopping your friend from talking.

HISTORY OF COMMUNICATION THEORY

The Academic Study of Communication

Communication has existed since the beginning of human beings, but it was not until the 20th century that people began to study the process. As communication technologies developed, so did the serious study of communication. When World War I ended, the interest in studying communication intensified. The social-science study was fully recognized as a legitimate discipline after World War II.

Before becoming simply communication, or communication studies, the discipline was formed from three other major studies: psychology, sociology, and anthropology. Psychology is the study of human behavior, Sociology is the study of society and social process, and anthropology is the study of communication as a factor which develops, maintains, and changes culture. Communication studies focus on communication as central to the human experience, which involves understanding how people behave in creating, exchanging, and interpreting messages.

Communication Theory has one universal law posited by S. F. Scudder (1980). The Universal Communication Law states that, "All living entities, beings and creatures communicate." All of the living communicates through movements, sounds, reactions, physical changes, gestures, languages, breath, etc. Communication is a means of survival. Examples - the cry of a child (communication that it is hungry, hurt, cold, etc.); the browning of a leaf (communication that it is dehydrated, thirsty per se, dying); the cry of an animal (communicating that it is injured, hungry, angry, etc.). Everything living communicates in its quest for survival."

Communication Theory Framework

It is helpful to examine communication and communication theory through one of the following viewpoints:

Mechanistic: This view considers communication as a perfect transaction of a message from the sender to the receiver.

Psychological: This view considers communication as the act of sending a message to a receiver, and the feelings and thoughts of the receiver upon interpreting the message.

Social Constructionist (Symbolic Interactionist): This view considers communication to be the product of the interactants sharing and creating meaning. The Constructionist View can also be defined as, how you say something determines what the message is. The Constructionist View assumes that "truth" and "ideas" are constructed or invented through the social process of communication. Robert T. Craig saw the Constructionist View or the constitutive view as it's called in his article, as "...an ongoing process that symbolically forms and re-forms our personal identities." (Craig, 125).

The other view of communication, the Transmission Model, sees communication as robotic and computer-like. The Transmission Model sees communication as a way of sending or receiving messages and the perfection of that. But, the Constructionist View sees communications as, "...in human life, info does not behave as simply as bits in an electronic stream. In human life, information flow is far more like an electric current running from one landmine to another" (Lanham, 7).

The Constructionist View is a more realistic view of communication because it involves the interacting of human beings and the free sharing of thoughts and ideas. Daniel Chandler looks to prove that the Transmission Model is a lesser way of communicating by saying "The transmission model is not merely a gross over-simplification but a dangerously misleading representation of the nature of human communication" (Chandler, 2).

Humans do not communicate simply as computers or robots so that's why it's essential to truly understand the Constructionist View of Communication well. We do not simply send facts and data to one another, but we take facts and data and they acquire meaning through the process of communication, or through interaction with others.

- Systemic: This view considers communication to be the new messages created via "through-put", or what happens as the message is being interpreted and re-interpreted as it travels through people.
- Critical: This view considers communication as a source of power and oppression of individuals and social groups.

Inspection of a particular theory on this level will provide a framework on the nature of communication as seen within the confines of that theory.

Theories can also be studied and organized according to the ontological, epistemological, and axiological framework imposed by the theorist.

Ontology essentially poses the question of what, exactly, it is the theorist is examining. One must consider the very nature of reality. The answer usually falls in one of three realms depending on whether the theorist sees the phenomena through the lens of a realist, nominalist, or social constructionist.

Realist perspective views the world objectively, believing that there is a world outside of our own experience and cognitions. Nominalists see the world subjectively, claiming that everything outside of one's cognitions is simply names and labels. Social constructionists straddle the fence between objective and subjective reality, claiming that reality is what we create together.

Epistemology is an examination of how the theorist studies the chosen phenomena. In studying epistemology, particularly from a positivist perspective, objective knowledge is said to be the result of a systematic look at the causal relationships of phenomena. This knowledge is usually attained through use of the scientific method.

Scholars often think that empirical evidence collected in an objective manner is most likely to reflect truth in the findings. Theories of this ilk are usually created to predict a phenomenon. Subjective theory holds that understanding is based on situated knowledge, typically found using interpretative methodology such as ethnography and also interviews. Subjective theories are typically developed to explain or understand phenomena in the social world.

Axiology is concerned with what values drive a theorist to develop a theory. Theorists must be mindful of potential biases so that they will not influence or skew their findings (Miller, 21-23).

Mapping the Theoretical Landscape

A discipline gets defined in large part by its theoretical structure. Communication studies often borrow theories from other social sciences. This theoretical variation makes it difficult to come to terms with the field as a whole. That said, some common taxonomies exist that serve to divide up the range of communication research. Two common mappings involve contexts and assumptions.

Contexts

Many authors and researchers divide communication by what they sometimes called **"contexts" or "levels"**, but which more often represent institutional histories. The study of communication in the US, while occurring within departments of psychology, sociology, linguistics, and anthropology (among others), generally developed from schools of rhetoric and from schools of journalism. While many of these have become "departments of communication", they often retain their historical roots, adhering largely to theories from speech communication in the former case, and from mass media in the latter.

The great divide between speech communication and mass communication becomes complicated by a number of smaller sub-areas of communication research, including intercultural and international communication, small group communication, communication technology, policy and legal studies of communication, telecommunication, and work done under a variety of other labels. Some of these departments take a largely social-scientific perspective, others tend more heavily toward the humanities, and still others gear themselves more toward production and professional preparation.

These "levels" of communication provide some way of grouping communication theories, but inevitably, some theories and concepts leak from one area to another, or fail to find a home at all.

The Constitutive Metamodel

Another way of dividing up the communication field emphasizes the assumptions that undergird particular theories, models, and approaches. While this approach also tends to have as its basis institutional divisions, theories within each of the **seven "traditions"** of communication theory that Robert T. Craig suggests tend to reinforce one another, and retain the same ground epistemological and axiological assumptions. His traditions include:

- rhetorical - practical art of discourse
- semiotic – intersubjective mediation through signs in order to mediate between different perspectives
- phenomenological - experience of otherness, dialogue
- cybernetic - information processing and explains how all kinds of complex systems, whether living or nonliving, macro or micro, are able to function, and why they often malfunction
- sociopsychological - expression, interaction and influence
- critical - discursive reflection
- sociocultural - reproduction of social order (Miller, 13)

Craig finds each of these clearly defined against the others, and remaining cohesive approaches to describing communicative behavior. As a taxonomic aid, these labels help to organize theory by its assumptions, and help researchers to understand why some theories may seem incommensurable.

Team Teaching

Team teaching involves a group of instructors working purposefully, regularly, and cooperatively to help a group of students of any age learn. Teachers together set goals for a course, design a syllabus, prepare individual lesson plans, teach students, and evaluate the results. They share insights, argue with one another, and perhaps even challenge students to decide which approach is better.

Teams can be single-discipline, interdisciplinary, or school-within-a-school teams that meet with a common set of students over an extended period of time. New teachers may be paired with veteran teachers. Innovations are encouraged, and modifications in class size, location, and time are permitted. Different personalities, voices, values, and approaches spark interest, keep attention, and prevent boredom.

The team-teaching approach allows for more interaction between teachers and students. Faculty evaluate students on their achievement of the learning goals; students evaluate faculty members on their teaching proficiency.

Emphasis is on student and faculty growth, balancing initiative and shared responsibility, specialization and broadening horizons, the clear and interesting presentation of content and student development, democratic participation and common expectations, and cognitive, affective, and behavioral outcomes. This combination of analysis, synthesis, critical thinking, and practical applications can be done on all levels of education, from kindergarten through graduate school.

Working as a team, teachers model respect for differences, interdependence, and conflict-resolution skills. Team members together set the course goals and content, select common materials such as texts and films, and develop tests and final examinations for all students. They set the sequence of topics and supplemental materials. They also give their own interpretations of the materials and use their own teaching styles. The greater the agreement on common objectives and interests, the more likely that teaching will be interdependent and coordinated.

Teaching periods can be scheduled side by side or consecutively. For example, teachers of two similar classes may team up during the same or adjacent periods so that each teacher may focus on that phase of the course that he or she can best handle. Students can sometimes meet all together, sometimes in small groups supervised by individual teachers or teaching assistants, or they can work singly or together on projects in the library, laboratory, or fieldwork. Teachers can be at different sites, linked by video-conferencing, satellites, or the Internet.

Breaking out of the taken-for-granted single-subject, single-course, single-teacher pattern encourages other innovations and experiments. For example, students can be split along or across lines of sex, age, culture, or other interests, then recombined to stimulate reflection.

Remedial programs and honors sections provide other attractive opportunities to make available appropriate and effective curricula for students with special needs or interests. They can address different study skills and learning techniques. Team teaching can also offset the danger of imposing ideas, values, and mindsets on minorities or less powerful ethnic groups. Teachers of different backgrounds can culturally enrich one another and students.

Pros

Students do not all learn at the same rate. Periods of equal length are not appropriate for all learning situations. Educators are no longer dealing primarily with top-down transmission of the tried and true by the mature and experienced teacher to the young, immature, and inexperienced pupil in the single-subject classroom. Schools are moving toward the inclusion of another whole dimension of learning: the lateral transmission to every sentient member of society of what has just been discovered, invented, created, manufactured, or marketed. For this, team members with different areas of expertise are invaluable.

Of course, team teaching is not the only answer to all problems plaguing teachers, students, and administrators. It requires planning, skilled management, willingness to risk change and even failure, humility, open-mindedness, imagination, and creativity. But the results are worth it.

Teamwork improves the quality of teaching as various experts approach the same topic from different angles: theory and practice, past and present, different genders or ethnic backgrounds. Teacher strengths are combined and weaknesses are remedied. Poor teachers can be observed, critiqued, and improved by the other team members in a nonthreatening, supportive context. The evaluation done by a team of teachers will be more insightful and balanced than the introspection and self-evaluation of an individual teacher.

Working in teams spreads responsibility, encourages creativity, deepens friendships, and builds community among teachers. Teachers complement one another. They share insights, propose new approaches, and challenge assumptions. They learn new perspectives and insights, techniques and values from watching one another. Students enter into conversations between them as they debate, disagree with premises or conclusions, raise new questions, and point out consequences. Contrasting viewpoints encourage more active class participation and independent thinking from students, especially if there is team balance for gender, race, culture, and age. Team teaching is particularly effective with older and underprepared students when it moves beyond communicating facts to tap into their life experience.

The team cuts teaching burdens and boosts morale. The presence of another teacher reduces student-teacher personality problems. In an emergency one team member can attend to the problem while the class goes on. Sharing in decision-making bolsters self-confidence. As teachers see the quality of teaching and learning improve, their self-esteem and happiness grow. This aids in recruiting and keeping faculty.

Cons

Team teaching is not always successful. Some teachers are rigid personality types or may be wedded to a single method. Some simply dislike the other teachers on the team. Some do not want to risk humiliation and discouragement at possible failures. Some fear they will be expected to do more work for the same salary. Others are unwilling to share the spotlight or their pet ideas or to lose total control.

Team teaching makes more demands on time and energy. Members must arrange mutually agreeable times for planning and evaluation. Discussions can be draining and group decisions take longer. Rethinking the courses to accommodate the team-teaching method is often inconvenient.

Opposition may also come from students, parents, and administrators who may resist change of any sort. Some students flourish in a highly structured environment that favors repetition. Some are confused by conflicting opinions. Too much variety may hinder habit formation.

Salaries may have to reflect the additional responsibilities undertaken by team members. Team leaders may need some form of bonus. Such costs could be met by enlarging some class sizes. Non-professional staff members could take over some responsibilities.

Lecture

A lecture is an oral presentation intended to present information or teach people about a particular subject, for example by a university or college teacher. Lectures are used to convey critical information, history, background, theories and equations. A politician's speech, a minister's sermon, or even a businessman's sales presentation may be similar in form to a lecture. Usually the lecturer will stand at the front of the room and recite information relevant to the lecture's content.

Though lectures are much criticised as a teaching method, universities have not yet found practical alternative teaching methods for the large majority of their courses. Critics point out that lecturing is mainly a one-way method of communication that does not involve significant audience participation. Therefore, lecturing is often contrasted to active learning. Lectures delivered by talented speakers can be highly stimulating; at the very least, lectures have survived in academia as a quick, cheap and efficient way of introducing large numbers of students to a particular field of study.

Lectures have a significant role outside the classroom, as well. Academic and scientific awards routinely include a lecture as part of the honor, and academic conferences often center around "keynote addresses", i.e., lectures. The public lecture has a long history in the sciences and in social movements. Union halls, for instance, historically have hosted numerous free and public lectures on a wide variety of matters. Similarly, churches, community centers, libraries, museums, and other organizations have hosted lectures in furtherance of their missions or their constituents' interests. Lectures represent a continuation of oral tradition in contrast to textual communication in books and other media.

The practice in the medieval university was for the instructor to read from an original source to a class of students who took notes on the lecture. The reading from original sources evolved into the reading of glosses on an original and then more generally to lecture notes. Throughout much of history, the diffusion of knowledge via handwritten lecture notes was an essential element of academic life.

Even in the twentieth century the lecture notes taken by students, or prepared by a scholar for a lecture, have sometimes achieved wide circulation. Many lecturers were, and still are, accustomed to simply reading their own notes from the lectern for exactly that purpose. Nevertheless, modern lectures generally incorporate additional activities, e.g. writing on a chalk-board, exercises, class questions and discussions, or student presentations.

The use of multimedia presentation software such as Microsoft PowerPoint has changed the form of lectures, e.g. video, graphics, websites, or prepared exercises may be included. Most commonly, however, only outlines composed of "bullet points" are presented. Critics such as Edward Tufte contend that this style of lecture bombards the audience with unnecessary and possibly distracting or confusing graphics.

Research

Bligh, in *What's the Use of Lectures?* argues that lectures "represent a conception of education in which teachers who know give knowledge to students who do not and are therefore supposed to have nothing worth contributing." Based on his review of numerous studies, he concludes that lecturing is as effective, but not more effective, as any other teaching method in transmitting information.

Nevertheless, lecturing is not the most effective method for promoting student thought, changing attitudes, or teaching behavioral skills. Bligh summarises research on memory to show the significance of the meaningfulness of material on retention (Marks and Miller 1964) and the importance of immediate rehearsal of information (Bassey 1968). He relates his own research on arousal during lectures to suggest a decrement in attention during the first 25 minutes.

Lloyd (1968) and Scerbo et al. (1992) showed that students take fewer and fewer notes as lectures proceed. Bligh shows that after a short break filled by buzz group discussion, attention will recover somewhat. The largest section of Bligh's book is devoted to lecturing technique, particularly the organisation of lectures, how to make a point, the effectiveness of taking notes, the use of handouts and ways of obtaining feedback. Early editions of the book contained a reply paid evaluation card. This research showed that the section on alternative teaching methods within lectures was the most highly praised.

Other forms

While lecture is generally accepted as an effective form of instruction, there have been some prominent educators who have succeeded without the help of lectures. Many university courses relying on lectures supplement them with smaller discussion sections, tutorials, or laboratory experiment sessions as a means of further actively involving students.

Often, these supplemental sections are led by graduate students, tutors, Teaching Assistants or Teaching Fellows rather than senior faculty. Those other forms of academic teaching include discussion (recitation if conducted by a Teaching Assistant), seminars, workshops, observation, practical application, case examples/ case study, experiential learning/active learning, computer-based instruction and tutorials.

In schools the prevalent mode of student-teacher interaction is lessons. The term "parlor lecture" gained currency throughout the British Commonwealth of Nations and the United States of America during the mid-19th century. It referred to the custom of inviting noted speakers to deliver private lectures, which were typically hosted in the parlors of wealthy and socially influential families.

Public Lecture

A public lecture is one means employed for educating the public in the sciences and medicine. The Royal Institution has a long history of public lectures and demonstrations given by prominent experts in the field. In the 19th century, the popularity of the public lectures given by Sir Humphry Davy at the Royal Institution was so great that the volume of carriage traffic in Albemarle Street caused it to become the first one way street in London. The Royal Institution's Christmas Lectures for young people are nowadays also shown on television. Alexander von Humboldt delivered a series of public lectures at the University of Berlin in the winter of 1827–1828, that formed the basis for his later work *Kosmos*.

Besides public lectures, public autopsies have been important in promoting knowledge of medicine. The public autopsy of Dr. Johann Gaspar Spurzheim, advocate of phrenology, was conducted after his death, and his brain, skull, and heart were removed, preserved in jars of alcohol, and put on display to the public.

Public autoposies have sometimes verged on entertainment: American showman P. T. Barnum held a public autopsy of Joice Heth after her death. Heth was a woman whom Barnum had been featuring as being over 160 years old. Barnum charged 50 cents admission. The autopsy demonstrated that she had in fact been between 76 and 80 years old.

The Reciprocal Category System (RCS) is an observational system used to record and assess teacher-student classroom verbal interaction. The RCS is composed of nine verbal categories which are applicable to either the student or teacher (and as such are numbered differently, thus producing 18 categories) and one additional category—silence or confusion.

The observer records the classroom verbal behavior not less than every three seconds by placing the number assigned to any of the 19 categories (such as number 1 for "'warms' the climate" or number 5 for "responds") on a tally sheet. The columns of raw data on the sheet are then bracketed into pairs and plotted on a 19 by 19 matrix for a visual representation of behavior patterns and the frequency of their occurrence.

The matrix is also used to determine percentage relationships among patterns, flexibility of classroom behavior, and the occurrence of behaviors in any of the four submatrices—teacher-teacher, teacher-student, student-teacher, and student-student talk. As a research tool, the RCS permits the conceptualization and measurement of many verbal behaviors; as a training tool which sensitizes teachers to subtle and uncommon verbal behaviors, it aids in producing teachers who are able to control or plan verbal behavior and who can use the RCS for feedback in their own classrooms.

Verbal Communication

The basis of communication is the interaction between people. Verbal communication is one way for people to communicate face-to-face. Some of the key components of verbal communication are sound, words, speaking, and language.

At birth, most people have vocal cords, which produce sounds. As a child grows it learns how to form these sounds into words. Some words may be imitative of natural sounds, but others may come from expressions of emotion, such as laughter or crying. Words alone have no meaning. Only people can put meaning into words. As meaning is assigned to words, language develops, which leads to the development of speaking.

The actual origin of language is subject to considerable speculation. Some theorists believe it is an outgrowth of group activities such as working together or dancing. Others believe that language developed from basic sounds and gestures.

Over 3,000 languages and major dialects are spoken in the world today. The development of languages reflects class, gender, profession, age group, and other social factors. The huge variety of languages usually creates difficulties between different languages, but even within a single language there can be many problems in understanding.

Through speaking we try to eliminate this misunderstanding, but sometimes this is a very hard thing to do. Just as we assume that our messages are clearly received, so we assume that because something is important to us, it is important to others. As time has proven this is not at all true. Many problems can arise is speaking and the only way to solve these problems is through experience.

Speaking can be looked at in two major areas: interpersonal and public speaking. Since the majority of speaking is an interpersonal process, to communicate effectively we must not simply clean up our language, but learn to relate to people.

In interpersonal speaking, etiquette is very important. To be an effective communicator one must speak in a manner that is not offending to the receiver. Etiquette also plays an important role in an area that has developed in most all business settings: hierarchical communication. In business today, hierarchical communication is of utmost importance to all members involved.

The other major area of speaking is public speaking. From the origin of time, it has been obvious that some people are just better public speakers than others. Because of this, today a good speaker can earn a living by speaking to people in a public setting. Some of the major areas of public speaking are speaking to persuade, speaking to inform, and speaking to inspire or motivate.

NON-VERBAL COMMUNICATION

Non verbal Communication is usually understood as the process of communication through sending and receiving wordless messages. i.e., language is not the only source of communication, there are other means also. Messages can be communicated through gestures and touch (Haptic communication), by body language or posture, by facial expression and eye contact. Meaning can also be communicated through object or artifacts (such as clothing, hairstyles or architecture), symbols, and icons (or graphics).

Speech contains nonverbal elements known as paralanguage, including voice quality, rate, pitch, volume, and speaking style, as well as prosodic features such as rhythm, intonation and stress. Dance is also regarded as a form of nonverbal communication. Likewise, written texts have nonverbal elements such as handwriting style, spatial arrangement of words, or the physical layout of a page.

However, much of the study of nonverbal communication has focused on face-to-face interaction, where it can be classified into three principal areas: environmental conditions where communication takes place, the physical characteristics of the communicators, and behaviors of communicators during interaction.

Verbal vs. Oral Communication

Scholars in this field usually use a strict sense of the term "verbal", meaning "of or concerned with words", and do not use "verbal communication" as a synonym for oral or spoken communication. Thus, vocal sounds that are not considered to be words, such as a grunt, or singing a wordless note, are nonverbal. Sign languages and writing are generally understood as forms of verbal communication, as both make use of words — although like speech, both may contain paralinguistic elements and often occur alongside nonverbal messages. Nonverbal communication can occur through any sensory channel — sight, sound, smell, touch or taste. Nonverbal communication is important as:

"When we speak (or listen), our attention is focused on words rather than body language. But our judgment includes both. An audience is simultaneously processing both verbal and nonverbal cues. Body movements are not usually positive or negative in and of themselves; rather, the situation and the message will determine the appraisal." (Givens, 2000, p. 4)

History

The first scientific study of nonverbal communication was Charles Darwin's book *The Expression of the Emotions in Man and Animals* (1872). He argued that all mammals show emotion reliably in their faces. Studies now range across a number of fields, including, linguistics, semiotics and social psychology.

Arbitrariness

While much nonverbal communication is based on arbitrary symbols, which differ from culture to culture, a large proportion is also to some extent iconic and may be universally understood. Paul Ekman's influential 1960s studies of facial expression determined that expressions of anger, disgust, fear, joy, sadness and surprise are universal.

Characteristics of Nonverbal Communication

1. Non-verbal messages primarily communicate emotions, attitudes.
2. Non-verbal cues substitute for, contradict, emphasize or regulate verbal message.
3. Non-verbal cues are often ambiguous.
4. Non-verbal cues are continuous.
5. Non-verbal cues are more reliable.
6. Non-verbal cues are culture bound.

Clothing and bodily characteristics

Elements such as physique, height, weight, hair, skin color, gender, odors, and clothing send nonverbal messages during interaction. For example, a study, carried out in Vienna, Austria, of the clothing worn by women attending discothèques showed that in certain groups of women (especially women who were in town without their partners) motivation for sex, and levels of sexual hormones, were correlated with aspects of the clothing, especially the amount of skin displayed, and the presence of sheer clothing, e.g. at the arms. Thus, to some degree, clothing sent signals about interest in courtship.

Research into height has generally found that taller people are perceived as being more impressive. Melamed & Bozionelos (1992) studied a sample of managers in the UK and found that height was a key factor affecting who was promoted. Often people try to make themselves taller, for example, standing on a platform, when they want to make more of an impact with their speaking.

Physical Environment

Environmental factors such as furniture, architectural style, interior decorating, lighting conditions, colors, temperature, noise, and music affect the behavior of communicators during interaction. The furniture itself can be seen as a nonverbal message

Proxemics: Physical Space in Communication

Proxemics is the study of how people use and perceive the physical space around them. The space between the sender and the receiver of a message influences the way the message is interpreted The perception and use of space varies significantly across cultures and different settings within cultures. Space in nonverbal communication may be divided into four main categories: intimate, social, personal, and public space.

The term territoriality is still used in the study of proxemics to explain human behavior regarding personal space. Hargie & Dickson (2004, p. 69) identify 4 such territories:

1. Primary territory: this refers to an area that is associated with someone who has exclusive use of it. For example, a house that others cannot enter without the owner's permission.
2. Secondary territory: unlike the previous type, there is no "right" to occupancy, but people may still feel some degree of ownership of a particular space. For example, someone may sit in the same seat on train every day and feel aggrieved if someone else sits there.
3. Public territory: this refers to an area that is available to all, but only for a set period, such as a parking space or a seat in a library. Although people have only a limited claim over that space, they often exceed that claim. For example, it was found that people take longer to leave a parking space when someone is waiting to take that space.
4. Interaction territory: this is space created by others when they are interacting. For example, when a group is talking to each other on a footpath, others will walk around the group rather than disturb it.

Chronemics: Time in Communication

Chronemics is the study of the use of time in nonverbal communication. The way we perceive time, structure our time and react to time is a powerful communication tool, and helps set the stage for communication. Time perceptions include punctuality and willingness to wait, the speed of speech and how long people are willing to listen. The timing and frequency of an action as well as the tempo and rhythm of communications within an interaction contributes to the interpretation of nonverbal messages. Gudykunst & Ting-Toomey (1988) identified 2 dominant time patterns:

Monochronic Time

A monochronic time system means that things are done one at a time and time is segmented into precise, small units. Under this system time is scheduled, arranged and managed. The United States is considered a monochronic society. This perception of time is learned and rooted in the Industrial Revolution, where "factory life required the labor force to be on hand and in place at an appointed hour" (Guerrero, DeVito & Hecht, 1999, p. 238). For Americans, time is a precious resource not to be wasted or taken lightly. "We buy time, save time, spend time and make time. Our time can be broken down into years, months, days, hours, minutes, seconds and even milliseconds. We use time to structure both our daily lives and events that we are planning for the future. We have schedules that we must follow: appointments that we must go to at a certain time, classes that start and end at certain times, work schedules that start and end at certain times, and even our favorite TV shows, that start and end at a certain time."

As communication scholar Edward T. Hall wrote regarding the American's viewpoint of time in the business world, "the schedule is sacred." Hall says that for monochronic cultures, such as the American culture, "time is tangible" and viewed as a commodity where "time is money" or "time is wasted." The result of this perspective is that Americans and other monochronic cultures, such as the German and Swiss, place a paramount value on schedules, tasks and "getting the job done." These cultures are committed to regimented schedules and may view those who do not subscribe to the same perception of time as disrespectful.

Monochronic cultures include Germany, Canada, Switzerland, United States, and Scandinavia.

Polychronic Time

A polychronic time system is a system where several things can be done at once, and a more fluid approach is taken to scheduling time. Unlike European-Americans and most northern and western European cultures, Native American, Latin American and Arabic cultures use the polychronic system of time.

These cultures are much less focused on the preciseness of accounting for each and every moment. As Raymond Cohen notes, polychronic cultures are deeply steeped in tradition rather than in tasks—a clear difference from their monochronic counterparts. Cohen notes that "Traditional societies have all the time in the world. The arbitrary divisions of the clock face have little saliency in cultures grounded in the cycle of the seasons, the invariant pattern of rural life, and the calendar of religious festivities" (Cohen, 1997, p. 34).

Instead, their culture is more focused on relationships, rather than watching the clock. They have no problem being "late" for an event if they are with family or friends, because the relationship is what really matters. As a result, polychronic cultures have a much less formal perception of time. They are not ruled by precise calendars and schedules. Rather, "cultures that use the polychronic time system often schedule multiple appointments simultaneously so keeping on schedule is an impossibility."

Polychronic cultures include Saudi Arabia, Egypt, Mexico, Philippines, India, and many in Africa.

Movement and Body Position

Kinesics

The term "Kinesics" was first used (in 1952) by Ray Birdwhistell, an anthropologist who wished to study how people communicate through posture, gesture, stance, and movement. Part of Birdwhistell's work involved making film of people in social situations and analyzing them to show different levels of communication not clearly seen otherwise. The study was joined by several other anthropologists, including Margaret Mead and Gregory Bateson.

Posture

Posture can be used to determine a participant's degree of attention or involvement, the difference in status between communicators, and the level of fondness a person has for the other communicator. Studies investigating the impact of posture on interpersonal relationships suggest that mirror-image congruent postures, where one person's left side is parallel to the other person's right side, leads to favorable perception of communicators and positive speech; a person who displays a forward lean or a decrease in a backwards lean also signify positive sentiment during communication. Posture is understood through such indicators as direction of lean, body orientation, arm position, and body openness.

Gesture

A gesture is a non-vocal bodily movement intended to express meaning. They may be articulated with the hands, arms or body, and also include movements of the head, face and eyes, such as winking, nodding, or rolling ones' eyes. The boundary between language and gesture, or verbal and nonverbal communication, can be hard to identify.

Although the study of gesture is still in its infancy, some broad categories of gestures have been identified by researchers. The most familiar are the so-called emblems or quotable gestures. These are conventional, culture-specific gestures that can be used as replacement for words, such as the hand-wave used in the US for "hello" and "goodbye". A single emblematic gesture can have a very different significance in different cultural contexts, ranging from complimentary to highly offensive. For a list of emblematic gestures, see list of gestures.

Another broad category of gestures comprises those gestures used spontaneously when we speak. These gestures are closely coordinated with speech. The so-called beat gestures are used in conjunction with speech and keep time with the rhythm of speech to emphasize certain words or phrases. These types of gestures are integrally connected to speech and thought processes. Other spontaneous gestures used when we speak are more contentful and may echo or elaborate the meaning of the co-occurring speech.For example, a gesture that depicts the act of throwing may be synchronous with the utterance, "He threw the ball right into the window."

Gestural languages such as American Sign Language and its regional siblings operate as complete natural languages that are gestural in modality. They should not be confused with finger spelling, in which a set of emblematic gestures are used to represent a written alphabet.

Gestures can also be categorized as either speech-independent or speech-related. Speech-independent gestures are dependent upon culturally accepted interpretation and have a direct verbal translation. A wave hello or a peace sign are examples of speech-independent gestures. Speech related gestures are used in parallel with verbal speech; this form of nonverbal communication is used to emphasize the message that is being communicated. Speech related gestures are intended to provide supplemental information to a verbal message such as pointing to an object of discussion.

Gestures such as Mudra (Sanskrit) encode sophisticated information accessible to initiates that are privy to the subtlety of elements encoded in their tradition.

Haptics: Touching in Communication

Haptics is the study of touching as nonverbal communication. Touches that can be defined as communication include handshakes, holding hands, kissing (cheek, lips, hand), back slapping, high fives, a pat on the shoulder, and brushing an arm. Touching of oneself may include licking, picking, holding, and scratching. These behaviors are referred to as "adapter" or "tells" and may send messages that reveal the intentions or feelings of a communicator. The meaning conveyed from touch is highly dependent upon the context of the situation, the relationship between communicators, and the manner of touch.

Humans communicate interpersonal closeness through a series of non-verbal actions known as immediacy behaviors. Examples of immediacy behaviors are: smiling, touching, open body positions, and eye contact. Cultures that display these immediacy behaviors are known to be high contact cultures.

Haptic communication is the means by which people and other animals communicate via touching. Touch is an extremely important sense for humans; as well as providing information about surfaces and textures it is a component of nonverbal communication in interpersonal relationships, and vital in conveying physical intimacy. It can be both sexual (such as kissing) and platonic (such as hugging or tickling).

Touch is the earliest sense to develop in the fetus. The development of an infant's haptic senses and how it relates to the development of the other senses such as vision has been the target of much research. Human babies have been observed to have enormous difficulty surviving if they do not possess a sense of touch, even if they retain sight and hearing. Babies who can perceive through touch, even without sight and hearing, tend to fare much better. Touch can be thought of as a basic sense in that most life forms have a response to being touched, while only a subset have sight and hearing.

In chimpanzees the sense of touch is highly developed. As newborns they see and hear poorly but cling strongly to their mothers. Harry Harlow conducted a controversial study involving rhesus monkeys and observed that monkeys reared with a "terry cloth mother", a wire feeding apparatus wrapped in softer terry cloth which provided a level of tactile stimulation and comfort, were considerably more emotionally stable as adults than those with a mere wire mother.(Harlow,1958)

Touching is treated differently from one country to another and socially acceptable levels of touching vary from one culture to another (Remland, 2009).

In the Thai culture, for example, touching someone's head may be thought rude. Remland and Jones (1995) studied groups of people communicating and found that in England (8%), France (5%) and the Netherlands (4%) touching was rare compared to their Italian (14%) and Greek (12.5%) sample.

Striking, pushing, pulling, pinching, kicking, strangling and hand-to-hand fighting are forms of touch in the context of physical abuse. In a sentence like "I never touched him/her" or "Don't you dare to touch him/her" the term touch may be meant as euphemism for either physical abuse or sexual touching. To 'touch oneself' is a euphemism for masturbation.

The word touch has many other metaphorical uses. One can be emotionally touched, referring to an action or object that evokes an emotional response. To say "I was touched by your letter" implies the reader felt a strong emotion when reading it. Usually does not include anger, disgust or other forms of emotional rejection unless used in a sarcastic manner.

Stoeltje (2003) wrote about how Americans are 'losing touch' with this important communication skill. During a study conducted by University of Miami School of Medicine, Touch Research Institutes, American children were said to be more aggressive than their French counterparts while playing at a playground. It was noted that French women touched their children more

Eye Gaze

The study of the role of eyes in nonverbal communication is sometimes referred to as "oculesics". Eye contact can indicate interest, attention, and involvement. Studies have found that people use their eyes to indicate their interest and with more than the frequently recognized actions of winking and slight movement of the eyebrows. Eye contact is an event when two people look at each other's eyes at the same time. It is a form of nonverbal communication and has a large influence on social behavior. Frequency and interpretation of eye contact vary between cultures and species. Eye aversion is the avoidance of eye contact. Eye contact and facial expressions provide important social and emotional information. People, perhaps without consciously doing so, probe each other's eyes and faces for positive or negative mood signs. Gaze comprises the actions of looking while talking, looking while listening, amount of gaze, and frequency of glances, patterns of fixation, pupil dilation, and blink rate.

Paralanguage: Nonverbal Cues of the Voice

Paralanguage (sometimes called vocalics) is the study of nonverbal cues of the voice. Various acoustic properties of speech such as tone, pitch and accent, collectively known as prosody, can all give off nonverbal cues. Paralanguage may change the meaning of words.

The linguist George L. Trager developed a classification system which consists of the voice set, voice qualities, and vocalization.

- The *voice set* is the context in which the speaker is speaking. This can include the situation, gender, mood, age and a person's culture.
- The *voice qualities* are volume, pitch, tempo, rhythm, articulation, resonance, nasality, and accent. They give each individual a unique "voice print".
- *Vocalization* consists of three subsections: characterizers, qualifiers and segregates. Characterizers are emotions expressed while speaking, such as laughing, crying, and yawning. A voice qualifier is the style of delivering a message - for example, yelling "Hey stop that!", as opposed to whispering "Hey stop that". Vocal segregates such as "uh-huh" notify the speaker that the listener is listening.

Functions of Nonverbal Communication

Argyle (1970) put forward the hypothesis that whereas spoken language is normally used for communicating information about events external to the speakers, non-verbal codes are used to establish and maintain interpersonal relationships. It is considered more polite or nicer to communicate attitudes towards others non-verbally rather than verbally, for instance in order to avoid embarrassing situations.

Argyle (1988) concluded there are five primary functions of nonverbal bodily behavior in human communication:

- Express emotions
- Express interpersonal attitudes
- To accompany speech in managing the cues of interaction between speakers and listeners
- Self-presentation of one's personality
- Rituals (greetings)

Concealing Deception

Nonverbal communication makes it easier to lie without being revealed. This is the conclusion of a study where people watched made-up interviews of persons accused of having stolen a wallet. The interviewees lied in about 50% of the cases. People had access to either written transcripts of the interviews, or audio tape recordings, or video recordings. The more clues that were available to those watching, the larger was the trend that interviewees who actually lied were judged to be truthful. That is, people that are clever at lying can use voice tone and face expression to give the impression that they are truthful.

However, there are many cited examples of 'leakage' cues, delivered via nonverbal (paraverbal and visual) communication channels, through which deceivers unwittingly provide clues to their concealed knowledge or actual opinions. Most studies examining the leakage hypothesis from visual cues rely upon hand coding of video footage (c.f. Vrij, 2008), a method that is open to coding errors. A recent study, however, demonstrated clear bodily movement differences between truth-tellers and liars using an automated body motion capture system: truth-tellers demonstrated greater overall bodily movement compared to liars in two different situations.

THE RELATION BETWEEN VERBAL AND NONVERBAL COMMUNICATION

The Relative Importance of Verbal and Nonverbal Communication

An interesting question is: When two people are communicating face-to-face, how much of the meaning is communicated verbally, and how much is communicated non-verbally? This was investigated by Albert Mehrabian and reported in two papers. The latter paper concluded: "It is suggested that the combined effect of simultaneous verbal, vocal, and facial attitude communications is a weighted sum of their independent effects - with coefficients of.07,.38, and.55, respectively." This "rule" that clues from spoken words, from the voice tone, and from the facial expression, contribute 7 %, 38 %, and 55 % respectively to the total meaning, is widely cited. It is presented on all types of popular courses with statements like "scientists have found out that... ". In reality, however, it is extremely weakly founded. First, it is based on the judgment of the meaning of single tape-recorded words, i.e. a very artificial context. Second, the figures are obtained by combining results from two different studies which potentially cannot be combined. Third, it relates only to the communication of positive versus negative emotions. Fourth, it relates only to women, as men did not participate in the study.

Since then, other studies have analysed the relative contribution of verbal and nonverbal signals under more naturalistic situations. Argyle, using video tapes shown to the subjects, analysed the communication of submissive/dominant attitude and found that non-verbal cues had 4.3 times the effect of verbal cues. The most important effect was that body posture communicated superior status in a very efficient way. On the other hand, a study by Hsee et al. had subjects judge a person on the dimension happy/sad and found that words spoken with minimal variation in intonation had an impact about 4 times larger than face expressions seen in a film without sound. Thus, the relative importance of spoken words and facial expressions may be very different in studies using different set-ups.

Interaction of Verbal and Nonverbal Communication

When communicating, nonverbal messages can interact with verbal messages in six ways: repeating, conflicting, complementing, substituting, regulating and accenting/moderating.

Repeating

"Repeating" consists of using gestures to strengthen a verbal message, such as pointing to the object of discussion.

Conflicting

Verbal and nonverbal messages within the same interaction can sometimes send opposing or conflicting messages. A person verbally expressing a statement of truth while simultaneously fidgeting or avoiding eye contact may convey a mixed message to the receiver in the interaction. Conflicting messages may occur for a variety of reasons often stemming from feelings of uncertainty, ambivalence, or frustration. When mixed messages occur, nonverbal communication becomes the primary tool people use to attain additional information to clarify the situation; great attention is placed on bodily movements and positioning when people perceive mixed messages during interactions.

Complementing

Accurate interpretation of messages is made easier when nonverbal and verbal communication complement each other. Nonverbal cues can be used to elaborate on verbal messages to reinforce the information sent when trying to achieve communicative goals; messages have been shown to be remembered better when nonverbal signals affirm the verbal exchange.

Substituting

Nonverbal behavior is sometimes used as the sole channel for communication of a message. People learn to identify facial expressions, body movements, and body positioning as corresponding with specific feelings and intentions. Nonverbal signals can be used without verbal communication to convey messages; when nonverbal behavior does not effectively communicate a message, verbal methods are used to enhance understanding.

Regulating

Nonverbal behavior also regulates our conversations. For example, touching someone's arm can signal that you want to talk next or interrupt.

Accenting/Moderating

Nonverbal signals are used to alter the interpretation of verbal messages. Touch, voice pitch, and gestures are some of the tools people use to accent or amplify the message that is sent; nonverbal behavior can also be used to moderate or tone down aspects of verbal messages as well. For example, a person who is verbally expressing anger may accent the verbal message by shaking a fist.

Dance and non-verbal Communication

Dance is a form of nonverbal communication that requires the same underlying faculty in the brain for conceptualization, creativity and memory as does verbal language in speaking and writing. Means of self-expression, both forms have vocabulary (steps and gestures in dance), grammar (rules for putting the vocabulary together) and meaning. Dance, however, assembles (choreographs) these elements in a manner that more often resembles poetry, with its ambiguity and multiple, symbolic and elusive meanings.

Clinical studies of Non-verbal Communication

From 1977 to 2004, the influence of disease and drugs on receptivity of nonverbal communication was studied by teams at three separate medical schools using a similar paradigm. Researchers at the University of Pittsburgh, Yale University and Ohio State University had subjects observe gamblers at a slot machine awaiting payoffs. The amount of this payoff was read by nonverbal transmission prior to reinforcement.

This technique was developed by and the studies directed by psychologist, Dr. Robert E. Miller and psychiatrist, Dr. A. James Giannini. These groups reported diminished receptive ability in heroin addicts and phencyclidine abusers was contrasted with increased receptivity in cocaine addicts. Men with major depression manifested significantly decreased ability to read nonverbal cues when compared with euthymic men.

Freitas-Magalhaes studied the effect of smile in the treatment of depression and concluded that depressive states decrease when you smile more often. Obese women and women with premenstrual syndrome were found to also possess diminished abilities to read these cues. In contradistinction, men with bipolar disorder possessed increased abilities. A woman with total paralysis of the nerves of facial expression was found unable to transmit any nonverbal facial cues whatsoever.

Because of the changes in levels of accuracy on the levels of nonverbal receptivity, the members of the research team hypothesized a biochemical site in the brain which was operative for reception of nonverbal cues. Because certain drugs enhanced ability while others diminished it, the neurotransmitters dopamine and endorphin were considered to be likely etiological candidate. Based on the available data, however, the primary cause and primary effect could not be sorted out on the basis of the paradigm employed.

A byproduct of the work of the Pittsburgh/Yale/ Ohio State team was an investigation of the role of nonverbal facial cues in heterosexual nondate rape. Males who were serial rapists of adult women were studied for nonverbal receptive abilities. Their scores were the highest of any subgroup. Rape victims were next tested.

It was reported that women who had been raped on at least two occasions by different perpetrators had a highly significant impairment in their abilities to read these cues in either male or female senders. These results were troubling, indicating a predator-prey model. The authors did note that whatever the nature of these preliminary findings the responsibility of the rapist was in no manner or level, diminished.

The final target of study for this group was the medical students they taught. Medical students at Ohio State University, Ohio University and Northest Ohio

Medical College were invited to serve as subjects. Students indicating a preference for the specialties of family practice, psychiatry, pediatrics and obstetrics-gynecology achieved significantly higher levels of accuracy than those students who planned to train as surgeons, radiologists, or pathologists. Internal medicine and plastic surgery candidates scored at levels near the mean.

Difficulties with non-verbal Communication

People vary in their ability to send and receive nonverbal communication. On average, to a moderate degree, women are better at nonverbal communication than are men.

Measurements of the ability to communicate nonverbally and the capacity to feel empathy have shown that the two abilities are independent of each other.

For people who have relatively large difficulties with nonverbal communication, this can pose significant challenges, especially in interpersonal relationships. There exist resources that are tailored specifically to these people, which attempt to assist those in understanding information which comes more easily to others. A specific group of persons that face these challenges are those with autism spectrum disorders, including Asperger syndrome.

Benefits of Interaction in Language Learning

There are many excellent reasons for using activities which promote classroom interaction. First and foremost, you make full use of your most valuable resource - the learners themselves. Not only are adults ready and willing to work together but they tend to learn better in a sociable environment and are more likely to stick to their studies when they feel part of a strong group.

The activities are designed to further their language learning in several ways:

Since the ostensible aim of the activities is to exchange information on a specific topic, your learners will focus on what they are saying rather than how they are saying it, helping to dispel any self-consciousness or inhibitions they might have about speaking a foreign language.

Repetition is vital to learning and retaining language but it can be tedious. During these activities key language elements have to be repeated in an interesting and natural way to communicate the required information.

People are far more likely to retain words and phrases they have used in a meaningful context rather than passively seen or heard. When scenarios are created in the classroom, the related interaction and the 'props' give your learners a hook on which to hang the vocabulary.

The language of the course is controlled but the activities allow an element of choice in the language used and are structured in a way that prepares your learners for the unpredictability inherent to language.

It is very motivating for learners to realise that, even at this early stage, they can communicate information successfully entirely in the target language. It promotes a tremendous feeling of achievement and gives them immediate confirmation that they are making progress.

Adults tend to lead busy lives, with work, family, social and other commitments having to take priority over their language learning. Since many adult classes take place in the evening, your learners may well be tired and stressed before they even start the class. On a purely practical level therefore, it makes sense to add variety and interest to the lesson and to ensure people participate in an enjoyable and motivating language learning experience.

BIBLIOGRAPHY

- Achterman, D (December 2006). "Beyond "Wikipedia"". Teacher Librarian 34 (2): 19-22.
- Al-Asfour, A (2012). "Online Teaching: Navigating Its Advantages, Disadvantages and Best Practices". Tribal College Journal of American Indian Higher Education 23: 3.
- Associated Press (August 28, 1989). "Most teachers think computers are boon to schools, poll says". The Deseret News.
- Baker, Celia. "Blended learning: Teachers plus computers equal success". Desert News. Retrieved 30 January 2014.
- Bates, A. (2005) Technology, e-Learning and Distance Education London: Routledge
- Bates, A. and Poole, G. Effective Teaching with Technology in Higher Education San Francisco: Jossey-Bass/John Wiley, 2003
- Bernard Luskin. "Think "Exciting": E-Learning and the Big "E"".
- Brooks, Laura (April-May 2008). "Old School Meet School Library 2.0". Library Media Connection 26 (7): 14-16.
- Brown, Jessamy; Jinkins, Shirley (February 25, 2010). "At tech-savvy DFW districts, netbooks are joining textbooks". Star Telegram. McClatchy Company. Retrieved May 19, 2010.
- Cahners In-stat Group (1999, December). Cable modem market: Moving to the masses. Boston: Author.
- Chen, M., & Hodder, L. (1997). A research overview of FASE productions' TV series on science, mathematics, and technology education. Unpublished manuscript.
- Craft, A (2012). "Childhood in a Digital Age: Creative Challenges for Educational Futures". London Review of Education 10 (2): 173-190. doi:10.1080/14748460.2012.691282.
- Crane,Beverly E. "Using Web 2.0 Tools in the K-12 Classroom". Neal-Schuman Publishers, Inc., 2009
- Crow, W. B. & Din, H. (2009). Unbound By Place or Time: Museums and Online Learning, Washington, DC: American Association of Museums, pp. 9-10

- Cuban, Larry (2001). Oversold and Underused: Computers in the Classroom. Cambridge, MA: Harvard University Press. p. 82. ISBN 978-0-674-00602-7. Retrieved May 19, 2010.
- Curriculum and Pedagogy in Technology Assisted Learning. Sero.co.uk. Retrieved 2013-10-22.
- David R. Woolley (12 February 2013). "PLATO: The Emergence of Online Community". Thinkofit.com. Retrieved 2013-10-22.
- deJong, T. (2010). "Cognitive Load Theory, Educational Research, and Instructional Design: Some Food for Thought". Instructional Science: An International Journal of the Learning Sciences: 38.
- DoD gives PTSD help 'second life' in virtual reality | Article | The United States Army. Army.mil. Retrieved 2013-10-22.
- Downes, S (2005) E-learning 2.0.Downes.ca
- Driscoll, K (May-June 2007). "Collaboration in Today's Classrooms: New Web Tools Change the Game". MultiMedia & Internet @ Schools 14 (3): 9-12.
- Eric Parks. "What's the "e" in e-Learning?". Askinternational.com. Retrieved 2013-10-22.
- Escuela 2.0. Ite.educacion.es. Retrieved 2013-10-22.
- Foundation for Advancements in Science and Education (1997). Classroom television: A useful resource for mathematics and science education. Evaluation of The Eddie Files. Los Angeles: FASE.
- Full text of Alberuni's India. An account of the religion, philosophy, literature, geography, chronology, astronomy, customs, laws and astrology of India about A.D. 1030"".
- Geer, R.; Sweeney, T. (2012). "Students' voices about learning with technology". Journal of social sciences 8 (2): 294-303.
- Graziadei, W. D., et al., 1997.Building Asynchronous and Synchronous Teaching-Learning Environments: Exploring a Course/Classroom Management System Solution
- Haney, Daniel Q (August 28, 1977), "Computers in the classroom- no match for real live teacher", The Modesto Bee
- Harasim, L., Hiltz, S., Teles, L. and Turoff, M. (1995) Learning Networks: A Field Guide to Teaching and Learning Online Cambridge, MA: MIT Press.

INDEX